1 *Stonewall Jackson*
From an engraving after a painting by Thomas Nast

STONEWALL JACKSON

as Military Commander

John Selby

B. T. BATSFORD LTD

D. VAN NOSTRAND COMPANY, INC

Made and printed in Great Britain
by William Clowes and Sons Ltd
London and Beccles, for the publishers
B. T. BATSFORD LTD
4 Fitzhardinge Street, Portman Square, London W1
D. VAN NOSTRAND COMPANY, INC
120 Alexander Street, Princeton, New Jersey

Contents

Confederate States Belt Buckle

Illustrations

7

Maps

9

Acknowledgment

Another book on Stonewall Jackson in this day and age requires some explanation. When I arrived in the United States to begin my research on it, the first person I met was Mr John Cook Wylie of the Alderman Library at the University of Virginia, Charlottesville. I was not used to the change in time between England and America, and arrived at the library very early in the morning, thus having to wait a short time for the librarian's arrival. On his appearance, I remarked nervously: 'As an Englishman, I feel rather presumptuous at attempting another life of Jackson.' 'Not at all,' he replied, comfortingly. 'It has to be a Westerner or an Englishman.' This led to a discussion on Henderson, and the expression of his opinion that a new book on the lines of Henderson would be welcome. He then conducted me to his Archives Department, and I started on the Fishburne Papers with renewed confidence in my project.

I also wish to acknowledge the help received from: Lieut-Col George B. Davis of the Preston Library at the Virginia Military Institute, Lexington, who put his library at my disposal, and who, with Mrs Davis, gave up so much time to entertain me; also Mrs Heiner who showed great interest in my book and took me round the museum there in such a friendly way; also Mr William J. van Schreeven of the Archives Department of the Virginia State Library, and Mr David C. Mearns, Manuscript Division Chief, Library of Congress for allowing me to study their manuscript collections.

I wish to thank Miss Ann K. Harlow, Chief, Readers' Services Division, The Library, United States Military Academy, West Point, who provided me with a comprehensive list of Universities, Institutes and Libraries having original material relating to Jackson. It was thanks to her that I was able to plan my visit to the United States and make it profitable. Also at the United States Academy, West Point, I would like to thank the Librarian, Colonel C. H. Schilling, and Mr Joseph M. O'Donnell, Chief, Archives and History Section USMA Library; the former for putting the West Point Library at my disposal, and the latter for producing for me photostats of the relevant Jackson records at West Point. I would also like to thank these members of West Point for entertaining me so hospitably.

Mr Jay W. Johns was kind enough to offer me the help of the Jackson Memorial Association, and arranged for Mr Monroe F. Cockrell to give me the benefit of his research into the few errors of Henderson's great book. Mr Cockrell was also kind enough to let me have copies of his maps of the railways in Virginia at the time of the Civil War and of Jackson's movements. I also wish to thank Mr Lowell H.

Harrison for allowing me to quote from his article in the *Civil War Times* of October, 1966, on Jackson's rating among the Southern Generals.

In Britain, I want to thank Mr J. McNaughtan, bookseller of Edinburgh, for lending me the *Confederate Record* and copies of the Hagerstown *Herald-Mail*. I wish to express my gratitude to Mr D. W. King, the Librarian of the Ministry of Defence (Army Department), who put his vast knowledge and the resources of his great library at my disposal, and whose staff were unfailingly helpful; to Lieut-Col Walter Young and Mr Oliver of the Staff College Library, Camberley, for allowing me almost exclusive use of the *War of the Rebellion, Official Records*, housed with them; to Lieut-Col L. H. Yates and Major W. Melia of the Prince Consort's Library, Aldershot, for their friendly cooperation; to Lieut-Col Alan Shepperd, Librarian of the Royal Military Academy, Sandhurst, and his Staff for their ever-ready help and support; to Brigadier Peter Young for his assistance with the illustrations, and to my colleague Mr John Keegan, for reading some of the script and making valuable suggestions.

Finally, I want to thank my Military History Set at Sandhurst for their help: G. S. Fenton and M. H. Kefford for their suggestions; P. J. Everingham, M. J. Steel and A. J. W. Powell for help with the appendices.

The publishers of *Battles and Leaders*, Thomas Yoseloff, Inc., of New York have been kind enough to allow me to quote from their books. The maps have been drawn by Arthur Banks from the author's designs; and the vignettes are by the author: the *Reb* from a statuette in his possession by Chas. C. Stadden produced by Norman Newton Ltd., and the 'old grey hat' from photographs—and a glimpse of it at the VMI Museum!

The R.M.A. Sandhurst
1 December 1967

The Author and Publishers wish to thank the following for permission to reproduce the illustrations which appear in this book: The Corcoran Gallery of Art, Washington, D.C. and Mrs Genevieve Plummer for Fig. 28; Library of Congress, Washington, D.C. for Figs. 9, 13–22, 24–27, 29–33; The Mansell Collection for Figs. 1 and 8; The National Archives and US War Dept. for Figs. 12 and 23; The National Archives and US Signal Corps (Brady Collection), for Figs. 2–7 and 11; US Department of the Interior, National Park Service, Washington, D.C. for Fig. 34, Valentine Museum (Cook Collection), Richmond, Virginia for Fig. 10.

Stonewall Jackson was of medium size and height, and had dark hair. He was rather pale, and his face lacked expression except when aroused, for example in battle. To strangers he appeared somewhat awkward and shy; but his kind smile made him attractive to children. His appearance was not imposing. He usually wore a stained old tunic of dingy grey, and his famous VMI cap (*see* sketch) was, if anything, more faded still. The sun had turned it quite yellow and it tilted over his forehead so far that he had to raise his chin to look at people. Often, he was to be seen sucking a bit of his favourite fruit, a lemon. Certainly, riding in his peculiar forward-leaning fashion with short stirrups on *Little Sorrel*, he could hardly be termed an imposing figure.

First Bull Run

It is said that Jackson won his nickname at Manassas and his immortality in the Shenandoah Valley. But he did more than gain a soubriquet at Manassas. He displayed in this first field battle of the American Civil War commendable staunchness as well as leadership of high quality; he chose a good defensive position on the beginning of a reverse slope, with his flanks protected by woods and Stuart's cavalry for additional protection of his left; and he massed his guns with skill. It was his brigade, consisting of the Second Virginia, the Fourth Virginia, the Fifth Virginia and the Twenty-Seventh Virginia, with the formerly non-brigaded Thirty-third Virginia Infantry, which, more than any others repulsed the Federal main attack.

What was more, Jackson knew that he had done well, and that his First Brigade had done well. In a letter[1] to his wife he wrote: 'When the official reports are published, if not before, I expect to see justice done to a noble body of patriots.'

The First Manassas (Bull Run) campaign began shortly after the outbreak of the war. 24 days after the attack by the South on the Federal-held Fort Sumter in Charleston Harbour on 12 April 1861, General Lee ordered the fortification of Manassas junction, 25 miles south-west of Washington; and a month later General Beauregard took command of the defences. Meanwhile the people of the North clamoured for a quick march on the Southern capital to end the war. 'On to Richmond!' was their cry; and this popular pressure forced General McDowell to launch his drive south prematurely.

[1] Henderson, i, 156.

As so often in the battles of the eastern plains the strategic influence of the Shenandoah Valley had an impact on the Battle of First Bull Run. The Appalachian Highlands system with the main Alleghany ridges in the south divided the war into two separate theatres of operations—the west and the east. But the eastern valleys of the great mountain system were linked strategically with the battles of Virginia and the east. The fertile Shenandoah Valley divided longitudinally by the Massanutton Mountains and separated from the eastern plains by the Blue Mountains, was not only the 'bread-basket of the Confederacy',[1] but provided a covered approach leading towards the rear of the Federal capital Washington. Its occupation by Southern troops in the north near the Potomac, on several occasions caused near panic to President Lincoln and the statesmen of the North; and time and time again they considered it necessary to divert to the Valley troops which could have been better employed attacking Richmond directly. When occupied by the North, however, it was tactically less of a menace, for the structure of its ridges and valleys led invaders away from the Southern capital, Richmond (*see* Map p. 16).

In the Manassas operation the military significance of the Manassas area lay in the junction of two railways there. The Orange and Alexandria, which offered the only rail connection between Washington and Richmond, was joined by the Manassas Gap Railway, a direct route to the Shenandoah Valley. By the seizure of the junction at Manassas the Federal army could follow the Orange and Alexandria Railway south-west to Gordonsville, and thence proceed by the Virginia Central eastward to Richmond (*see* Map p. 16). This, with good supporting roads, would assure an overland approach that would avoid many of the natural barriers found in the shorter route by Fredericksburg, where the Occoquan and Aquia creeks and the Rappahannock river, had to be crossed (*see* Map p. 16).

Beauregard says of Manassas Junction : 'Its strategic value was that, being close to the Federal capital, it held in observation the chief army then being assembled by Gen. McDowell, under the immediate eye of the commander-in-chief, General Scott, for an offensive movement against Richmond.'[2] It was also important in another way as Colonel Cocke, commanding in the area before the arrival of Beauregard, points out in a despatch to Lee : 'It is obvious, sir, with a strong corps d'armée at Manassas, and at least a division at Winchester (in the Valley), these two bodies being connected by a continuous railway through Manassas Gap, two columns—one at Manassas and

[1] 'The fertile valley of the Shenandoah was then teeming with livestock and cereal subsistence, as well as with other resources essential to the Confederates.' B & L, i, 196.
[2] B & L, i, 196.

2 General Beauregard
Commander of the Confederate Army
at First Bull Run

3 General Joseph E. Johnston
Jackson's Commander before and, nominally,
during the Shenandoah Valley Campaign

4 General McClellan
In Jackson's class at West Point. Commanded
the Federal Army in the Seven Days' Battles
and in the Maryland Campaign

5 General McDowell
Commander of the Federal Army
at First Bull Run

6 *General Banks*
Jackson said of him: 'He is always ready to fight and generally gets whipped.'
He was Jackson's opponent in 'The Valley' and at Cedar Run

7 *Stonewall Jackson as a corps commander, taken two weeks before he was mortally wounded at Chancellorsville*

one at Winchester—could readily cooperate and concentrate upon one point or the other.'[1]

McDowell's plan was to attack the 22,000[2] Confederates under Beauregard at Manassas with nearly 36,000 men under his own command, while General Patterson with 18,000 men in the north of Shenandoah Valley prevented a Confederate Army of 12,000 under General J. E. Johnston from leaving Winchester and reinforcing Beauregard. In the event Patterson failed to keep Johnston's forces in the Valley, and the brigades of Jackson, Bartow, Bee and Kirby Smith, of the Army of the Shenandoah, all came by rail and road to Manassas Junction to reinforce the Army of the Potomac and play a vital part in the Confederate victory.

Beauregard drew up and partially entrenched his forces along the Bull Run River which ran like the ditch of a fortress across his front. Action began on 18 July 1861, when a part of McDowell's army was smartly repulsed at Blackburn's Ford[3] by Longstreet's Fourth Brigade of the Army of the Potomac. This action had a depressing effect on Union morale but greatly boosted that of the Confederates. There followed two days of costly delay for McDowell while he brought up more supplies; and the Confederates made good use of the respite by building abattis and road blocks of felled trees on the Warrenton road near Stone Bridge and in general strengthening their defences. More important still, the delay gave Johnston time to reach Manassas. On the 19th Jackson arrived with 2,500 men, having covered approximately 55 miles in 25 hours, his infantry using the railway for the section from Piedmont to Manassas Junction, his cavalry, artillery and wagons coming all the way by road (Map p. 16). At sunrise on the 20th more of Johnston's reinforcements came in—the 7th and 8th Georgia regiments of Bartow's brigade numbering 1,400 men. About noon Johnston himself arrived accompanied by Bee, the 4th Alabama, the 2nd Mississippi, and two companies of the 11th Mississippi. At this stage Beauregard with Johnston's approval planned an offensive involving an attack on McDowell's left flank towards Centreville. Through a miscarriage of orders and the hold-up of the reserves required on the Manassas Gap Railway, coupled with the Federal attack on Stone Bridge which forestalled it, this Confederate offensive never got properly under way. General Beauregard explains it as follows in his report:[4]

[1] *Manassas*, Historical Handbook Series, National Park Service, 2.
[2] The figure on map 1, 32,000, includes reinforcements from 'the Valley'.
[3] This action is called the Battle of Bull Run by the Confederates and the main action Manassas, B & L, i, 179. The main battle is now called by both names.
[4] O.R., ii, 486.

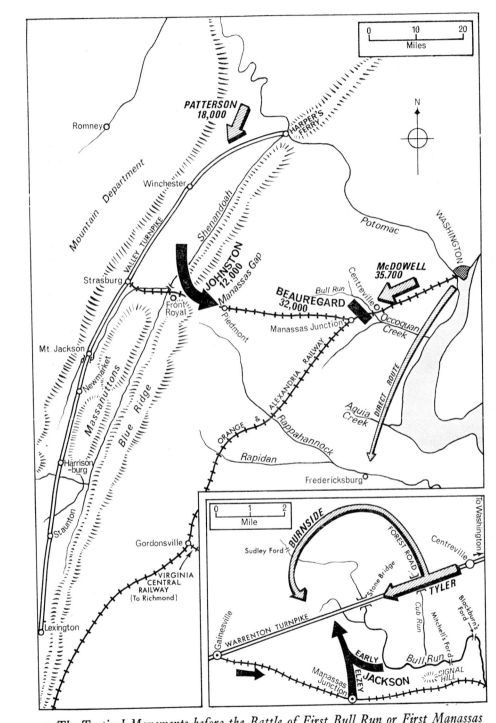

1 The Tactical Movements before the Battle of First Bull Run or First Manassas

16

In consequence of the untoward detention of some five thousand of General Johnston's army corps, resulting from the inadequate and imperfect means of transportation for so many troops at the disposition of the Manassas Gap Railway, it became necessary, on the morning of the 21st, before daylight, to modify the plan accepted to suit the contingency of an immediate attack on our lines by the main force of the enemy, then plainly at hand.

The enemy's forces, reported by their best informed journals to be fifty-five thousand strong,[1] I had learned from reliable sources on the night of the 20th were being concentrated in and around Centreville and along the Warrenton turnpike road to Bull Run, near which our respective pickets were in immediate proximity. This fact, with the conviction that after his signal discomfiture on the 18th of July before Blackburn's Ford—the centre of my lines—he would not renew the attack in that quarter, induced me at once to look for an attempt on my left flank, resting on the stone bridge, which was weakly guarded by men, as well as but slightly provided with artificial defensive appliances and artillery. In view of these palpable military conditions, by 4.30 a.m. on the 21st July I had prepared and dispatched orders directing the whole of the Confederate forces within the lines of Bull Run, including the brigades and regiments of General Johnston, which had arrived at that time, to be held in readiness to march (north-west), at a moment's notice.

In this way the whole form of the battle altered; instead of carrying out a strong attack towards Centreville (Beauregard's first plan) or on the main Warrenton road nearer Stone Bridge (Beauregard's second plan) the Confederates, leaving small bodies of men to guard the southern Bull Run fords swung in force north-west to meet the main Federal attack crossing Sudley Ford in the north. The Confederates moving north comprised Holmes' force of 1,250 which had come across originally from Aquia Creek, the bulk of Beauregard's Army of the Potomac, and the brigades of General Johnston from the Army of the Shenandoah. Thus it came about that Jackson's First Brigade played a vital part at Bull Run, fighting furiously in the small sector which turned out to be the key to the battle.

The main battle began at 5.30 a.m. with the arrival of some shells from a Federal 30-pounder Parrott gun in front of Evans' position at Stone Bridge. The second shot passed through the tent of Beauregard's signal officer, Captain E. P. Alexander, at headquarters half a mile in the rear of Mitchell's Ford. Later from Signal Hill Alexander scanned the horizon for any evidence of a flanking movement. With telescope in hand he was examining the area of Sudley Ford when about 8.45 a.m. his attention was arrested by the glint of the morning sun on a brass field piece. Closer observation revealed the glitter of bayonets and musket barrels. Quickly he signalled Evans at Stone Bridge, 'Look out for your left; you are turned!'[2] This message, which was

---

[1] An overestimate: there were 35,700.   [2] *Manassas Handbook*, 10.

to play an important part in the tactical development of the battle, represents probably the first use in battle of the 'wig-wag' system of signalling. Under this, messages were sent by waving a signal flag from up to the right to left and back (one) or down to the right and up (two). Combinations of these numbers stood for letters, and phrases. The flags were white, with a red square; black, which could be seen against snow; or red with a white square.[1]

The Federal attack consisted of a thrust by Tyler's First Division at Stone Bridge including a minor right flanking movement over a Bull Run ford north of Stone Bridge by Sherman's Third Brigade; and a main attack well to the north by Hunter's and Heintzelman's divisions (*see* Map p. 20). These two divisions were held up on the Warrenton road by Tyler's troops, and when they did move off to the north on a forest road, they made very slow progress. In fact, McDowell's advance was ponderous throughout. When they left Washington, the various regiments were brilliantly uniformed, some in Federal blue, some in gaudy Zouave dress copying the French, and their silk banners flung to the breeze were unsoiled and untorn. But the men were mostly civilians in uniform, and were not yet soldiers. Unused to marching, by the time they reached Centreville they were hot, weary, bedraggled and footsore and dropped down as soon as they halted. Another cause of delay was the throng of visitors from Washington, official and unofficial, who came in carriages to see the fun, and cluttered up roads which should have been reserved for troop movements.

McDowell had waited in the morning at the point on the Warrenton road where his flanking columns turned to the right, until the troops, except Howard's brigade which he halted at this point, had passed. He gazed silently and with evident pride upon the regiments as they filed by, lively again in the freshness of the morning. Later he conducted, with some success, the battle in the north where his troops drove back Evans' forces from Matthews Hill and put to flight the reinforcements from Bee's and Bartow's joint brigade.

The early part of the battle is described in General Beauregard's report[2] as follows:

Colonel Evans, having become satisfied of the counterfeit character of the movement on his front (Tyler's), and persuaded of an attempt to turn his flank, decided to change his position to meet the enemy, and for this purpose immediately put in motion to his left and rear six companies of Sloan's Fourth Carolina Regiment, Wheat's Louisiana Battalion's five companies, and two 6-pounders (howitzers) of Latham's battery, leaving four companies of Sloan's regiment under cover as the

---

[1] Coggins, 107. [2] O.R., ii, 488.

sole immediate defence of the stone bridge, but giving information to General Cocke (in command of the area) of his change of position and the reasons that impelled it.

Following a road to Carter's mansion (*see* Map p. 20), Colonel Evans formed a line of battle some 400 yards behind that house, his guns to the front. Finding, however, that the enemy did not appear, he turned abruptly to the left and marching across the fields for about three quarters of a mile, took up a position in line of battle, his left, Sloan's Carolinians, resting on the main Sudley road in a shallow ravine, and Major Wheat's Louisiana Tigers to the right, a rectangular copse of wood separating them. One of his guns was planted on a hill 700 yards to the rear of Wheat's battalion, and the other on a ridge in the rear of Sloan's position, commanding a reach of the road just in front. In this order he awaited the coming of the masses of the enemy, numbering over 16,000 men of all arms with 24 pieces of artillery, and led by Burnside's brigade.

In the meantime, nearly 3,000 of the troops of Bee's and Bartow's brigades now united, were moving up to support Evans; and Jackson was sent to take up a position along Bull Run in the north (*see* Map p. 20).

When the Federals came out of the woods into the open fields in front of Evans, Wheat's Louisiana Tigers fired volleys at the skirmishers, and Sloan's Carolinians did the same into the Rhode Island Regiment which was advancing on them; while the two 6-pounder howitzers in the rear flung their grape shot upon the attacking line. Burnside's entire brigade was now sent forward in a second charge, including eight regular companies under Major Sykes and many pieces of artillery, some of them the North's vaunted rifled guns.[1] After an hour, having suffered severe casualties, Evans sought reinforcements from General Bee. General Bee had borrowed Imboden's battery from Jackson's brigade and placed it with a brigade of infantry on either side on the north-west edge of the Henry House plateau where it could support Evans by fire over the depression caused by Young's Branch (*see* Map p. 20). Bee answered Evans' request by suggesting that Evans should fall back on his own stronger position; but Evans pressed him to

[1] B & L, i, note 233: 'I venture the opinion, after a good deal of observation during the war, that in open ground, at 1000 yards, a 6-pounder battery of smooth guns, or, at 1500 to 1800 yards, a similar battery of 12-pounder Napoleons, well handled, will in one hour discomfit double the number of the best rifles (rifled guns) ever put in the field. A smooth-bore gun never buries its projectiles in the ground, as the rifle does invariably when fired against sloping ground. Of course, this advantage of the smooth-bore gun is limited to its shorter range, and to an open field fight, defensive works not being considered'. (Imboden.)

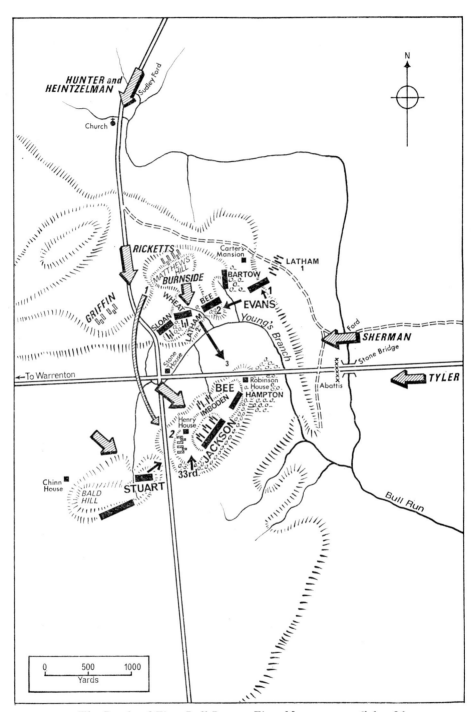

2 The Battle of First Bull Run or First Manassas, 21 July 1861

come forward, and against his better judgment, he agreed, leaving Imboden and his guns but moving forward his infantry to prolong Evans' line on the right—one regiment in the copse held by Evans, two along a fence on the right, and two under General Bartow extended forward at right-angles along the edge of another wood (*see* Map p. 20).

At first the Federals, although in superior numbers, failed to make any headway against the Confederate forces, but when Heintzelman's two strong brigades added their fire to Hunter's, and Sherman, crossing a ford over Bull Run north of Stone Bridge, struck at their right flank, the Confederates were forced back in confusion.

While the Confederates were retreating, closely followed by the Federals swarming after them, Hampton's Legion [1] formed up by Robinson House to cover the retirement of the discomfited brigade. Meanwhile Imboden's battery was left isolated and alone, shattered by shells which fell in quick succession from Ricketts' and Griffin's regular Federal batteries. The day seemed lost. Strong masses of Northern infantry could be seen moving past Stone House and across the Warrenton road, Hampton's Legion was beginning to retire from Robinson House, and Imboden's battery with only three rounds left for each piece had hooked in and was galloping back across the plateau of Henry House Hill. Then help came from Jackson. Hearing the heavy fire increasing in intensity, he turned the head of his column in its direction. As he pushed forward, part of the troops he intended to support swept by in disorder to the rear. Imboden's battery came dashing back, and met Jackson and his men coming up. Imboden writes: [2] 'When I met Jackson I felt very angry at what I then regarded as bad treatment from General Bee in leaving us so long exposed to capture, and I expressed myself with some profanity, which I could see was displeasing to Jackson. He remarked, "I'll support your battery. Unlimber right here."'

At that moment General Bee appeared, approaching at full gallop, and he and Jackson met face to face. The latter cool and composed; Bee covered with dust and sweat, his sword in his hand, and his horse foaming. 'General', he said, 'they are beating us back!' 'Then, sir, we will give them the bayonet,' [3] Jackson replied; and he formed up the First Brigade in line on the eastern edge of Henry House Hill to carry this out.

Jackson's determined bearing inspired Bee with renewed confidence. He turned and galloped back towards Robinson House where his officers were attempting to reform their broken companies. Riding into the confused

---

[1] A regiment of gentlemen raised and commanded by a wealthy planter from South Carolina.

[2] B & L, i, 234.   [3] Henderson, i, 145.

throng while the fate of the battle seemed hung in the balance, there occurred one of the dramatic moments of the war. Bee, desperately attempting to rally his men, glanced towards Henry House Hill where he saw Jackson and his men standing bold and resolute. Catching the inspiration of the moment, Bee leaned forward in his stirrups. 'Look!' he shouted, pointing with his sword. 'There is Jackson standing like a stone wall! Rally behind the Virginians!'[1] Bee's men echoed the shout and formed on their colours, and the tide of battle turned at the moment 'Stonewall' Jackson won his immortal name![2]

The second part of the Battle of Bull Run shows Jackson leading his forces in the field with confident skill, and thereby inspiring the broken regiments forming up on their colours to the right of him, and allowing the reinforcing troops of Early and Elzey (when Kirby Smith was wounded Elzey replaced him) to form up on the left on a new firm line of battle.

General Beauregard also played a part personally in rallying the disordered regiments on Henry House Hill. 'The disorder seemed irretrievable', he wrote, 'but happily the thought came to me that if the colours were planted out to the front the men might rally on them, and I gave the order to carry the standards forward some forty yards, which was promptly executed by the regimental officers, thus drawing the common eye of the troops. They now received easily the orders to advance and form on the line of their colours, which they obeyed with a general movement; and as General Johnston and myself rode forward shortly after with the colours of the 4th Alabama by our side, the line that had fought all morning, and had fled, routed and disordered, now advanced again as stately as veterans.'[3]

As an artillery officer, Jackson made full use of his guns. To Captain Imboden's battery, with only three rounds left per gun and so cut up that it was waiting to be sent to the rear, he brought up the Rockbridge Artillery and the Leesburg Artillery, and all these were placed out in front of the infantry, as well as several other batteries. By the time the two Federal regular rifled batteries of Griffin and Ricketts had placed themselves in a position a few hundred yards away near Henry House, there were 26 fresh guns ready for them. Imboden described the scene thus: 'During the lull in front, my men lay about, exhausted from want of water and food, and black with powder, smoke and dust. Lieutenant Harman and I amused ourselves training one of the guns on a heavy column of the enemy who were advancing towards us, in the direction of Chinn House (*see* Map p. 20), but were still

---

[1] Henderson, i, 145.   [2] See note, p. 28.   [3] B & L, i, 210.

1200 to 1500 yards away. While we were still engaged, General Jackson rode up and said that three or four batteries were approaching rapidly (to replace Imboden's). I asked permission to fire the three rounds of shrapnel left to us, and he said, "Go ahead" . . . The contest that ensued was terrific. Jackson ordered me to go from battery to battery and see that the guns were properly aimed and fuses cut to the right length. This was the work of but a few minutes. On returning to the left of the line of guns, I stopped to ask General Jackson's permission to rejoin my battery (now in the rear). The fight was just then hot enough to make him feel well. His eyes fairly blazed. He had a way of throwing up his left hand with the open palm toward the person he was addressing. And as he told me to go, he made this gesture. The air was full of flying missiles, and as he spoke he jerked down his hand and I saw that blood was streaming from it. I exclaimed, "General, you are wounded." He replied, as he drew a handkerchief from his breast-pocket, and began to bind it up, "Only a scratch—a mere scratch", and galloped away along the line.'[1]

The battle was being conducted by General Beauregard. General Johnston, his senior, having only recently arrived from the Shenandoah, allowed Beauregard to remain in command in the field, and was persuaded, a little unwillingly, to go back and organise the flow of reinforcements to the main battle on Henry House Hill. Beauregard ordered up the 49th and 8th Virginia regiments from Cocke's neighbouring brigade, and placed the 7th Georgia on the left of Jackson's brigade, along the belt of pines occupied by the latter on the eastern rim of the plateau (*see* Map p. 20). As the 49th came up, their Colonel pointed out Beauregard, and the men and some of Jackson's brigade gave him a cheer. Pleased with this sign of confidence, he placed the 49th on the extreme left next to the 7th Georgia, and returning, paused to say a few words to Jackson.

A steady fire of the musketry told severely on the Federal ranks, particularly on the left where the Confederates were continually being reinforced; the troops in this quarter confronting each other at very short range.

Next followed three charges. Griffin's and Ricketts' Batteries, with a body of Fire Zouaves[2] in blue and scarlet with white turbans, were placed well forward south of Henry House in an exposed position. Jeb Stuart and the cavalry, seeing their opportunity, charged them and rode the Zouaves down. Almost at the same moment the 33rd Virginia on Jackson's left charged from the copse in which they were hidden (*see* Map p. 20). Mistaking these latter

[1] B & L, i, 235, 236.
[2] 11th New York—recruited from New York fire brigade, or volunteers connected with it.

for their own men,[1] the officers in charge of the Federal batteries withheld their fire. This brought about their doom. At 70 yards the 33rd fired a deadly volley; every gunner was shot down; the teams were almost annihilated, and several officers fell killed or wounded. Meanwhile the Zouaves, already shaken by Stuart's charge, turned and fled. Beauregard now ordered a general advance, and this was so successful that the open surface of the plateau was swept clear of the Federals. But the Federals again pushed up the slope, and Henry and Robinson houses were once more taken into their possession, as well as the unmanned guns. A second general Confederate charge, however, was made with such dash that the Federals were driven this time right across the turnpike and Young's Branch, never to return.

Henderson described Jackson's First Brigade's part in one[2] of these charges as follows: 'Jackson's men were lying beneath the crest of the plateau. Only one of his regiments—the 33rd—had as yet been engaged in the open . . . riding to the centre of the line . . . he gave orders for a counter-stroke. "Reserve your fire till they come within fifty yards, then fire and give them the bayonet; and when you charge, yell like furies."' This was the famous 'Rebel Yell' much encouraged by Jackson and music to his ears.

The second combined attack, delivered about 3.45 a.m. proved overwhelming. A brief rally north of Young's Branch was broken up by artillery fire. The Federals had had enough; they made for home as best they could, covered by Sykes' regulars and Palmer's cavalry. A lucky shot from Kemper's battery hit the bridge over Cub Run, upsetting a wagon which had just driven upon it. This blocked the bridge and caused panic and confusion which was increased by the throngs of sightseers also making their way back to Washington along the crowded narrow roads. All through the night and the rain of the next day the soldiers and civilians streamed into Washington. Attempts by McDowell to rally the soldiers were in vain. But the exhausted battle-weary Confederates made no effective pursuit. Early's brigade and Stuart's cavalry did succeed in capturing a number of prisoners, but the main Union forces escaped. By 22 July both armies were back in the positions they had occupied prior to the battle.

---

[1] 'Less than two hundred yards to the right of the guns a body of infantry appeared which Griffin quickly decided to face and meet with canister; but Major Barry, who was directing the two batteries, declared it was a supporting regiment and must not be fired on. There was much confusion all through the battle owing to the fact that there were some blue uniforms among the Confederates.' With no wind stirring, the flags were also difficult to distinguish. Johnston, 217.

[2] Henderson, i, 151. Henderson seems to telescope the two charges into one.

It is generally believed that the Confederates might have made more of their pursuit. As Dr Hunter McGuire was dressing his wound, Jackson is reported as having said: 'Give me 10,000 fresh troops and I would be in Washington tomorrow.'[1] A present-day authority[2] (1964), however, writes:

I do not believe Jackson said any such thing. He fought furiously in a very small sector which turned out to be the key to the battle where he had no way of knowing the effective strength, condition or placements of the Confederate army, its supply of food, ammunition and wagon trains, if any.

His record at VMI[3] and throughout the war shows that he was a taciturn man. If he said anything at all, it could have been nothing more than an emotional outburst. Let's examine the conditions.

In the first place, it had been a long full-daylight battle on an intensely hot day; both opponents had suffered crippling losses; no time for noon rations; both armies were deficient in organisation, training and discipline; when the battle ended at about five o'clock both armies were badly disorganised and exhausted; the Federals were in wild flight back to Sudley Springs while some crossed the Stone Bridge and followed the shorter Warrenton turnpike to Centreville where stood in battle array the Federal reserves of the 4th and part of the 5th divisions.

The Confederates were scattered into mixed commands; no ammunition wagons were ready for a forward movement; attention to the wounded seemed more important than furious pursuit of the defeated Federals.

Where were the fresh Confederate troops to come from? None were handy. The nearest were spread out on guard duty some two miles away at Ball's Ford; the regiments of Bonham, Longstreet and Jones were some two miles further along and dispersed on their defence line of Bull Run around Mitchell's Ford, in turn about three miles from the Federal base at Centreville. All these troops were too far away from Jackson on Henry House Hill where he had no fresh troops, supplies or ammunition.

On hearing three days after the fight that Jackson was still suffering from his wound, which had become inflamed, Captain J. D. Imboden rode to his quarters in a farm near Centreville. Imboden writes:

Although it was barely sunrise, he was out under the trees, bathing the hand with spring water. It was much swollen and very painful, but he bore himself stoically. His wife had arrived the night before. Of course, the battle was the only topic discussed at breakfast. I remarked, in Mrs Jackson's hearing: 'General, how is it that you can keep so cool and appear so utterly insensible to danger in such a storm of shell and bullets as rained about you when your hand was hit?' He instantly became grave and reverential in his manner and answered in a low tone of great earnestness: 'Captain, my religious belief teaches me to feel as safe in battle as in bed. God has fixed the time for my death. I do not concern myself about *that*, but to

[1] Henderson, i, 154 and E. P. Alexander's *Military Memoirs*.
[2] Monroe F. Cockrell, researcher for Jackson Memorial Trust.
[3] Virginia Military Institute, Lexington.

be always ready, no matter when it may overtake me.' He added, after a pause, looking me full in the face: 'Captain, that is the way all men should live, and then all would be equally brave.'

I felt that this remark was intended as a rebuke for my profanity, when I complained to him on the field of the apparent abandonment of my battery to capture, and I apologised. He heard me, and simply said, 'Nothing can justify profanity.'[1]

After the battle of Bull Run Jackson showed his qualities as an administrator. The camp he occupied with the First Brigade was an unhealthy one; the water was bad and the site depressing. Explaining to General Johnston that a change of camp would increase the efficiency of his brigade, he moved it to a new site near Centreville. Next he got some new tents, 'chased up' the arrears of pay for his men and pressed, with some success, the ordnance to supply fresh arms and new clothes. Fortunately food could be had in abundance, and with a little money it was possible for the men to buy a few luxuries like chickens, butter and eggs.[2]

General Jackson earned renown at Bull Run. General Johnston's report said:

Our victory was as complete as one gained by infantry and artillery alone can be. An adequate force of cavalry would have made it decisive. (His reason for the failure of the pursuit). It is due under Almighty God, to the skill and resolution of General Beauregard, the admirable conduct of Generals Bee, Kirby Smith, and Jackson, and of the Colonels (commanding brigades) Evans, Cocke, Early and Elzey, and the courage, and unyielding firmness of our patriotic volunteers.'[3] General Beauregard was more generous: 'The conduct of General Jackson also requires mention as eminently that of an able, fearless soldier and sagacious commander, one fit to lead his efficient brigade. His prompt, timely arrival before the plateau of the Henry house, and his judicious disposition of his troops, contributed much to the success of the day. Although painfully wounded in the hand, he remained on the field to the end of the battle, rendering valuable assistance.[4]

In view of his performance at Bull Run Jackson was promoted Major-General on 4 November 1861, and given the command of the Shenandoah Valley. Thus he no longer continued to command the First Brigade directly as before. Whether he or his soldiers felt the parting most, it is hard to say. Certain it is that the men had now a warm regard for their leader. The Stonewall Brigade had made Jackson a hero, and he had won from them more than admiration. His care for their comfort and well being, the thorough way he had trained them, and what was more, the success his methods had

---

[1] B & L, i, 238.   [2] Vandiver, 168.
[3] O.R., vol. 11, 477.   [4] O.R., vol. 11, 500.

26

achieved, had won their affection. Even his peculiarities became endearing, and 'Old Jack' or 'Stonewall' were now his nicknames.

His farewell to the First Brigade was a striking one:[1]

On the morning of the 4th of October, 1861, the gallant 'Stonewall Brigade' was drawn up near its encampment at Centreville. All the regiments except the Fifth, which was on picket, were present. Drawn up in close columns, the officers and soldiers who had, on the immortal 21st of July, won such glory under the guidance of their gallant general, stood with sad hearts and sorrowful countenances to bid him farewell, while thousands of troops from other portions of the army stood in respectful silence. Until this moment his appearance had never failed to draw from his men the most enthusiastic cheers. But now, not a sound was heard! A deep and painful silence reigned over everything; every heart was full. And this silence was more eloquent than cheers could have been.

As they reached the centre of the line the staff halted, and the general rode slowly forward to within a few paces of his men. Then pausing, he gazed for a moment wistfully up and down the line. Beneath the calm, quiet exterior of the hero there throbbed a warm and generous heart, and this parting filled it with inexpressible pain. After a silence of a few moments, General Jackson turned to his men and addressed them as follows:

'Officers and Soldiers of the First Brigade! I am not here to make a speech, but simply to say farewell. I first met you at Harper's Ferry, in the commencement of this war, and I cannot take leave of you without giving expression to my admiration of your conduct from that day to this, whether on the march, the bivouac, the tented field, or on the bloody plains of Manassas, where you gained the well-deserved reputation of having decided the fate of the battle. Throughout the broad extent of the country over which you have marched, by your respect for the rights and property of citizens, you have shown that you were soldiers, not only to defend, but able and willing both to defend and protect. You have already gained a brilliant and deservedly high reputation throughout the army of the whole Confederacy, and I trust, in the future, by your deeds on the field, and by the assistance of the same kind Providence who has heretofore favoured our cause, you will gain more victories and add additional lustre to the reputation you enjoy. You have already gained a proud position in the future history of this our second war of independence. I shall look with great anxiety to your future movements; and I trust, whenever I shall hear of the *First Brigade* on the field of battle, it will be of still nobler deeds achieved and higher reputation won.'

Having uttered these words, Jackson paused for an instant, and his eye passed slowly along the line, as though he wished thus to bid farewell individually to every old familiar face, so often seen in the heat of battle, and so dear to him. The thoughts which crowded upon him seemed more than he could bear—he could not leave them with such formal words only—and

[1] *Confederate Scrap Book*, L. C. Daniel, 1893, 121, 122, 123.

that iron lip which had never trembled in the hour of the deadliest peril, now quivered. Mastered by an uncontrollable impulse, the great soldier rose in his stirrups, threw the reins on the neck of his horse with an emphasis which sent a thrill through every heart, and extending his arm, added, in tones of the deepest feeling :

In the army of the Shenadoàh you were the *First Brigade*! In the army of the Potomac you were the *First Brigade*! In the second corps of the army you were the *First Brigade*! You are the *First Brigade* in the affections of your general; and I hope by your future deeds and bearing you will be handed down as the *First Brigade* in this our second war of independence. Farewell!

For a moment there was a pause, and then there arose cheer after cheer, so wild and thrilling that the very heavens rang with them. Unable to bear calmly such affecting evidence of attachment, General Jackson hastily waved farewell to his men, and gathering his reins rode rapidly away.

Note

As in many military legends there are several versions of the origin of the name *Stonewall*. Henderson, vol i, p. 145, and J. D. Adams in *Stonewall*, p. 77, give the version above, as does the brochure of the Manassas (Bull Run) National Battlefield Park, and *Manassas* in the National Park Service Historical Handbook Series. On Jackson's statue in the Park is written' There stands Jackson like a stone wall.' Beauregard is recorded as saying, *Battles and Leaders*, vol i, p. 210, that Bee cried: ' "Look at Jackson's brigade! It stands like a stone wall"—a name passed from the brigade to its immortal commander.' The version given by the *Charleston Mercury* of 25 July 1861 was: 'There is Jackson standing like a stone wall. Let us determine to die here and we will conquer. Follow me!' Frank E. Vandiver in his fully documented, scholarly biography of Jackson (1957) adopts the *Mercury's* version; and *The Life of Jackson* by J. D. McCabe has something close to it. In *The Life and Military Career of T. J. Jackson* by M. Addey, p. 33, is found a slightly different rendering: 'Beauregard fancying that his troops were raw, asked Jackson if he thought they would be likely to stand. "Yes", replied he, "like a stone wall!"' John G. Gittings in *Personal Recollections of Stonewall Jackson*, p. 30, has, 'Rally men, on the Virginians! There stands Jackson like a stone wall.' The Rev R. L. Dabney, Jackson's cleric chief of staff, in the first major biography, p. 222, combines both versions with: 'There is Jackson standing like a stone wall. Rally behind the Virginians. Let us determine to die here, and we will conquer.' D. S. Freeman in *Lee's*

Lieutenants, vol i, appendix V, p. 733, goes into the origin of the name *Stonewall* in some detail, as does R. M. Johnston in *Bull Run, Its Strategy and Tactics*.[1] Johnston says that General D. H. Hill 'rejected the whole story as fabulous;' while Freeman infers that Hill believed only that 'something was said by somebody during or immediately after the battle that likened Jackson, or his men, or both, to a stone wall.' They both, however, think this is going too far.

Certainly it is established that the story was circulating in Richmond within three days of the battle, and appeared in a South Carolina newspaper[2] unlikely to go out of its way to praise a little known Virginian. Also, Jackson himself believed that Bee spoke of a stone wall. Freeman also mentions an entirely different theory put forward in the *Reminiscences of Col. J. C. Haskell* that 'the fact was that Bee said that his and Bartow's brigades were hard pressed and that Jackson refused to move to their relief and in a passionate expression of anger he denounced him for standing like a stone wall, and allowing them to be sacrificed.'

All in all, except for Haskell, Henderson's version seems fairly near to the norm of this varied assortment, and as such is adopted here.

The 'give them the bayonet' story also has other versions: the one in the text is Henderson's. J. D. McCabe's, p. 40, is more dramatic. 'Riding up to General Jackson who sat on his horse calm and unmoved though severely wounded in the hand, General Bee exclaimed in a voice of anguish : "General they are beating us back!" General Jackson glanced around him for a moment. His large eyes flashed and his features shone with a glorious light. Turning to General Bee, he said calmly : "Sir, we'll give them the bayonet." Then placing himself at the head of his brigade, he thundered, "Forward!"'

In an article in the *Southern Bivouac*, entitled *Use the Bayonet, Colonel*, Thomas M. Boyd writes : 'He was extremely pale, but his eyes glared with an unnatural brilliancy. It was on that occasion that Col. Baylor of Augusta County rode hurriedly up to him and said, "General, my men are armed with the old flint lock musket, and not half of them will fire." He replied, "If you will examine it, you will find that the old musket has the best bayonet in the world. Use the bayonet, Colonel."' I have seen the statement that General Bee said to him, 'General, they are beating us back', and Jackson's reply was, 'We will give them the bayonet, sir.' (Another version adds 'I'm tired of this long range work').[3] This may be true but it is probable that the remark made to Col Baylor was afterwards claimed to have been made to General Bee.

---

[1] Johnston: Note 202, 203.   [2] *Charleston Mercury*, 25 July 1861.
[3] Douglas, p. 21.

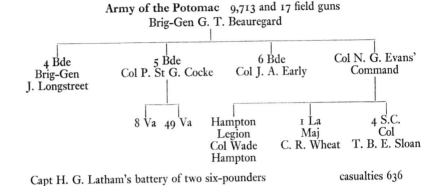

Army of the Potomac 9,713 and 17 field guns
Brig-Gen G. T. Beauregard

| 4 Bde Brig-Gen J. Longstreet | 5 Bde Col P. St G. Cocke | 6 Bde Col J. A. Early | Col N. G. Evans' Command |

8 Va 49 Va   Hampton Legion Col Wade Hampton   1 La Maj C. R. Wheat   4 S.C. Col T. B. E. Sloan

Capt H. G. Latham's battery of two six-pounders   casualties 636

Maj-Gen T. H. Holmes' Force 1,250

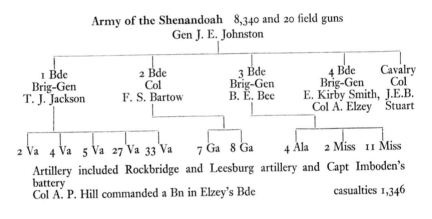

Army of the Shenandoah 8,340 and 20 field guns
Gen J. E. Johnston

| 1 Bde Brig-Gen T. J. Jackson | 2 Bde Col F. S. Bartow | 3 Bde Brig-Gen B. E. Bee | 4 Bde Brig-Gen E. Kirby Smith, Col A. Elzey | Cavalry Col J.E.B. Stuart |

2 Va 4 Va 5 Va 27 Va 33 Va   7 Ga 8 Ga   4 Ala 2 Miss 11 Miss

Artillery included Rockbridge and Leesburg artillery and Capt Imboden's battery
Col A. P. Hill commanded a Bn in Elzey's Bde   casualties 1,346

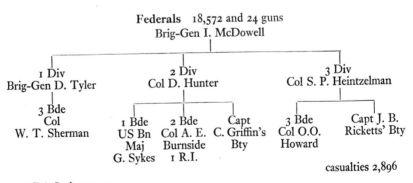

Federals 18,572 and 24 guns
Brig-Gen I. McDowell

| 1 Div Brig-Gen D. Tyler | 2 Div Col D. Hunter | 3 Div Col S. P. Heintzelman |

3 Bde Col W. T. Sherman

1 Bde US Bn Maj G. Sykes   2 Bde Col A. E. Burnside 1 R.I.   Capt C. Griffin's Bty   3 Bde Col O.O. Howard   Capt J. B. Ricketts' Bty

casualties 2,896

[1] B & L, i, 194, 195.

30

Early Life

'No one could have had any reason before the war of 1861 to predict for him the glorious career which opened to him then', Jackson's brother-in-law, Professor C. D. Fishburne is reported as having said. [1] Fishburne married Julia Junkin, sister of Eleanor Junkin, Jackson's first wife; but he first met Jackson at J. B. Lyle's bookshop in Lexington when Jackson was a professor at the Virginia Military Institute. He did not know much about Jackson's boyhood, or his West Point career, or his exploits in the Mexican War; and, in fact, contrary to Fishburne's belief as expressed above, Jackson's early life had shown promise of future greatness.

CHILDHOOD

Thomas Jackson was born at Clarksburg, Harrison County, Virginia, now West Virginia, on 21 January 1824. Both his parents died young, and after staying with his grandmother until her death, Jackson and his surviving brothers and sister lived with various relatives. From the age of seven until he went to West Point Jackson lived with his well-to-do bachelor uncle, Cummings Jackson at his farm and mill in Lewis County, West Virginia. 'Cummings Jackson', in Jackson's own hand with the second 'm' added as an afterthought, appears as his parent or guardian, and Weston P.O., Lewis, Virginia, as his place of residence, on the Descriptive List [2] of new cadets for the year 1842 at West Point.

[1] *Fishburne Papers.*   [2] *West Point Records.*

In his early 'teens' he took part with his elder brother Warren in a strange escapade. In an unsuccessful quest for fortune they travelled as far as the south-west corner of Kentucky, where they remained for a winter and spring.

At the age of 17 Jackson, through the influence of his uncle, was appointed to the office of constable of Freeman's Creek District of Lewis County. The ledger in which he recorded his judgments and fee bills is now in the manuscripts section of the Alderman Library of the University of Virginia, Charlottesville. The six by eight inch ledger contains a hundred pages. It gives the transactions of the constable, and is a record of the debts and interest Jackson collected and turned over to another county official. His duties as constable do not appear to have been very important, but the fact that he carried them out satisfactorily for two years shows that he had great determination even at an early age. Although he appears to have been an energetic constable—once even leading a horse through a doorway to force its owner to dismount so as to levy the horse against the adjudged debt—he left several uncollected judgments for his successor when he joined West Point on 20 June 1862—then being aged 19 years and 5 months, according to the Descriptive List of new cadets for the year 1842 already mentioned.

WEST POINT

Uncle Cummings was a good guardian to Thomas Jackson, and in his home 'Thomas received all the privileges of a son of the family'.[1] An able and kind man, he brought up Jackson to be trustworthy and reliable. But that was not all. He gave his nephew the best education of its kind open to the youth of America. In the period in which Jackson was a constable, a vacancy occurred at The United States Military Academy at West Point for a cadetship from his District. Through Uncle Cummings' intimate friend the Hon Samuel Hayes, Member of Congress for the said District, Jackson was appointed in 1842 to fill the vacancy. Then by sheer determination in the very short time available, although lacking formal schooling, he passed the preliminary examination for admission to the academy.

West Point suited Jackson. Although he found the work there very difficult, the combination of formal academic studies with military training and severe discipline fitted his philosophy of life. He firmly 'believed in system, method and discipline in every phase of life'[2] and was intensely ambitious. This made him weigh, as it were, the possibilities of every hour, and give to his

[1] Arnold, p. 55.   [2] Arnold, 14.

work all his intelligence and effort. Just as later he evolved military maxims, at West Point he kept a book in which he penned moral and ethical axioms. One of the soundest was : 'You may be whatever you resolve to be.' This he certainly lived up to. Surrounded by cadets who had much more education, and hampered by being slow to learn, he got through his first year at West Point by sheer force of will. Rigid study rules brought about his success, and his study habits became a West Point legend.[1] Everyone knew that *The General* (his first nickname) almost never went to bed. At first he 'would pile his grate high with anthracite coal',[2] stretch out on the floor and study long into the night. But this posture revived an old stomach complaint, and later he took to sitting bolt upright while reading, as this put less strain on his alimentary system. The posture became an ingrained habit which he retained all his life ; and the people of Lexington, when he was a professor at the VMI, spoke of him sitting in just the same way, and thinking him eccentric because of it.

Among the cadets of his class, or with him at West Point, were many who became famous in the American Civil War, fighting on his side or against him. McClellan, Pickett, A. P. Hill and Stoneham were of his class ; Grant, Longstreet and Bee in others. Jackson's relentless studiousness made him aloof and gruff at West Point ; but he was not unpopular there.

With a rigid attention to every detail, a complete list is kept at West Point of all merits and demerits, good marks and delinquencies, of every cadet for every day of every term. I have before me the list of Thomas J. Jackson's Delinquencies for his four years at West Point. There are 32 of them—very few indeed by West Point standards. To give a random sample : 9 July 1842, Late at morning parade ; 4 August 1842, Inattention at morning drill ; 21 August 1842, Coat torn at camp inspection ; 18 July 1843, Shoes not properly blacked at inspection ; 24 August 1843, Firing before command ; 4 June 1844, Bedding not properly arranged ; and strange indeed for Jackson of all people, 24 May 1845, Late for church (with a further note—excused by superintendent).

The steady upward progress which characterised his academic life may be summarised as follows : in the order of merit he rose from 51st out of 83[3] in his first year to 30th in his second, then to 20th in his third year, and finally to 17th in his last year, indicating 'an abundance of energy, industry, application and ambition',[4] the last being one of his most striking characteristics. 'It was a frequent remark among his brother cadets that if the course had been a year longer he would have come out first' ;[5] but in any case his high standing

[1] Vandiver, 16. [2] Maury, 23. [3] See following note.

[4] Arnold, 75. [5] Henderson, i, 16.

33

in the class list earned him his own choice of arm. 'Brevet Second Lieutenant Thomas Jonathan Jackson requested assignment in the artillery—an honoured and active arm which had also been Napoleon's choice.'[1]

Note[2]

CADET RECORD OF THOMAS JONATHAN JACKSON

The 'West Point Hotel Register' shows that a T. J. Jackson registered at the hotel around noon Sunday, 19 June 1842; he stayed in room 48 located in the 'Attick'. The next day Cadet Candidate Thomas J. Jackson reported to the Adjutant's Office and signed his name in the 'Descriptive List of New Cadets for the year 1842.' The Cadet Candidates were examined for admission on 23, 24 and 25 June. At 3.0 p.m. Saturday 25 June, the Academic Board announced the names of the Cadet Candidates found qualified for admission as Cadets of the United States Military Academy. Thomas J. Jackson's name was last on the list.

Thomas Jonathan Jackson was admitted to the United States Military Academy as a Cadet, 1 July 1842, aged 19 years and 5 months. His legal residence on date of admission was Weston Post Office, Lewis County, Virginia. Cummings E. Jackson of Weston Post Office, Virginia was his parent or guardian.

During his Cadet career, Thomas J. Jackson raised his over-all class standing from number 51 in a class of 83 members during his Fourth Class Year to number 17 in a class of 59[3] members in June of his First Class Year. Cadet Jackson was graduated and commissioned a Brevet 2nd Lieutenant in the 1st Artillery 1 July 1846.

Cadet Jackson arrived at the Military Academy with a very meagre academic background. However, he marshalled all his talents and waged a war with academics, winning top quarter standings in Third Class Year Mathematics; Second Class Year Philosophy; and First Class Year Ethics, Artillery, Mineralogy and Geology and Engineering. His standing in Conduct over the four year period was excellent. During his Second Class Year, Cadet Jackson received no demerits and was rated number 1 in the United States Corps of Cadets in conduct for that year. Militarily, Cadet Jackson served as a Sergeant, Company 'D.' United States Corps of Cadets during his Second Class Year.

[1] Vandiver, 18.   [2] *West Point Records.*
[3] The numbers in the class diminished as members fell out.

In the history of the Military Academy, Thomas J. Jackson is one of the Cadets who so remarkably raised his academic standings from one of an average student to a place in the top third of his class. More remarkable was the constancy of the struggle he waged against academics. His record at the Academy mirrors the fighting character, devotion to duty and the will to succeed of the man.

MEXICAN WAR

After West Point Jackson saw service in the Mexican War. General Zachary Taylor had advanced on Mexico from the north over the Rio Grande; but progress was slow, and instead of continuing the drive there in more strength, an amphibious expedition under General Winfield Scott was planned to land near Vera Cruz on the east coast of Mexico, and march up the National Road on the capital, Mexico City. Jackson, posted to the First Artillery, joined this expedition; and with the First Artillery acting as infantry, took part in the storming of Vera Cruz. The American forces marching inland were then forced to fight a series of actions against Mexicans in defence positions on mountain barriers across the National Road. At one of these, the Cerro Gordo, General Scott carried out a model operation to clear the way. First, Captain Robert Lee[1] scouted round the Mexican left flank and discovered a route by which the Mexican position could be turned. Then a flanking column swung round by it and cut the National Road, while a frontal attack kept the Mexican defenders occupied.

Although Jackson did not take an active part in the battle, he learnt several lessons from watching its progress. General Scott made full use of his engineers[2] to find out all they could about the Mexican position and plot the flanking route round it. Next, Scott carried through a successful surprise flank attack—the Mexican General Santa Anna is reported as saying that 'he had not believed a goat could approach his lines' that way.[3] Finally, although hampered by a shortage of cavalry, he followed up with a quick and vigorous pursuit. Scout, flank, pursue—here was a formula to become familiar as Jackson's own trademark in the future.[4] He also learnt the limitations of volunteers. The United States Army was a very small one. Even in this

---

[1] Later Commander-in-chief of the Confederate Forces in Virginia.
[2] Used for reconnaissance. [3] Henderson, i, 31.
[4] Vandiver, 29.

restricted operation in Mexico, General Scott had to rely on a proportion of volunteers. Some of these were enlisted only for three months, and had to be sent home in the middle of the campaign—a feature to be repeated in the early days of the American Civil War. Also, they did not show up well in action. At Cerro Gordo, for example, 'the volunteers, badly disciplined, soon got into complete confusion' . . . 'the First Tennessee Regiment had seen service at Monterey and was fairly disciplined; but the other troops of the brigade were eminently raw, and the check which had been received shook the nerves of many so that a large number fled from the colours.'[1]

Major Magruder of the First Artillery captured four guns at Cerro Gordo, and General Scott presented them to him in recognition of his gallantry.[2] Jackson, eager to return to his own arm, volunteered to serve with Magruder when he reverted to artillery. This turned out to be a fortunate move. Approaching Mexico City from the south-west, having skirted the great lakes of Chalco and Yochisilco, the Americans were held up at the fortress of Chapultepec on the outskirts of the capital. In the storming of the fortress on its high hill, Jackson played a distinguished part. In a force on the left under Colonel William Trousdale he was in independent command of two of Magruder's guns. 'The position to which Trousdale advanced was exposed to fire from the castle causing serious annoyance. Believing he saw reinforcements entering the castle, he determined to advance. Lieutenant Jackson was ordered to move forward with the guns, and a part of the 14th regiment to follow in support. Before the pieces were unlimbered, a heavy fire of cannon and musketry was opened from the barricades, besides that from the castle above. Under it, the horses of the pieces were nearly all killed and disabled, the drivers and cannoneers much cut up, and the supporting force instantly checked. The soldiers found some shelter and held their ground (other authorities say that except for a doughty sergeant they ran away); and, with great exertion, Jackson got one of his pieces from under the direct fire, and opened in reply to the enemy. With this the point was held until the castle was carried, and the Mexicans around the barricades commenced the retreat.'[3]

Jackson's share in the glory of the victories in the Mexican War was considerable. Highly praised by Magruder and General Scott, within 18 months from joining his regiment he was breveted major. Such promotion was phenomenal even in the Mexican War, and none of his West Point comrades made so great a stride in rank.[4]

[1] Ripley, ii, 73   [2] Henderson, i, 32.   [3] Ripley, i, 429.
[4] Henderson, i, 47.

VMI

The glory of Mexico was followed by some of the least successful years of Jackson's life. Worse even than the ten years which followed at Lexington, they showed the hypochrondriac, cantankerous and litigious side of his character, and provided, as far as the last aspect, a foretaste of his habit of preferring charges against his comrades in arms.

During his service at Fort Hamilton on Long Island, he devoted his time profitably: getting to know New York and some of its citizens, studying Napoleon's campaigns and other histories, playing a part on courts martial at his station and at Carlisle Barracks, Pennsylvania, commanding his company when Captain Frank Taylor his superior was away, and serving as commissary and quarter-master. But unfortunately that was not all. What concerned him most was his health; and this in its turn produced almost a religious mania. The cause of his discomfort is obscure; but the ailment was probably some sort of circulatory or stomach complaint. Consultations with a series of doctors, including one of the first medical men of New York City,[1] brought no relief, and Jackson resorted to his own cure. This consisted in a rigid schedule of diet and exercises which did bring some improvement in his condition. But much more significantly, he came to believe that the betterment in his health was the result of Divine Ordinance; and he began to link his illness with Divine Providence until, in time, the two subjects became inseparable.

Although not religious in his youth, and not sure whether he had ever been baptised, he had come under the influence of the devout Captain Frank Taylor in Mexico, and after the end of hostilities had studied seriously the tenets of the Roman Catholic Church.[2]

At Fort Hamilton the sacrament of baptism was administered to him on Sunday, 29 April 1849 at St John's Episcopal Church, and from then on there was an almost mystical identification in his mind between God and his own physical condition.[3] 'My afflictions' he wrote to his sister Laura,[4] 'I believe were decreed by Heaven's Sovereign as a punishment for my offences against his *Holy Laws*; and have probably been the instrument of turning me from the path of eternal death, to that of everlasting life.' His illness was such as to cause him to behave very strangely to get relief from it. At West Point he had sat rigidly to allow his alimentary ducts to function freely. Now he adopted,

[1] Letter to sister Laura, Arnold, 150.
[2] He eventually turned to the Protestant Church.   [3] Vandiver, 52.
[4] Letter dated Fort Hamilton, 8 March 1850, in T. J. Jackson papers, VMI.

in addition, stranger habits still. Maury, who was a fellow cadet at West Point, when back there as an instructor writes:

One day while at West Point we were surprised by a visit from young Major Stonewall Jackson, who had been serving since the war with an artillery company on duty in New York harbour. At that time he was convinced that one of his legs was bigger than the other, and that one of his arms was likewise unduly heavy. He had acquired the habit of raising the heavy arm straight up so that, as he said, the blood would run back into his body and lighten it. I believe he never after relinquished this peculiar practice, even upon the battlefield—(he was wounded in the hand when holding it up like this at Bull Run). He told us he had procured a year's furlough to try a professorship which had been offered him at the Virginia Military Institute. He remained there until the outbreak of the war between the States brought him before the world as the great Christian soldier of his time. His was the most remarkable character I have ever known. Cold and impassive of aspect, he was tenderly affectionate and full of fire. Filled with conscientious scruples, he was at times cruelly unjust. His arrests of Hill, Winder, and General Richard Garnett, three of the noblest officers in our service, were inexcusable, especially that of Garnett, whom he arrested for not charging Shields' victorious army with the bayonet when his ammunition failed. [1]

Jackson also believed that one side of his body did not perspire and was less well nourished than the other, and he would spend long hours rubbing it. Certainly his odd habits seemed to have provided a reasonable cause for some people to have considered him a bit 'touched'.

From New York he was posted to Florida, where a number of Seminole Indians were eluding deportation to Indian Territory and making the lives of the Florida settlers hazardous. He joined a company of the First Artillery commanded by Brevet-Major French, senior but of the same rank as himself; and this was to cause trouble between them. Jackson carried out his duties as a commissary and quartermaster efficiently; but he wished to assume greater responsibilities than French would allow. The first quarrel developed over whether Jackson was to have sole charge of constructing the new public buildings on the post. French won this round. When the matter was referred to the general commanding the troops in Florida, Jackson received a reprimand, being told that French, as commander of the post, was responsible for everything done there. The second dispute was more serious. There were rumours that French was having an affair with the nurse of his children. Jackson considered it his duty to investigate the rumour and, if necessary, bring the facts to the attention of higher authority. He interviewed a number of enlisted men about it, and they in their turn, through their sergeant, reported what Jackson had done. French now put Jackson under arrest, and

[1] Maury, 71, 72; also p. 219 of this book.

all Fort Meade and Florida became involved in an unwholesome quarrel. This time matters went against French who was considered to have shown himself incapable of commanding his post satisfactorily. French was transferred to Fort Myers, and all should have been well; but more changes were in the wind. Jackson was offered the position of Professor of Natural and Experimental Philosophy and Artillery Tactics at the Virginia Military Institute at Lexington. In March 1851 he was appointed to that post.

The cadets of the Virginia Military Institute, although they wore uniform, were taught by officers of the regular army, were disciplined as soldiers, and spent some of their time in camp, were not then usually destined for a military career.[1] Still, in all essential respects the VMI was little behind West Point. The discipline was strict and the drill precise. The cadets had their own officers and sergeants, and the whole establishment was administered on a military footing.[2]

Jackson's duties there were peculiar. As Professor of Artillery he was responsible for little more than the drill of the cadets and their instruction in the theory of gunnery. But as Professor of Natural and Experimental Philosophy: optics, mechanics and astronomy were his allotted subjects; and he was strangely out of place in expounding their dry formulas.

In fact, he had little success in either of his main professorial activities; and the tales that are told of this period make him out as a figure of fun.

In the *History of the VMI, 1839–65*, Jennings Wise relates: 'Jackson did not make a very favourable impression on the cadets, and he was the recipient of a thousand jests upon his peculiarities of mind and demeanour . . . he was frequently occupied rubbing one side of himself under the impression (confided to a select few) that one side of his body was not as well nourished as the other and was wasting away.'

There is also a story which illustrates his trials at the hands of the cadets as professor of artillery. 'The battery used in drilling was managed by dragropes which the plebs wagon class manhandled. Sometimes a linchpin would be secretly abstracted, and then the piece or caisson would break down in the middle of the drill. A more mirth-provoking device even than this, however, was hit upon. A small bell was adroitly suspended inside the limber-box, and the conspirators demurely took their places at the drag-ropes. The commander of the battery gave the order "Forward" and the piece began to

---

[1] Now (1966) about 25 per cent of the cadets join the regular armed services. In the Second World War, 1939–45, two distinguished alumni were: Generals George C. Marshall and George S. Patton. In the American Civil War 1861–65 many VMI cadets became officers in the CS Army.

[2] Henderson, i, 57.

move. Suddenly a mysterious tinkling was heard, and the cadets burst out laughing. The professor looked astonished, halted the battery, and with great earnestness instituted an enquiry into the phenomenon. It was in vain; nothing was discovered, and the order was given for the piece to move forward with the same result. This was not greatly enjoyed by Professor Jackson!'

Dr J. William Jones, formerly Chaplain of the Army of Northern Virginia, in his Recollections on Major Jackson at the VMI writes: 'I used to hear the cadets of the Virginia Military Institute speak of a quiet, eccentric, but hard-working professor, whom they called "Old Jack", or "Fool Tom Jackson", and upon whom they delighted to play all sorts of pranks. Stories of his eccentricities were rife—such as wearing a thick uniform in the sweltering heat of summer because he had "received no orders to change it", or of his pacing up and down in front of the superintendent's office in a pelting hail storm because he would not deliver his report one minute before the appointed time.' [1]

In the classroom it was the same; and Jackson had to use all his disciplinary powers to maintain order there. The professor's tasks were heavy. He taught the second-class, Optics and Analytical Mechanics, and the first-class, Optics, Acoustics and Astronomy. Almost wholly ignorant of these subjects, Jackson had to spend long hours preparing for his classes. Most of the cadets displayed a healthy dislike for these abstract sciences and soon spotted that Jackson knew little more about them than they did. They disliked subject and poor teaching equally, and despite his severity—he seldom let a misdemeanour pass—ragged him unmercifully.

Letters and textbooks of the period bear witness to this. 'I find the studies this year a great deal more interesting (except for) Optics which (is) so very difficult and taught by such a hell of a fool, whose name is Jackson;' [2] and scrawled across a text book now in the VMI Museum, 'Major T. J. Jackson is crazy as damnation to-day (God-damn him) and the old scoundrel marked me accordingly. Oho, how I hope that he may sink in Hell-flames before January.'

Complaints about his bad teaching reached the VMI Alumni Society (Old Boys' Society) who brought the matter before the authorities; but Superintendent Smith supported Jackson, and nothing came of it except the provision of some new equipment to try to make his instruction more realistic.

[1] *Richmond Times*, July 19, 21, 22, 1891.
[2] Letter of C. M. Barton of VMI, 28 September, 1865.

The death of his first wife, daughter of the Rev Dr Junkin, President of Washington College, Lexington, after they had been married only 14 months; his reception into the Presbyterian Church at Lexington; a five months tour of Europe; his marriage to Miss Anna Morrison, daughter of a North Carolina clergyman: such were the landmarks of his life at Lexington during his ten years at the VMI.

Outside the Institute his life was somewhat happier. Admitted a member of the local Presbyterian Church, he became a devout and tireless deacon and ran a successful Sunday School for negroes. By this time his Church and Faith dominated every action, and proved a rock on which he could lean during the sad periods of the deaths of his first wife and of the young child of his second wife.

In society he was shy and silent and anything but a convivial companion. He never smoked, he was a strict teetotaller, and he never touched a card. His diet, for reasons of health, was of the most sparing kind, and for many years he abstained from both tea and coffee. He drew the line at dancing, and musical parties became the limit of his dissipation. His observance of the Sabbath was well nigh complete. He took the Bible as his guide, and his rigid literal interpretations of its precepts caused him to be regarded by some as having religious mania.

Yet among his few friends and in his own family circle, he was known as a sensible, pleasant companion, fond of children, kind to those in need, and loved by his negro servants. His nephew Tom Arnold, who stayed at the Jackson home for nine months when he was 12 years old, wrote:

Major Jackson took part in the usual conversation in the home, as much as any one ordinarily would. When there was company, which was not infrequent, he talked freely, and was entertaining in conversation, and seemed perfectly at ease. I do not recall a single circumstance during my residence there, or in fact at any other time, that could be termed eccentric on his part. I do not think he was so.[1]

The limitations of his knowledge of the subjects which he had to teach at the VMI, combined with another symptom of ill health, in this case weakness of the eyes, caused him to adopt strange daily habits, which, in Henderson's view had a bearing on his future success as a general. He rose at six for private prayer, and had a cold bath. Household prayers followed by breakfast came at seven; and he was off to the VMI for his classes at eight. Returning at eleven, he spent the rest of the morning preparing his lessons, standing erect at a high desk in his study. In the evening, as in his opinion his

[1] Vandiver, p. 123.

eyes were too weak to work with artificial light, he carried out an hour's meditation, studying without books, and going over his prepared lessons of the morning in his mind. To do this, at the time of his first wife Eleanor (Junkin), he would go to the study, shade the light, and sit bolt upright in a chair facing the wall. In the time of Anna (Morrison) his second wife, he still continued the practice, but as she did not like being left alone, and never interrupted his nightly meditation, he took to doing his studies facing the wall in the sitting-room. Henderson considers that a good general should possess strategic insight, tactical skill, administrative ability, and personal leadership qualities in battle of a high order. Jackson proved that he possessed the last during his service in Mexico. He showed tactical skill at First Manassas, and displayed administrative ability after the battle, while camping near Centreville. But Henderson also suggests that the strategic insight that Jackson showed in the Valley campaign, mystifying and misleading the enemy by carefully planned manoeuvres, stemmed from the academic theoretical training that he gave himself while preparing his lessons mentally each night when he was at the VMI. He may have been a bad teacher of cadets; but the prodigious mental effort which he put into memorising his lectures during his strange nightly meditations so disciplined his thought processes that he was able to adopt similar methods to prepare his long-range plans as a general in the field.

Falling Waters

The Civil War really began long before the shelling of Fort Sumter in Charleston Harbour by the Confederates under General Beauregard on 12 April 1861. The negro was the main point at issue. The economy of the South depended on him; while the institution of slavery was abhorrent to many people in the North where his labour was unnecessary. The trouble began slowly with a war of words and legal actions. Then violence broke out. Abolitionist settlements were sacked and burned in Kansas, and, for the other side, John Brown tried to seize the arsenal at Harper's Ferry to equip slaves for an armed rising against their Southern masters.

When Lincoln became President on 6 November 1860, matters took a turn for the worse. The feeling in the South was that abolitionists would now control the country. On 20 December 1860 South Carolina seceded from the Union, and other states followed their lead, including Jackson's state Virginia on 17 April 1861.

Jackson played a part in the story of John Brown before the war; and in seizing United States' Government property at Harper's Ferry on behalf of seceding Virginia, after the war had begun.

The Government of Virginia thought it necessary to muster as many troops as possible for the hanging of John Brown; and a body of the VMI cadets, including an artillery detachment under Major Jackson, was ordered to Charles Town near Harper's Ferry. [1] Jackson described the hanging most graphically to Anna his wife, something like this:

[1] The story of the hanging of John Brown is very well told in the Prologue of Burke Davis' book *They Called Him Stonewall*, New York, 1961.

John Brown was hung to-day. He behaved with unflinching firmness. The arrangements were well made and well executed under the direction of Colonel Smith. The gibbet was erected in a large field, south-east of the town. Brown rode on the head of his coffin from the prison to the place of execution. The coffin was of black walnut, enclosed in a box of poplar of the same shape as the coffin. He was dressed in a black frock-coat, black pantaloons, black waistcoat, black slouch hat, white socks, and slippers of predominating red. The open wagon in which he rode was strongly guarded on all sides. The gaoler, the high-sheriff, and several others rode in the same wagon with the prisoner. Brown had his arms tied behind him, and ascended the scaffold with apparent cheerfulness. After reaching the top of the platform, he shook hands with several who were standing around him. The sheriff placed the rope round his neck, then threw a white cap over his head, and asked if he wished to be told when everything was ready. He replied that it made no difference, provided he was not kept waiting too long. In this condition he stood for about ten minutes on the trap-door, which was supported on one side by hinges and on the other side by a rope. Colonel Smith then announced to the sheriff 'all ready', which apparently was not comprehended by him, and the colonel had to repeat the order. Then the rope was cut by a single blow, and Brown dropped several inches, his knees falling to the level occupied by his feet before the rope was cut. With the fall, his arms below the elbows flew up horizontally, his hands clenched; but soon his arms gradually fell by spasmodic motions. There was very little motion for several moments; then the wind started to blow his lifeless body too and fro.

Characteristically, Jackson offered up a prayer for his salvation; but Brown had refused the services of a minister and Jackson feared he was unprepared to meet his Maker. The cadets were determined to show they were not affected by the grim ceremony, and made rude jokes to each other about their eccentric leader; but even they had to admit that he had a martial air sitting on his horse in front of them.

John Brown had died, but his memory lingers on, for, as the words of the song still tell us:

> *John Brown's body lies a-mouldering in the grave;*
> *John Brown's body lies a-mouldering in the grave;*
> *John Brown's body lies a-mouldering in the grave;*
> *But his soul goes marching on.*

Nevertheless, the whole incident is probably a great deal less important than this perpetual memory suggests.

When war was declared, Jackson was despatched from Lexington on another mission; and this time he was not to return again until he was brought back to be buried in the cemetery there. The most important military training camp was in the western suburbs of Richmond; the Southern Government thought that the senior cadets of the VMI would make

suitable drill sergeants for the rush of volunteers assembling in the capital; and Jackson was given the task of conducting them there by rail.

During Jackson's stay in Richmond he tried to get an appointment for himself in the army, and was first offered one in the engineer department with the rank of major. 'For placing a battery or a line of battle, indeed, his judgment was almost infallible', writes Dabney;[1] 'but he was no draughtsman, and to set him to the drudgery of compiling maps, was a sacrifice of his reputation and of his high capacities for command.' Fortunately, at this time, friends in Virginia, including Governor Letcher, made recommendations to the Convention appointing officers into the Confederate army to make him the commander of the Virginia force at Harper's Ferry. When the recommendation was sent to the Convention for their approval, someone asked, 'Who is this Major Jackson that we are asked to commit to him so responsible a post?' 'He is one', replied the member for Rockbridge where Lexington lies, 'who, if you order him to hold a post, will never leave it alive to be occupied by the enemy.'[2]

On 27 April 1861, the Convention handed Jackson his commission as Colonel in the Confederate army, and he departed at once for Harper's Ferry. Harper's Ferry had been evacuated by the Federal forces, and was thus open to occupation by the Confederates. It is a village on a tongue of land on the west bank of the Shenandoah river just where it joins the Potomac. It was used by the Federal Government for the manufacture and storage of firearms; and the place had a number of factories where muskets were made, as well as several arsenals in which to store them. At the western, wider end of the triangle of land on which Harper's Ferry lies, stands the Bolivar Heights. East of the Shenandoah is more high ground consisting of the Loudoun Heights which are part of the Blue Ridge. North of Harper's Ferry, across the Potomac, are the Maryland Heights, rising to about the same height as the others and commanding the valley of the Potomac from the North.

Harper's Ferry, although difficult to defend, was a focal point of rivers and roads. The railway from Washington to the West also passed through it, as well as the Chesapeake and Ohio canal; and a branch line diverged from it to Winchester. Hence the Confederate Government considered it a valuable place to occupy as an advanced post, as well as for the supply of arms that might be had from it.

The Virginia Militia were assembled to capture the place. Unfortunately, they arrived almost too late; when they entered the village, the storehouses containing the arms were wrapped in flames. Most of the muskets, however,

---

[1] Dabney, i, 215.   [2] *Ibid*, 215.

had already been stolen and hidden by the inhabitants; and many of these were discovered and gathered in. The machinery for making arms in several of the factories was also unharmed.

Meanwhile, a large number of volunteers had poured into Harper's Ferry. General Lee ordered Jackson to arm, organise and drill them; and this was Jackson's first task in the Valley. He proved himself a good commander and organiser; and with the help of two colleagues from the VMI 'speedily reduced the crude rabble to order and consistency'.

To secure the defence of his station Jackson seized the dominating Maryland Heights; and he showed himself a good engineer by constructing personally the block-houses for the outlying pickets he left there.

Even at this stage he was reticent concerning military affairs, and disliked to be questioned about them. For example, when asked how many troops he had, he was said to have replied: 'I should be glad if Lincoln thought I had fifteen thousand.'[1]

On 23 May 1861, however, Major-General J. E. Johnston was appointed to command in the Valley, and Jackson's first short period of command ended. When Johnston arrived at Harper's Ferry, Jackson showed the rigidity of mind concerning orders and regulations for which he later became renowned. Jackson had received no directions from the Virginian Government to hand over his command, and refused to do so. Only when a personal letter came from Lee endorsing Johnston's claim did Jackson agree to transfer his powers.

Johnston now made Jackson commander of the brigade of Virginian regiments which later became so famous as *The Stonewall Brigade*. This consisted of the 4th, 5th, 27th and a little later the 33rd Virginia, with the Rockbridge Artillery under the Rev Dr W. N. Pendleton,[2] father of young Sandy Pendleton who became one of Jackson's staff officers. Other officers who joined his staff at this time included Dr Hunter McGuire, medical director, Major William Hawks, chief commissary, and Major John Harman, quartermaster. The last was said to understand the management of wagons as well as Jackson did that of soldiers.

The Federal commander, General Patterson, now approached Harper's Ferry from the north, while another army threatened to do the same from Romney in the Mountain Department; and Johnston decided that the village was too difficult to defend, and a better defensive position could be found further south around Winchester. With this in mind, he evacuated Harper's

[1] Dabney, i, 224 . . . he had 4,500.
[2] Captain the Rev Dr William N. Pendleton was rector of the Episcopal Church in Lexington, having previously been through West Point.

Ferry and withdrew towards Winchester; but he ordered Jackson to move against the enemy, who were now between Martinsburg and Williamsport, to try and delay their advance.

Jackson was delighted to move forward instead of retreating; and equally disappointed when a counter-order brought him back to Winchester without firing a shot.

About this time, Colonel A. P. Hill, a familiar figure in operations with Jackson to come, appeared on the scene and was sent towards Romney with a detachment of Confederate troops. In that area Hill did good work destroying bridges and driving back the Federals, and in conjunction with Hill's expedition Jackson was ordered forward again to Martinsburg where he succeeded in destroying a number of Federal locomotives and wagons in the railway yards. Afterwards, Jackson remained with his brigade a little north of Martinsburg, with the cavalry under the later famous Colonel Jeb Stuart out to his front.

Then, on 2 July 1861, came Jackson's first contact with the enemy. He had been told to observe the Federals, and if they advanced in full force, to retire on the main body behind him. Near Falling Waters Church his 5th Virginia, a few cavalry and Pendleton's battery brushed with them. Jackson's men got the better of the first engagement, and of a second one which immediately followed. Then, the Federals developed a double turning movement against Jackson's force which was posted in the buildings and barns of Haine's Farm. Here, with 380 men and one gun, he repulsed attacks by nearly ten times as many Federals, and held his position for three hours. During this engagement, in which Jackson's force inflicted fairly heavy casualties, Stuart's cavalry captured 45 prisoners. Jackson's loss was only two men killed and ten wounded. He was probably the only man among the infantry who had ever been under fire; but he declared that 'both officers and men behaved beautifully'.

After this neither Johnston nor Patterson made any move. Patterson, in fact, was now preparing merely to hold Johnston's force in the Valley while General McDowell attacked General Beauregard in the neighbourhood of Manassas—the scene of the Battle of First Manassas, or First Bull Run as the Federals call it—the battle which has already been described in the prologue of this book. To this battle on 21 July 1861, Jackson proceeded as a brigadier-general, a promotion awarded on the recommendation of General Johnston immediately after the affair of Haine's Farm; after it, as a major-general, he moved back to the Valley to conduct the operations which brought him his greatest fame.

The Valley

ROMNEY

It has been said that brilliant as were the achievements of Jackson during the succeeding months of his too brief career, it was the Valley campaign which first lifted him into great fame; nor do any of his subsequent deeds show more strikingly the characteristics of his genius. [1]

The nucleus of Jackson's command in the Shenandoah Valley in November 1816 consisted of some regiments of militia, the greater part armed with flintlock muskets, [2] and a few squadrons of irregular cavalry. Jackson wanted to enter western Virginia, advancing from the north-east up the tributaries of the Potomac, to try to cut the Federal communications between the West and Washington, and to bring about the evacuation of west Virginia. To carry out this plan he asked for his old brigade, which had been left at Manassas, and the Confederate forces in the Alleghany Mountain District to be added to his command. This would have brought his force up to 16,000 men. The Secretary of War, J. P. Benjamin, contrary to General J. E. Johnston's wishes [3] (Jackson was still under Johnston), allotted the Stonewall Brigade to Jackson, as well as three brigades of Brigadier-General Loring from Huntersville; but he did not give him Brigadier-General Edward Johnson's mountain force. This was left west of Staunton to guard the back door into the Shenandoah Valley. Jackson thus had only 11,000 men, [4] not sufficient to carry out his original plan.

Jackson took prompt measures to equip and discipline his forces; and

[1] Allan, 216.
[2] Henderson, i, 171—Governor Letcher of Virginia soon replaced these with 1,550 percussion muskets, OR, v, 389.
[3] O.R., v, 940.   [4] Allan, 9.

8 *General Pope*

*He said unwisely when taken from the West to command the Federal Army
in the East: 'I have come to you from the West where we have always seen
the backs of our enemies'; and thus alienated many of his new command*

9 *General A. P. Hill*
In Jackson's class at West Point.
Placed under arrest by Jackson
on the march into Maryland

10 *General J. E. B. Stuart*
A splendid cavalry leader and an admirer of
Jackson. He presented Jackson with a new
uniform coat before the Battle of Fredericksburg

11 *General 'Fighting Joe' Hooker astride his horse*
He said before Chancellorsville: 'My plans are perfect. May God have mercy
on General Lee, for I will have none!' But he lost the battle

while waiting for Loring's troops, sent expeditions north from his head-quarters at Winchester to break the dams on the Chesapeake and Ohio Canal, which ran alongside the Potomac River, and, together with the Baltimore and Ohio Railway, formed a valuable means of communication by which coal, hay and forage reached Washington from the West. The railway was broken in several places between Harper's Ferry and Bath; but attempts on the canal were less successful. Nevertheless, breaches were made in the canal near Williamsport, which let out some of the water, and rendered stretches of the canal useless for a time.

After Jackson's return to Winchester from the canal-breaking expedition he found General Loring and his brigades awaiting him. General Loring was permitted by Jackson to remain in command of his own troops, and these were allowed to keep their title of the Army of the North West; but in spite of Loring's initial willingness to join Jackson, the two generals did not co-operate well. In fact the whole Romney campaign, which is about to be de-scribed in terms of the dispute between them, shows that Jackson was not basically a good leader or man-manager. His success in this field came only as a concomitant of winning battles and outwitting the enemy. Realising his supreme talent, his men gradually came to accept the trials and tribulations which they had to suffer while serving with him. Even at Romney the men of the Stonewall brigade, remembering Manassas and Jackson's farewell to them afterwards, were well on the way to such a state of mind. They had acquired the habit of cheering him whenever he appeared. Loring's men thought them as crazy as Jackson himself. [1]

The short spells at Winchester before and after the Romney expedition made up a happy period in Jackson's life. His second wife Anna was with him and they lodged with Dr Graham, the Presbyterian minister, at his manse, a short distance from Jackson's headquarters. Anna soon became part of the social life of Winchester. She loved the ladies who entertained her and who formed the circle of her friends. But above all she and her husband loved the Grahams, the Graham children, and the Graham home. 'We spent as happy a winter as ever falls to the lot of mortals on this earth,'[2] she was later to write. The Reverend Doctor Graham found his boarder the most devout and humble Christian he had ever met; and Jackson for his part seems to have had his already firm faith strengthened by such close contact with a kindred soul of his own Church. But after his time at Winchester the connection between his illness and his God was less in evidence. He was too busy to think much of his illness, and it was his victories which now became linked with Divine Providence. Due note of this is always found in his reports. For

[1] 23 S.H.S.P., 124.   [2] Mrs Jackson, 212, *Memoirs*.

example there is the typical despatch to General Cooper on the 9 May 1862:
'God blessed our arms with victory at M'Dowell yesterday.'

Although Christmas was approaching and the season was so far advanced that a mountain campaign would be attended with great difficulties, Jackson was anxious to make an effort to recover some of west Virginia from the Federals. His original plan had envisaged an attempt to reclaim and occupy all north-west Virginia, and even to move north-west and destroy the United States arsenal at Pittsburgh on the other side of the Alleghanies. With a force of only 11,000 he had to be content with less. A plan to attack the Federal force at Romney was thus put forward; and this was approved by the Confederate President Davis.

There were 22,000 men and 40 guns under General Rosecrans in the area. They were very dispersed, however, with detachments at Bath, Hancock, Moorefield, Franklin, Beverley and Cumberland, besides the 5,000 men under Kelley at Romney. To the north-east on the far side of the Potomac were 16,000 more men under Banks. These were around Frederick in winter quarters. On 1 January 1862, 9,000 Confederates under Jackson left Winchester and marched northwards towards the Potomac. Jackson wished, both to disperse the garrisons at Bath and Hancock and prevent support being sent to Romney, his main objective, and to cut the telegraph and break the rail connection between Banks and Frederick and Rosecrans' scattered detachments in the Alleghany valleys.

The weather was bright and pleasant at first, but soon underwent a sudden change, with a fierce storm of snow and hail. It was unusual, and some thought unwise, to conduct operations in winter, and Jackson was taking considerable risks in doing so. He took the chance; he was successful; but he nearly ended his military career in the process.

In order to conceal the march as far as possible from enemy observation, the troops used country roads; and, delayed by steep gradients and slippery surfaces, the supply wagons fell far behind. The troops, used to comfortable winter quarters, suffered accordingly; and that night had to huddle without food around their camp fires in conditions more miserable than those of the march. Loring left his troops to be settled in by his inspector-general in order to go back himself and see Jackson.[1] This led Jackson to make the charge against him that 'he failed to be with his command and see that it was properly encamped and cared for on the evening of the 1st of January, 1862, near Pughtown, Va.'[2] This charge seems to indicate that Jackson cared for the comfort of his men. But he did not hesitate to press them forward in

---

[1] O.R., v, 1070.   [2] O.R., v, 1065.

wintry conditions regardless of the consequences. Because of this, their spirits and their fighting qualities were speedily reduced. The third day out, the commander of the Stonewall Brigade took it upon himself to halt his wearied men. Riding along the column Jackson found his old regiments stationary by the roadside, and asked the reason for the delay. 'I have halted to let the men cook their rations,' was General Garnett's reply. 'There is no time for that.' 'But it is impossible for the men to march further without them.' 'I never found anything impossible with this brigade!'[1] replied Jackson and rode on.

A few miles short of Bath Federal scouts were encountered by an advanced guard made up of Loring's troops; but, according to Jackson in another charge preferred against Loring later, Loring neglected to give orders to 'attack and press forward with requisite promptness'.[2] An officer of Jackson's staff, however, got some of Loring's companies (Gilham's) moving, and these killed four of the enemy and took eight prisoners. With night coming on and a snowstorm brewing, orders were given to bivouac, and the assault on Bath was postponed until next morning. On Saturday, 4 January, Jackson made his dispositions to surround the town. The plans were sound enough. It was the execution of them that was at fault. Again Loring was the culprit. Jackson charged him that 'he did permit the head of his column, without sufficient cause, repeatedly to halt and lose so much time as to induce Maj. Gen. T. J. Jackson to order forward other troops of General Loring's command for the purpose of at least securing the town of Bath before night.'[3] In the attack on Bath, a detachment was sent over the mountain to the west to approach the town from the rear, and the main body pushed along the road, with regiments making smaller flanking thrusts on either side. It was not only Loring's fault that things proceeded slowly. All the troops made slow progress along the bad roads and over ground covered with ice, under their inexperienced leaders. They were too exhausted by the cold and suffering of the preceding night to move very fast. The result was that the day was nearly out before the Confederates entered the town, from which, after a little skirmishing, the enemy hastily retired, leaving their stores and camping equipment behind. That night some of the Confederates revelled for a short time in unwonted warmth and luxury; but the next day they were all marching on again under their relentless commander towards the Potomac. When they reached the river they halted opposite Hancock on the far bank. Jackson demanded the surrender of the town, stating that if his demand was not acceded to he would subject it to a bombardment. The commanding

---

[1] Henderson, i, 190.   [2] O.R., v, 1066.   [3] *Ibid.*, 1066.

officer refused to comply, and after allowing two hours for the removal of non-combatants, the Confederate batteries opened on it. An attempt was made to construct a bridge two miles above the town, but this was not completed when the Federals appeared likely to be strongly reinforced before it would be finished. Colonel Rust of Loring's Division, in command of his own and Fulkerson's regiment and one section of Shumaker's battery, was sent to destroy the railway bridge over the Capacon River west of Bath. He did not manage to complete this task until the next day when, reinforced by one of Gilham's regiments, and under the command of Loring, their artillery was employed to drive off the enemy defending the bridge. Then they destroyed the bridge, demolished the railway buildings, cut the telegraph for some distance alongside the track, and rejoined Jackson at Hancock. A working party was also sent to enlarge the gap in the broken canal dam over to the east towards Williamsport.

On 6 January the Federals were reinforced to such an extent that Jackson came to the conclusion that nothing more of value could be achieved by his forces before Hancock without risking a large number of casualties. As Jackson himself said, 'the invader having been defeated and driven across the Potomac, the telegraph line broken at several points, and the railroad bridge across Big Capacon destroyed, thus throwing material obstacles in the way not only of transmitting intelligence from Romney to Hancock, but also of receiving reinforcements from the east, arrangements were made for moving to Romney.'[1]

The march to Romney started badly. Cavalry patrols had been sent out in all directions, and a detachment of militia, acting as a flank guard in the direction of Romney while the main body was moving back towards Unger's Store, was surprised and defeated with a loss of two guns at Hanging Rock, a narrow pass by which the main road from Winchester to Romney goes over the mountains. 'The weather, too, grew colder and colder, and the mountain roads were little more than sheets of ice. The sleet beat fiercely down upon the crawling column. The men stumbled and fell on the slippery tracks; many wagons were overturned, and the bloody knees and muzzles of the horses bore painful witness to the severity of the march. The bivouacs were more comfortless than before.'[2] The intense cold caused the bivouacs on the night of 7 January 1862, to be long remembered. The privations endured began to cause discontent and murmuring, especially among Loring's troops. They were in part the cause of the mutinies which were to follow. On arriving at Unger's Store, it was impossible to continue the march until the horses

had been roughshod, and Jackson, though reluctant, was obliged to remain some days at Unger's for this purpose. The provision train lagged far in rear. Axes there were none; and had not the fence rails afforded a supply of firewood, the sufferings of the troops would have been intense. As it was, despite the example of their commander, they pushed forward but slowly through the bitter winter. Jackson was everywhere; here, putting his shoulder to the wheel of a gun that the exhausted team could no longer move; there, urging the wearied soldiers, or rebuking the officers for want of energy. Attentive as he was to the health and comfort of his men in quarters, on the line of march he looked only to the success of the Confederate arms. The hardships of the winter operations were to him but a necessary concomitant of his designs, and it mattered but little if the weak and sickly should succumb. Commanders who are over-chary of their soldiers' lives, who forget that their men have voluntarily offered themselves as food for powder, often miss great opportunities. To die doing his duty was to Jackson the most desirable consummation of the soldier's existence, and where duty was concerned or victory in doubt he was as careless of life and suffering as Napoleon himself. The well-being of an individual or even of an army were as nothing as compared with the interest of Virginia. And, in the end his indomitable will triumphed over every obstacle. Romney village came at length in sight, lonely and deserted amid the mountain snows, for the Federal garrison had vanished, abandoning its camp equipment and its magazines. [1] The Federals evacuated Romney on 10 January. It was occupied by the Confederates on 14 January.

During this operation one of the qualities which make Jackson a great general is brought to light. He displayed great determination, a capacity for carrying the task through regardless of difficulties. He had shown this iron will at West Point. It had been embodied in his maxim: 'You may be what you resolve to be.' Now he was showing that he could do whatever he resolved to do. Nothing is impossible to determined men—or at least, very little. 'The possible we can do at once, the impossible may take a little longer' was a maxim adopted by units of the Allied forces in the Second World War, 1939–45; it has been the axiom, in some form or another, of all great leaders throughout the ages. But in spite of this Jackson cannot be classed as a good leader at this time. A determined leader, yes; a good leader, no. As Henderson says, 'there are occasions when both officers and men are the better for a little humouring, and the march to Romney was one. A few words of hearty praise, a stirring approach to their nobler instincts, a touch of sympathy, might have worked wonders. But whatever of personal magnetism existed in Stonewall Jackson, it found no utterance in words. Whilst

[1] Henderson, i, 193.

his soldiers struggled painfully towards Romney in the teeth of the winter storm, his lips were never opened save for sharp rebuke or peremptory order, and Loring's men had some reason to complain of his fanatical regard for the letter of the law.'

On the most inclement of those January nights the captain of a Virginia company, on whose property they happened to have halted, had allowed them to use the fence rails for camp fires. Jackson, ever careful of private rights, had issued an order that fences should not be burnt, and the generous donor was suspended from duty on the charge of giving away his own property without first asking leave! Well might the soldiers think that their commander regarded them as mere machines.

The Romney operation was a success; but its success was limited. When Jackson planned to move on Cumberland and destroy the railway bridges over the Potomac on either side of that town, he found Loring's men unwilling to move. He had a mutiny on his hands. Allan describes the situation as follows:

Now it was that a new difficulty confronted the Confederate leader, and forced him to relinquish for the time all further movements. The severe privations of the soldiers at Bath and Hancock had not been endured without murmuring; the painful march to Unger's Store had not allayed the dissatisfaction, and that to Romney, in still more severe weather, had caused the discontent, expecially in Gen. Loring's command, to become open and outspoken. Many men were in hospital from the effects of the exposure. It was commonly declared that the cold was more fatal than the enemy. A campaign at such a season, among inhospitable mountains, was pronounced madness. This feeling was not confined to the men. Many of the officers, under Jackson for the first time, sympathised with it, or did nothing to repress it. Rain and a partial thaw were converting the ice-bound roads into slush and mire. The sufferings of the march, now proposed, promised to be greater than those already endured. The result was that when Jackson was ready to set out he found the troops, and especially Taliaferro's brigade (one of Loring's brigades), so discontented, and opposition to further movements with the present roads and weather so widespread, as to render his proposed undertaking inexpedient. [1]

Jackson in preferring Specification 4 of Charge I against Loring later wrote:

Brig. Gen. W. W. Loring permitted part of his command to become so demoralised as not to be in a condition for active service at Romney, Va., on the 18th of January, 1862, and thus, though the troops of other commanders were in a condition for

[1] Allan, 24, 25.

active service, it was necessary to abandon an important expedition against the enemy in consequence of such inefficiency in Brig. Gen. W. W. Loring's command preventing his efficient co-operation.[1]

Jackson thus proceeded to place his army in winter quarters. Detachments were left at Moorefield to link with General Edward Johnson's forces west of Staunton, at Bath, and at Martinsburg. Ashby's cavalry were to patrol the line of the Potomac. The Stonewall Brigade under Brigadier-General Garnett was ordered to Winchester where Jackson was to have his headquarters again; and Brigadier-General Loring's three brigades and 13 pieces of artillery were quartered around Romney. A line of telegraph was to put Jackson in communication with Romney; and with Garnett's brigade at hand, to resist any movement of Banks force which menaced the front from Harper's Ferry to Williamsport, or to go the assistance of Loring, preparations against any Federal attack in north-west Virginia seemed adequate.

Jackson returned to Winchester on 24 January expecting some weeks of quiet, undisturbed by any important military movements. He was not, however, to have a quiet time. Worse trouble than ever broke out in Loring's command. The officers and men complained bitterly of the campaign which had been conducted at the expense of so much suffering; a campaign now suspended, they said, only to leave them in an exposed and dangerous position, in the midst of an inhospitable mountain region, out of reach of adequate supplies and help in need. They declared their position untenable in case of attack, and even attributed the removal of the Stonewall Brigade in Winchester as favouritism.[2] One of Loring's colonels (Fulkerson) sent a complaint forwarded by Taliaferro, his brigade commander, to the Hon Walter R. Staples, an eminent politician in Richmond;[3] and officers on leave in Richmond made complaints which reached the ears of the Administration. A round robin[4] asking for the withdrawal of the command to Winchester was signed by eleven officers, indorsed by Loring, and respectfully forwarded, but disapproved, by Jackson to the Secretary of War, J. P. Benjamin. This was seen by the Confederate President Jefferson Davis; but even before it reached the Administration, on 30 January, at the President's instance, and on few grounds except the complaints mentioned, Benjamin telegraphed Jackson: 'Our news indicates that a movement is being made to cut off General Loring's command. Order him back to Winchester immediately.'[5]

Jackson was furious at this political interference with his military plans. On 31 January 1862, he replied to Secretary of War Benjamin:

[1] O.R., v, 1066. [2] Allan, 26. [3] O.R., v, 1040.
[4] O.R., v, 1046, 47, 48. [5] O.R., v, 1053.

Sir: Your order requiring me to direct General Loring to return with his command to Winchester immediately has been received and promptly complied with.

With such interference in my command I cannot expect to be of much service in the field, and accordingly respectfully request to be ordered to report for duty to the superintendent of the Virginia Military Institute at Lexington, as has been done in the case of other professors. Should this application not be granted, I respectfully request that the President will accept my resignation from the Army. [1]

This went through Johnston who was still overall commander of the Valley District. He was appalled at the resignation of a general he could ill afford to lose, and did not indorse the letter of resignation or send it on for a week. He was also annoyed on his own behalf at being missed out in the chain of command—Benjamin did not inform Johnston of his direct order to Jackson to recall Loring's command until 3 February. [2] Johnston wrote to Jackson a letter begging him in noble terms to reconsider the matter:

My Dear Friend: I have just read, and with profound regret, your letter to the Secretary of War, asking to be relieved from your present command either by an order to the Virginia Military Institute or the acceptance of your resignation. Let me beg you to reconsider this matter. Under ordinary circumstances a due sense of one's own dignity, as well as care for professional character and official rights, would demand such a course as yours, but the character of this war, the energy exhibited by the Government of the United States, the danger in which our very existence as an independent people lies, requires sacrifices from us all who have been educated as soldiers.

I received my information of the order of which you have such cause to complain from your letter. Is not this as great an official wrong to me as the order itself to you? Let us dispassionately reason with the Government on this subject of command, and if we fail to influence its practice, then ask to be relieved from positions the authority of which is exercised by the War Department, while the responsibilities are left to us.

I have taken the liberty to detain your letter to make this appeal to your patriotism, not merely from warm feelings of personal regard, but from the official opinion which makes me regard you as necessary to the service of the country in your present position. [3]

Jackson had also written to Governor Letcher of Virginia, and it was this gentleman who finally got Jackson to withdraw his resignation. Although Jackson's resignation reached Benjamin before the letter to Letcher arrived, the Governor went immediately to the War Department and found that that Benjamin had done as yet nothing about it and was entirely disposed to listen to reason. Agreement was reached that the resignation would be disregarded until Letcher had time to approach Jackson.

[1] O.R., v, 1053.   [2] O.R., v, 1059.   [3] Ibid., 1060.

Romney Operation: Commanders and Formations [1]

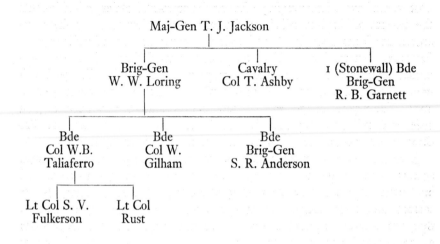

Maj-Gen T. J. Jackson

Brig-Gen W. W. Loring   Cavalry Col T. Ashby   1 (Stonewall) Bde Brig-Gen R. B. Garnett

Bde Col W.B. Taliaferro   Bde Col W. Gilham   Bde Brig-Gen S. R. Anderson

Lt Col S. V. Fulkerson   Lt Col Rust

Artillery (Loring)	
Shumaker's battery	4 guns
Marye's battery	4 guns

Artillery (Jackson)	
McLaughlin's (Rockbridge) battery	6 guns
Waters' battery	4 guns
Carpenter's battery	4 guns
Cutshaw's battery (lost 7 Jan.)	2 guns
A section of 24-pdr Parrotts	2 guns

Jackson was opposed by very scattered Federal forces: 16,000 men under Banks with headquarters at Frederick, Md; and 22,000 men under Rosecrans in the Mountain Department of West Virginia.

The casualties in the Romney operation were trifling, but Jackson had placed the troops opposing him, while preparing for an aggressive movement, upon the defensive; had expelled them virtually from his whole district; had liberated three counties from their rule, and secured supplies in them for the subsistence of his own troops. [2]

[1] Allan, 224.
[2] *Ibid*, 225.

Finally a letter from Letcher, supported by some verbal arguments on the part of Colonel Boteler, who brought it to Jackson, persuaded Jackson to withdraw his resignation. Letcher had said that Jackson's abandonment of his post would have a discouraging effect on the country. Boteler had added that the defence of Virginia called for the service of all her sons. To these two arguments Jackson yielded;[1] but he did not forget his personal indictment of Brigadier-General Loring. To the Specifications of Charge I already mentioned in the account of the Romney campaign, he now added Charge II with two more Specifications. The summary of the first charge was neglect of duty. The second charge was the new one of conduct subversive to good order and military discipline, particularly that he 'did forward to the War Department without disapproval'[2] the mutinous petition of his officers.

Jackson's letter of resignation was returned to him. Jackson's charges against Loring were not entertained. Although the charge of operational inefficiency was not very completely countered by Loring, Loring's plea against the second charge was more substantial. He rather sourly asserted that, 'an intimate acquaintance with the Army regulations and the customs of the service for some twenty-six years has failed to inform me of the fact that a respectful and truthful statement by commanders of the conditions of their commands was other than a duty.'[3]

The authorities at Richmond seem to have been convinced by this defence. They not only failed to punish Loring; they moved him to another theatre and promoted him major-general.

KERNSTOWN

By the end of 1861 it was evident that the Confederates would have to fall back from their advanced position around Manassas. General Johnston was not strong enough to face McClellan's huge force near Washington. He needed the protection of the Rappahannock River between him and his enemy, as well as the advantage of being closer to his base at Richmond. If Johnston moved back, Jackson in the Valley would have to pull back in sympathy to be out of reach of Banks' forces which faced him. The advantage in numbers for the Federals opposing Jackson north of the Potomac was enormous. There were 38,000 Northerners being assembled there while

[1] Freeman, LL, i, 129.   [2] O.R., v, 1066.
[3] O.R., v, 1070.

Jackson could muster only three brigades to make 4,600 men. But the Federals were slow to get moving. Their large armies beyond the Potomac did not show any signs of advancing until the end of February 1862, and war did not come to the Valley again until early in March. Then, obeying President Lincoln's order for a general advance, Banks threw a pontoon bridge across the Potomac at Harper's Ferry and pushed southwards.

Jackson had been in no hurry to abandon Winchester, and through Johnston [1] had asked the President for reinforcements to strike a blow near Winchester which he thought would cause alarm in Washington. But no aid was sent him. He was ordered to defend the Valley as best he could with the 4,600 men encamped at Winchester, to use his own judgment as to his own position, and to endeavour to employ the invaders in the Valley without exposing himself to the danger of defeat, by keeping so near the enemy as to prevent his making any considerable detachment to reinforce McClellan, but not so near that he might be compelled to fight [2] at a disadvantage.

When menaced by Banks, Jackson thus fell back 30 miles from Winchester to Woodstock, leaving behind him a rear guard and Ashby's cavalry screen. Jackson's cavalry leader, Ashby, was 'the beau-ideal of a captain of light horse. His reckless daring, both across country and under fire made him the idol of the army.' Jackson's cavalry, comprising horse-loving Virginians of good standing, was better than the Federal cavalry; and Jackson demanded more of it. It was not sufficient for him just to receive a warning that the enemy was advancing. He expected to be given an estimate of its strength and details of its every movement. To penetrate the enemy's lines, to approach his camps, and observe his columns—these were the tasks of Ashby's riders and in them they were unrivalled. They were acquainted with every country lane and woodland track. They had friends in every village, and their names were known to every farmer. 'We thought no more of riding through the enemy bivouacs than of riding round our fathers' farms,' was how they put it.

After Jackson's retreat, Banks became confident that the Valley could be controlled by only a token force. He started to obey his instructions to reinforce McClellan, and he began to move some of his troops over the Blue Ridge towards Manassas to help McClellan in his drive against Johnston and Richmond.

On the evening of 21 April 1862, Ashby reported to Jackson that the enemy was retreating and that Banks' whole force seemed to be leaving the Valley: 'Having followed the enemy in his hasty retreat from Strasburg on Saturday evening, I came upon the forces remaining at Winchester within a

[1] O.R., v, 1095.
[2] J. E. Johnston's Narrative, Henderson, i, 220.

mile of that place and became satisfied that he had but four regiments, and learned that they had orders to march in the direction of Harper's Ferry.'[1] In accordance with his instructions to hold the enemy in the Valley, Jackson at once pushed northwards. On 22 April, Ashby and his cavalry with three horse artillery guns struck some Federal pickets about a mile south of Winchester. A skirmish followed, and Ashby still considered that only four regiments besides the guns and cavalry remained around Winchester. The local inhabitants also gave a similar estimate of the enemy's strength, and Jackson decided to attack. He wrote: 'after arriving near Kernstown I learned from a source which had been remarkable for its reliability that the enemy's infantry force at Winchester did not exceed four regiments. A large Federal force was leaving the valley, and had already reached Castleman's Ferry on the Shenandoah. Though it was very desirable to prevent the enemy leaving the valley, yet I deemed it best not to attack until morning [Jackson also shrank from fighting on Sunday]. But subsequently ascertaining that the Federals had a position from which our forces could be seen, I concluded that it would be dangerous to postpone it until the next day, as reinforcements might be brought up during the night.'[2] With regard to being in a position from which his forces could be seen, 'the staff appear to have been at fault,'[3] for selecting a halting and assembly place in full view of the enemy. This coupled with the wrong information about the enemy's strength —Shields had his whole division 9,000 strong in the neighbourhood not just four infantry regiments—goes some way to explain Jackson's failure at Kernstown. For failure it was in spite of the sound tactical plan on which he based his attack.

The Federal force under Kimball—Shields the divisional commander having been wounded in the skirmish with Ashby—extended on both sides of the main Valley turnpike which runs up from Staunton through Harrisonburg, Woodstock and Strasburg to Winchester. To the east, where a large portion of the Federal troops and several guns were posted, was grassland; and in front around Kernstown there were fields under plough. To the north-west stretching from the narrow valley of the Opequon towards Winchester was a low ridge covered with woods called Sandy Ridge. Just beside the turnpike on the west side between Kernstown and Winchester, but nearer to the former, was a detached hill with a few trees on it called Pritchard's Hill. This was the site of two Federal batteries and had Federal skirmishers along its base.

The open fields and meadows, heavy from the recent rains, would not

[1] O.R., XII, i, p. 385—Ashby's report.   [2] O.R., XII, i, 381.
[3] Henderson, i, 237, footnote.

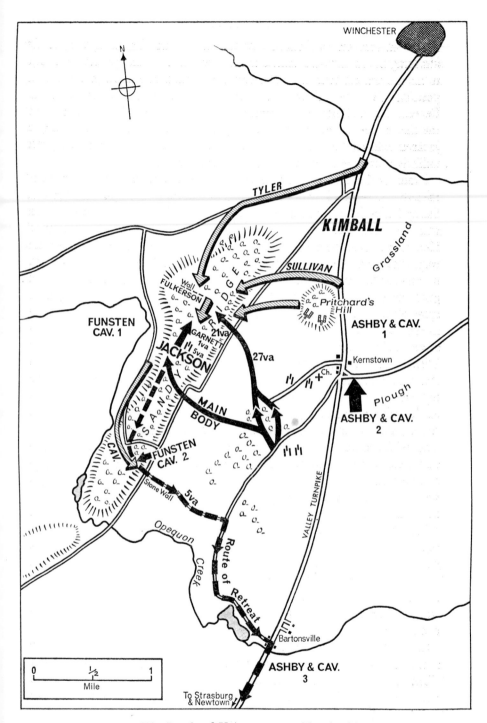

WINCHESTER

N

TYLER

KIMBALL

Grassland

FULKERSON
Wall
R I D G E
SULLIVAN

Pritchard's
Hill

FUNSTEN
CAV. 1

21va
GARNETT
1va
5va
JACKSON

27va

ASHBY & CAV.
1

Kernstown

Ch.

ASHBY & CAV.
2

Plough

MAIN
BODY

S A N D Y

CAV.

FUNSTEN
CAV. 2

VALLEY TURNPIKE

Stone Wall
5va

Opequon

Creek

Route of Retreat

Bartonsville

ASHBY & CAV.
3

0   ½   1
Mile

To Strasburg
& Newtown

3 The Battle of Kernstown, 23 March 1862

61

favour an attacker, so Jackson determined to turn the enemy's right. By attacking the enemy's unmanned flank he would make his opponent conform to his movements instead of awaiting the Confederate attack in a prepared position. To seize the wooded Sandy Ridge while the cavalry held the Federals fast in front; to pass round the west of Pritchard's Hill, and to cut the line of the Federal retreat to Winchester, seemed no difficult task, as Jackson believed the force confronting him to be no more than a rear-guard unlikely to involve itself in a desperate engagement.

From the Confederate position south of Kernstown an advanced guard of the 27th Va Regt with two guns marched westwards by a wagon track towards Sandy Ridge led by guides recruited from Winchester, who were familiar with the locality. At the same time Ashby pressed the Federals in front of Kernstown. Later the main body in two columns followed—one by the same wagon track and the other by a track further south. The northerly track was in range of the batteries on Pritchard's Hill, and the guns with the advanced guard were brought into action by Opequon Church to distract their aim. In spite of this enemy artillery fire from Pritchard's Hill, the Confederate infantry with most of their guns managed to get through and establish themselves, largely unscathed, on a line across Sandy Ridge facing towards Winchester. The 5th Va Regt from Garnett's Stonewall Brigade remained to start with at the foot of the ridge (it was later brought up), on the right at the top were the 21st Va from Burks' Brigade and the 27th from Garnett's, and on the left was Fulkerson's Brigade. The other three regiments of Garnett's Brigade and the 1st Va (Irish Regulars) from Burks' were in the second line.

Kimball conducted the battle for the Federals with great skill. He recognised quickly that Ashby's frontal attack was nothing more than a demonstration, and moved over to the ridge nearly the whole of his own brigade as well as the brigades of Tyler and Sullivan. Thus it was on Sandy Ridge that the main battle took place. On the Confederate side Fulkerson did best. In an open space on his front a stone wall ran across a field; and in the race to secure its protection Fulkerson's men beat the Federals. From behind this barrier the Confederates were able to produce such heavy fire that the stubble in front of the wall on the Federal side was soon strewn with Federal dead. A Pennsylvanian regiment abandoned its colour and fled in panic, and the whole enemy force retreated back to the shelter of the woods on the far side of the open space.

In the centre, however, where the Federals were in greatly superior numbers, the Confederates fared worse. The right, too, was hardly pressed. When the ammunition began to give out and more and more Federal reinforcements arrived, and regiments from Pritchard's Hill attacked the

Confederate flank, Garnett commanding the Stonewall Brigade finally gave the order to fall back. Fulkerson, whose right was now exposed, was obliged to conform to this rearward movement, and the whole Confederate line composed now of various regiments much mixed up, fell back, still fighting, through the woods.

Jackson had not been consulted, and watching the progress of the action on the left was amazed and angered to see his old brigade falter and fall back. One of Jackson's 'Foot Cavalry' described it in this way: 'All our ammunition being gone we gradually retired, passing through the 5th Va Regt that had formed in the rear. Our artillery had taken position and were firing on the enemy, but when we retreated they were compelled to do so. In going through a gap in a stone wall one of the guns became entangled and disabled and was lost. One of our company in going to the rear encountered Gen. Jackson who inquired where he was going. He answered, that he had shot all his ammunition away, and did not know where to get more. Old Stonewall rose in his stirrups, and gave the command, "Then go back and give them the bayonet", and rode off to the front.'[1] He galloped up to Garnett and ordered him to hold his ground to no avail, and then turned to try and restore the fight himself. 'Seizing a drummer by the shoulder, he dragged him to a rise of ground in full view of the troops, and bade him in curt terms to "Beat the rally!" The drum rolled at his order, and with his hand on the frightened boy's shoulder, amidst a storm of balls, he tried to check the flight of his defeated troops.'[2] His efforts proved useless. It was impossible to stop the rout. The 5th and 42nd Va Regts had been halted by Garnett in a position well behind so that a new front could be established for the shattered troops, and to this arrangement Jackson had unwillingly to agree.

There followed more severe fighting on the new line. In front of the 5th Va Regt one of the colours of the 5th Ohio changed hands no less than six times and was pierced by 84 bullets. But although most of the Confederates got away from the ridge, even this new line could not long be held. As night began to fall the 5th Va, retiring steadily towards the turnpike, filed into a narrow lane fenced by a stone wall nearly a mile from their last position, and took post for a final stand. Up from the Opequon Valley beyond the ridge appeared the Northern Cavalry; but it was now too dark for the horsemen to charge the 5th Va, and Funsten's squadrons were able to drive them off. Thus, with the Federal infantry stuck in the darkened pathless woods, the 5th were able to retire unmolested.

It was now night, and the Federals had full possession of the field. They had picked up 200 or 300 prisoners from the Confederates as the latter fell

[1] Worsham, 68.　　　　[2] Henderson, i, 244.

back, and also two guns, both of which had been disabled. The Confederates, with the exception of Ashby and the cavalry who halted at Bartonsville, a farm two miles south of Kernstown, fell back to Newtown three miles further south, where the wagon trains had been parked. They had marched 14 miles; they had attacked a force more than double their size and fought them for three hours; by this time they were utterly worn out. 'In the fence-corners, under the trees, and around the wagons they threw themselves down, many too weary to eat, and forgot in profound slumber the trials, dangers and disappointments of the day.'[1] Jackson shared the open-air bivouac with his men. Next morning he and his forces retired before the advancing enemy to Mount Jackson, from where they had set out.

The bold attack of Jackson at Kernstown, in which, like the Federals, he lost about 600 men killed and wounded, although unsuccessful, had important results. It led to the recall to the Valley of the Federal troops which had been sent to reinforce McClellan. Shields writes: 'Though the battle had been won, still I could not believe that Jackson would have hazarded a decisive engagement at such a distance from the main body without expecting re-inforcements. So, to be prepared for such a contingency, I set to work during the night to bring together all the troops within my reach. I sent an express after Williams' division, requesting the rear brigade, about twenty miles distant, to march all night and join me in the morning.'[2] Eventually all Williams' division of 8,000 men were withdrawn from the force covering Washington. Blenker's division was transferred from McClellan to the Valley, and the Ist Army Corps, 37,000 strong, under General McDowell was left at Manassas to guard Washington instead of embarking with McClellan to the Peninsula for his attack on Richmond from the east coast.

Kernstown illustrates many of Jackson's characteristics as a general. Acting on faulty information, he decided to attack and keep the enemy in the Valley. This was his main task, and Jackson always tried to carry out to the letter what he was order to do.[3] His plans and general tactics for the conduct of the battle were sound. No one could fault the principle which he applied of hurling what he thought were overwhelming numbers at the spot where the enemy least expected it. This surprised the Federals and very nearly beat them. Only the fact that there was a full division facing Jackson instead of four regiments and the quick reaction of Kimball, the temporary Federal commander, thwarted Jackson's left flanking attack. Jackson always expected the highest standards from his officers. At Kernstown, he believed that Garnett, by ordering an unnecessary retreat on his own responsibility, had failed in his duty. Characteristically, he placed Garnett under arrest and

[1] Allan, 62.   [2] O.R., XII, i, 341.   [3] See p. 116.

12 *Ruin of Stone Bridge over Bull Run after the battle there*

13 *Sudley Springs Ford over which General McDowell's flank attack came*
on Beauregard's army, at First Bull Run (Manassas), 21 July 1861

14 *The Battle of Cross Keys—8 June 1862*
From a drawing by Edwin Forbes (1839–1894)

*1 Blue Ridge 2 and 3 Ewell's position 4 Federal batteries ready to move
5 Federal Infantry advancing 6 Ambulances 7 Field Hospital 8 Ridge
west of Cower Mill Creek 9 Road from Harrisonburgh to Port Republic*

15 *The Battle of Kernstown—23 March 1862*
*Federal troops charge the stone wall on Sandy Ridge. From a drawing by
Alfred R. Waud (1828–1891)*

Kernstown: Commanders and Formations[1]

Confederates 3,087 of whom 2,742 were engaged

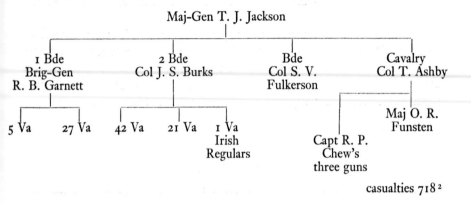

Maj-Gen T. J. Jackson

1 Bde	2 Bde	Bde	Cavalry
Brig-Gen R. B. Garnett	Col J. S. Burks	Col S. V. Fulkerson	Col T. Ashby

5 Va   27 Va   42 Va   21 Va   1 Va Irish Regulars

Maj O. R. Funsten

Capt R. P. Chew's three guns

casualties 718[2]

Federals 7,000

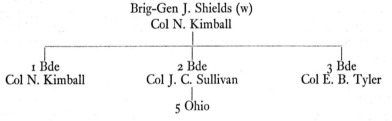

Brig-Gen J. Shields (w)
Col N. Kimball

1 Bde	2 Bde	3 Bde
Col N. Kimball	Col J. C. Sullivan	Col E. B. Tyler

5 Ohio

casualties 590[3]

[1] Allan, note 231.
[2] B & L ii, 300.
[3] *Ibid.*, 299.

framed charges for his trial by court martial, although the officers of his brigade always declared he was perfectly justified in ordering a retreat, as did General Maury.[1] Jackson would not accept the excuse that the ammunition had run out. At the time the Stonewall Brigade gave way, the 5th and 42nd Va were at hand, 'and the bayonet, his favourite, yet remained to them; and he did not consider the means of victory as exhausted, until the naked steel was employed.'[2]

No battle is ever perfectly conducted, and Kernstown offers some openings to the critics. For example, Jackson, it is said, attacked with tired troops on insufficient information. Be that as it may, the results seem to justify his action, for, as has already been indicated, although a tactical defeat Kernstown was undoubtedly a strategic victory for the Confederates.

M'DOWELL

Jackson describes his movements after Kernstown as follows:

After the battle of Kernstown I retreated in the direction of Harrisonburg. My rear guard—comprising Ashby's cavalry, Captain Clew's battery, and from time to time other forces—was placed under the direction of Col Turner Ashby, an officer whose judgment, coolness, and courage eminently qualified him for the delicate and important trust. Although pursued by a greatly superior force under General Banks, we were enabled to halt for more than a fortnight in the vicinity of Mount Jackson.

After reaching Harrisonburg we turned toward the Blue Ridge, and on April 19 crossed the South Fork of the Shenandoah, and took position between that river and Swift Run Gap in Elk Run Valley (a small tributary, one branch of which has its source in Swift Run Gap, which joins the Shenandoah near Conrad's Store, see map facing p. 96).

General R. S. Ewell, having been directed to join my command (with some 8,000 men), left the vicintiy of Gordonsville, and on the 30th arrived with his division west of the Blue Ridge.

The main body (19,000) of General Banks' pursuing army did not proceed further south than the vicinity of Harrisonburg; but a considerable force, under the command of General Milroy was moving toward Staunton . . . the positions of these two Federal armies were now such that if left unmolested they would readily form a junction . . . At this time Brig-Gen. Edward Johnson, with his (3,000 Confederate) troops was west of Staunton.[3]

[1] See p. 38; Maury 71, 72.   [2] Dabney, ii, 47.
[3] O.R., XII, i, 470.

Jackson, who had 6,000 men of his own not counting Ewell's and Johnston's, thought he should fight either Milroy[1] or Banks before they could join; and he sent a report to General Lee, President Davis' military adviser, putting forward alternative plans. Lee replied that he wanted a diversion in the Valley, but he left the choice of opponents and all other details to Jackson.

Jackson's final choice brought into being a typical Jackson manoeuvre. Jackson planned to fall upon Frémont's advanced body under Milroy before Schenck and Frémont could join it, or Banks join up from Harrisonburg.

The route for this movement was chosen to mislead the enemy as well as to give security from attack. Leaving Ewell in Elk Run Valley to watch Banks, Jackson marched his own forces up the east side of the Shenandoah River to Port Republic, a distance of 16 miles, and then across the Blue Ridge through Brown's Gap to Mechum's River station on the Virginia Central railway. From here he sent his artillery and wagons by road to Staunton while the troops were sent by railway.

The first part of the route was made with the Shenandoah River as protection to Jackson's flank. Crossing the Blue Ridge seemed to suggest that he was off to join Johnston near Richmond. 'He was never in the habit of informing his subordinates, even those of highest rank, of his plans, and his staff were frequently more ignorant of them than otherwise. On this occasion only one or two, whose duties made it necessary, knew the General's designs, so that friends as well as foes were mystified.'[2]

Meanwhile Ashby and the cavalry made demonstrations in force in the direction of Harrisonburg, and a scouting party under Major Hotchkiss[3] went to the top of Peaked Mountain, the south-west end of the Massanutton Mountains, to observe the enemy, whom they found quietly camped about Harrisonburg.

From Elk Run Valley—where Ewell had placed his 8,000 men in the camps Jackson evacuated—Jackson followed an unpaved country road which from the heavy rain had become very muddy. 1 May was very wet again, and the men and horses found themselves floundering through what seemed to be a quagmire. The guns sank axle deep; and it was only by the help of large detachments of pioneers, organised by Jackson for the purpose, that the heavy wagons were able to move at all. The pioneers strewed piles of stones and brushwood on the roadway, but even with this help the column made

---

[1] Behind Milroy in The Mountain Department were Schenck and the senior Commander Frémont, in all 15,000 men.
[2] Allan, 80.
[3] Hotchkiss Papers.

only five miles on the first day. The next day and the following one the struggle with mud and rain continued. The staff dismounted and lent a hand, and Jackson, his uniform bespattered with mud, carried stones and brushwood with the rest. On the third day the column reached the hard mountain road winding up Brown's Gap, and to add to the men's relief the sun heralded a glorious May day. The worst of the journey was now over.

Jackson reached Staunton on Sunday 4 May, and by that evening all the troops, by rail and by road, had arrived in the town and been placed in camp around it. So secret had Jackson been about his plans that the people of Staunton were taken completely by surprise, 'and when they had convinced themselves that Jackson was on his way to Richmond were astonished by his appearance in their midst'.[1] After a day's rest the advance continued. Led by General Edward Johnson's Brigade, who had been there already, and followed by the Stonewall Brigade, and a detachment of cadets from the Virginia Military Institute [2]—'the natty appearance of these youthful soldiers affording a striking contrast to the seedy and dilapidated veterans'[3]—the Confederates set off to meet Milroy in the mountains west of Staunton.

Jackson considered the Battle of M'Dowell a Confederate success. 'God blessed our arms with victory at M'Dowell yesterday' was the despatch he sent to Richmond after it. But as will be seen on studying its features, it was far from being a significant victory on the field. The repulse of 2,500 men by 4,000 was not a remarkable feat. Its success lay in its achievement of the strategic and tactical results which Jackson sought.

Milroy concentrated his whole brigade of 3,700 men at M'Dowell, a little village at the foot of Bull Pasture Mountain, and sent back for reinforcements. Frémont's command was much strung out. Schenck's brigade had not advanced beyond Franklin, 34 miles north of M'Dowell. Frémont himself, with a couple of battalions, was as far away again beyond Franklin; and Blenker's division, still further to the rear, had not quitted Romney. Amidst Bull Pasture Mountains and short of Bull Pasture River which separated the Confederates from the Federals in M'Dowell, Johnson with a small party went up to the top of Sitlington's Hill to view the enemy position. The Federals sent a body of skirmishers against them, but these were driven back. The hill was then secured by a larger Confederate force.

The enemy position was so strong that Jackson decided against a direct assault on it. From the rugged plateau on top of Sitlington's hill the ground dropped sharply to the protective Bull Pasture River swollen by rain directly

---

[1] Allan, 83.   [2] Dabney, ii, 65.   [3] Douglas, 56.

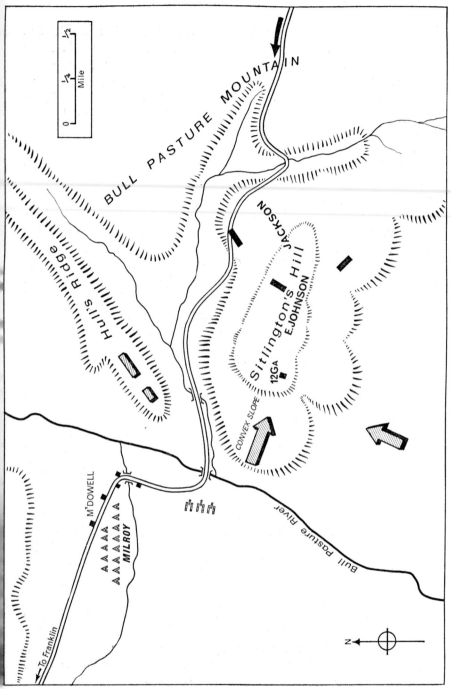

4 The Battle of M'Dowell, 8 May 1862

in front. On the Confederates' right the main road followed a ravine down to the river bridge, commanded by Federal guns. On the other side of the ravine was Hull's Ridge occupied by the Federals, almost out of range.

Jackson planned to hold Sitlington's Hill with infantry alone, and to get his staff to reconnoitre a route around the Federal position to take it in the rear. On the outflanking route he proposed to send all his artillery and a force from his reserve brigades. But Milroy decided to attack Sitlington's Hill at once in force, and thus there followed a battle for the hill in which the Confederate artillery played no part. Even the Federal guns achieved little. They found the steep elevation of the hill made effective fire impossible; and it is reckoned that only one man on Sitlington's Hill was struck by a piece of shell. It was a fierce encounter all the same. Two Federal regiments attacked the Confederate front; and three others, bringing the numbers of the attackers up to 2,500 rifles, assaulted the left. The convex slope favoured the attackers, who advanced at first in dead ground. 'The 12th Georgia, holding the centre of Johnson's line, displayed more valour than judgment. Having advanced in front of the crest to get a sight of the attackers, they could not be persuaded to retire to the reverse of the slope where other regiments found partial protection without sacrificing the efficiency of their fire. Their commander, perceiving their useless exposure, endeavoured again and again to withdraw them; but amidst the roar of the musketry his voice was lifted in vain, and when passing along the ranks he persuaded one wing of the regiment to recede, they rushed again to the front while he was gone to expostulate with the other.'[1] A tall Georgian youth expressed the spirit of his comrades when he replied to the question why they did not retreat to the shelter of the ridge: 'We did not come all this way to Virginia to run before Yankees.'[2] The action became so fierce that Jackson had to call up another of his brigades in support of Johnson's men. Then after four hours' fighting, and with the onset of darkness, the Federals fell back in good order. They had been repulsed at every point; but they had inflicted more casualties than they had received— 498 to 256, with the 12th Georgia making up 175 of the Confederate total.

During the night the camp fires of the Federals could be seen blazing ostentatiously in long and regular lines, and the troops seemed wrapped in sleep. In the morning, however, when Jackson rode out at dawn to reconnoitre, the Federals had disappeared.

News of the Confederate success was received by the people of Virginia with rejoicing. The war had been going badly elsewhere at this stage. New Orleans had fallen; Johnston was being pursued by McClellan up the Peninsula towards Richmond; the ironclad Confederate vessel, the *Merrimac*, had

[1] Henderson, i, 298, 299   [2] Dabney ii, 73.

been grounded in the James River and destroyed by its commander. 'The victory of M'Dowell was one gleam of brightness athwart the clouds.'[1]

The Confederate pursuit after M'Dowell was not very successful. It was delayed by a Federal smokescreen. 'The Federals resorted to the expedient of setting fire to the forests upon the mountain sides, in order to envelop their flight in obscurity. Soon the sky was overcast with volumes of smoke, which almost hid the scene, and wrapped every distant object in a veil, impenetrable alike to the eyes and telescopes of the officers. Through the sultry fog the pursuing army felt its way cautiously along, cannonaded by the enemy from every advantageous position; while it was protected from ambuscades only by detachments of skirmishers who scoured the burning woods on each side of the highway. As fast as these could scramble over the precipitous hills, and through the blazing thickets, the great column crept along the main road, like a lazy serpent; their General often in advance of its head, in his eagerness to overtake the foe.'[2] Jackson acknowledged this clever manoeuvre by the Federals. He said that it produced for him all the disadvantages of a night attack. By slow stages with constant skirmishing the Federals were followed up as far as Franklin, where, deciding nothing more could be gained in this area, Jackson called a halt and resolved to return to the Valley. His object was not really the destruction of Frémont's advanced guard in front of him, but Banks' army back at Harrisonburg watched over by Ewell. No great results could be expected from further operations in as distant an area as Franklin. He appeared to have frustrated Frémont's plans by defeating his advanced guard under Milroy at M'Dowell. Now he felt it was time to join with Ewell and tackle Banks. To make sure that Frémont did not come down from the Mountain District and intervene and support Banks, he had already sent Major Hotchkiss with a detachment of cavalry to block the passes further north by which Frémont could cross the mountains and support his colleague. North River Gap, Dry River Gap and Brook's Gap were all blocked by this party; and their success is shown by this extract from Frémont's report: 'Of the different roads leading from Franklin to Harrisonburg all but one had been obstructed by Jackson . . . Bridges and culverts had been destroyed, rocks rolled down and in one instance trees felled across the way for the distance of nearly a mile. The road still left open ran southerly reaching Harrisonburg by a long détour. Granting, however, that loss of time by removal of obstacles, or by taking the longer route, were no consideration, tending to lengthen my line of supplies, was little better than a physical impossibility.'[3]

M'Dowell illustrates Jackson's strategic skill, and his understanding of the

[1] Dabney, ii, 75.　　　　[2] *Ibid.*, 76, 77.　　　　[3] O.R., Vol. xii, i, 11.

basic principles for conducting war successfully. In this operation he moved his armies in strange directions so that friend and foe alike were surprised by his manoeuvres. He has been criticised for keeping his own people in the dark. When Jackson was informed of the irritation of his generals he merely smiled, and said: 'If I can deceive my own friends I can make certain of deceiving the enemy.' Nothing shook his faith in Frederick the Great's maxim, which he was fond of quoting: 'If I thought my coat knew my plans, I would take it off and burn it.'[1] He displayed great skill in placing his armies in Elk Run Valley; it was not only a strong defensive position; it was also a splendid place from which to pounce on Banks' flank and cut his line of supplies, if the latter were to advance on Staunton to link with Frémont's advance guard. He showed his appreciation of the importance of attacking with his forces concentrated, by joining his own with Johnson's troops at Staunton to defeat Milroy. He recognised the necessity of keeping Frémont away from Banks so that the Federals could not concentrate in their turn, both by the battle at M'Dowell itself, and by his action in getting the passes from the Mountain Department blocked. The M'Dowell operation also shows Jackson in a good light as a leader, helping his wagons through the mud on the road to Port Republic, and in the van urging on the pursuit through the smoke towards Franklin. Finally, this period ends with incidents not yet related, which show very clearly his attitude to discipline:

A part of the men of the 27th Regiment, in the Stonewall Brigade, who had volunteered for twelve months, now found their year just expired. Assuming that the application of the last conscription act was a breach of faith to them, they demanded their discharge, and laying down their arms refused to serve another day. Their Colonel, Grigsby, referred the case to General Jackson for instructions. On hearing it detailed, he exclaimed, his eye flashing, and his brow rigid with a portentous sternness, 'What is this but mutiny? Why does Colonel Grigsby refer to me to know what to do with a mutiny? He should shoot them where they stand.' He then turned to his adjutant, and dictated an order to the Colonel to parade his regiment instantly, with loaded muskets, to draw up the insubordinate companies in front of them, disarmed, and offer them the alternative of returning to duty, or being fusiladed on the spot. The order was obeyed, and the mutineers, when confronted with instant death, promptly reconsidered their resolution. They could not afterwards be distinguished from the rest of the regiment in their soldierly behaviour.[2]

In the administration of discipline Jackson was far stricter than General Lee, or indeed than any other of the generals in Virginia.

Once on the march, fearing lest his men might stray from the ranks and commit acts of pillage, he had issued an order that the soldiers should not enter private

---

[1] Henderson, i, 441. [2] Dabney, ii, 79, 80.

M'Dowell: Commanders and Formations[1]

Confederates 6000

Maj-Gen T. J. Jackson

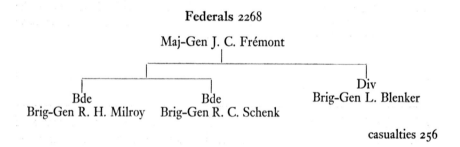

1 Bde
(not engaged)

Bde
Col J. A. Campbell

Bde
Brig-Gen
W. B. Taliaferro

Army of the
North-West
Brig-Gen
Edward Johnson

27 Va
Col A. J. Grigsby

1 Bde

Bde

12 Ga

casualties 499

Federals 2268

Maj-Gen J. C. Frémont

Bde
Brig-Gen R. H. Milroy

Bde
Brig-Gen R. C. Schenk

Div
Brig-Gen L. Blenker

casualties 256

[1] Allan, note 243 & B & L, ii, 299–301.

dwellings. Disregarding the order, a soldier entered a house, and even used insulting language to the women of the family. This was reported to Jackson, who had the man arrested, tried by court-martial, and shot in twenty minutes. [1]

He seldom failed to confirm the sentences of death passed by courts-martial on deserters. It was in vain that his oldest friends, or even chaplains, appealed for a mitigation of the extreme penalty. The Rev Dr Graham, with whom Jackson stayed with his wife at Winchester, says:

While he was in command at Winchester, in December 1861, a soldier who was charged with striking his captain was tried by court-martial and sentenced to be shot. Knowing that the breach of discipline had been attended with many extenuating circumstances, some of us endeavoured to secure his pardon. Possessing ourselves of all the facts, we waited upon the general, who evinced the deepest interest in the object of our visit, and listened with evident sympathy to our plea. There was moisture in his eyes when we repeated the poor fellow's pitiful appeal that he be allowed to die for his country as a soldier on the field of battle but not as a dog by the muskets of his own comrades. Such solicitude for the success of our efforts did he manifest that he even suggested some things to be done which we had not thought of. At the same time he warned us not to be too hopeful. He said: 'It is unquestionably a case of great hardship. Resistance to lawful authority is a grave offence in a soldier. To pardon this man would be to encourage insubordination throughout the army, and so ruin our cause. Still', he added, 'I will review the whole case, and no man will be happier than myself if I can reach the same conclusions as you have done.' The soldier was shot. [2]

FRONT ROYAL WINCHESTER

After the Confederate pursuit reached Franklin following the battle of M'Dowell, Jackson turned back, and joining the main Valley turnpike, reached Harrisonburg where he learned that Banks had returned to Strasburg and was entrenching. Shields' division had been detached from Banks' command and was on its way to join General McDowell at Fredericksburg. Lincoln had recovered somewhat from his initial fear of the threat from the Valley on Maryland and Washington, and in response to McClellan's appeals had agreed to permit McDowell to join McClellan's army in its attack on Richmond. Banks was thus left with only about 8,000 men, his main force at Strasburg blocking the Valley turnpike, and a detachment at Front Royal under Kenly guarding the Luray road to Winchester.

It was at this stage that a distinctive Confederate strategy for the Valley began to evolve. This was the idea of playing by design on the fears of

[1] Field, 286.   [2] Henderson, ii, 365.

Lincoln for the safety of his capital by striking in the Valley. 'If Banks is defeated it may directly retard McClellan's movement,' Lee wrote; and, 'Whatever movements you make against Banks, do it speedily, and if successful drive him back towards the Potomac, and create the impression, as far as possible, that you design threatening that line.'[1]

In his advance against Banks Jackson employed manoeuvres to mystify the enemy similar to the ones he used before the battle of M'Dowell. General Richard Taylor's Louisiana brigade from Ewell's division was marched from Ewell's camp in Elk Run Valley round the south end of the Massanuttons through Keezletown up to Jackson's force on the Valley turnpike near Newmarket. 'This detachment seems to have been made with the view of inducing Banks to believe, should information filter through Ashby's pickets, that the whole Confederate force was advancing directly to Strasburg.'[2] Banks certainly gained that impression whatever the cause. He writes to Stanton, the Federal Secretary of War: 'The return of the rebel forces of General Jackson to the valley, after his forced march against Generals Milroy and Schenck (M'Dowell operation) increased my anxiety for the safety of the position I occupy and that of the troops under my command . . . From all the information I can gather—and I do not wish to excite alarm unnecessarily—I am compelled to believe that he meditates attack here (Strasburg).'[3]

General Taylor was a man after Jackson's own heart, eager to carry out any instruction given him, willing to tackle with his disciplined Louisiana troops the hardest of assignments. The brigade was made up of roughs from New Orleans—Wheat's *Tigers*—planters and sons of planters, Irishmen, and Acadians of French extraction, the last, the 8th Louisianians, born cooks and having a splendid regimental band. So villainous was the reputation of the *Tigers* battalion that every commander desired to be rid of it. General Taylor, however, proved himself capable of dealing with the *Tigers* by exacting, in the fashion of Jackson himself, a high degree of discipline from the start. Early in his command,

For some disorder after tattoo, several *Tigers* were arrested and placed in charge of the brigade guard. Their comrades attempted to force the guard and release them. The attempt failed, and two ringleaders were captured and put in irons for the night. On the ensuing morning an order for a general court-martial was obtained from army headquarters, and the court met at 10 a.m. The prisoners were found guilty and sentenced to be shot at sunset. I ordered the firing party to be detailed from their own company; but Wheat and his officers begged to be spared this hard duty, fearing that the *Tigers* would refuse to fire on their own comrades. I insisted for the

---

[1] Henderson, i, 306. [2] *Ibid.*, 309. [3] O.R., XII, i, 524.

sake of the example, and pointed out the serious consequences of disobedience by their men. The brigade, under arms, was marched out; and as the news spread many thousands from other commands flocked to witness the scene. The firing party, ten *Tigers*, was drawn up fifteen paces from the prisoners, the brigade provost gave the command to fire, and the unhappy men fell dead without a struggle. This account is given because it was the first military execution in the Army of Northern Virginia; and punishment, so clearly following offence, produced a marked effect. [1]

Taylor's men made a favourable impression on Jackson and Jackson's men, when they caught up with the main body lying on either side of the turnpike near Newmarket. The Louisianians were 'over three thousand strong, neat in fresh clothing of grey with white gaiters, bands playing at the head of their regiments, not a straggler, but every man in his place, stepping jauntily as on parade, though they had marched twenty miles or more.' After settling his men in their camp beside the turnpike, Taylor sought Jackson to report. He found him sitting on a fence overlooking the road. Taylor says:

Approaching, I saluted and declared my name and rank, then waited for a response. Before this came I had time to see a pair of cavalry boots covering feet of gigantic size, a mangy cap with visor drawn low, a heavy, dark beard, and weary eyes—eyes I afterward saw filled with intense but never brilliant light. A low, gentle voice inquired the road and distance marched that day. 'Keezletown road, six and twenty miles.' 'You seem to have no stragglers.' 'Never allow straggling.' 'You must teach my people; they straggle badly.' A bow in reply. Just then my creoles started their band and a waltz. After a contemplative suck at a lemon (he was rarely without one), 'Thoughtless fellows for serious work' came forth. I expressed a hope that the work would not be less well done because of the gaiety. A return to the lemon gave me the opportunity to retire. [2]

The next day soon after dawn the whole of Jackson's force moved north with Taylor's Louisianians in the van. Reaching the crossroads at Newmarket the head of the column was turned to the right, and the troops, who had confidently expected that Strasburg would be the scene of their next engagement, found themselves moving eastwards across the Massanuttons. Reaching Luray on the east side and expecting to continue on across Blue Ridge, they were equally surprised when they found themselves turned northwards, and, together with the rest of Ewell's force from Elk Run Valley, set on the road towards Front Royal, a combined force of nearly 17,000 men.

Front Royal was guarded by only 1,000 men with two 10-pounder Parrott guns, under Colonel Kenly. They were completely surprised and overwhelmed. Kenly writes: 'Not having a single cavalry soldier (The New York cavalry joined him from Strasburg later) attached to my command to warn the pickets or the company in town of the approach of the enemy, I had

[1] Taylor, 25.　　　　　　　　[2] *Ibid.*, 49, 50.

ordered them, in case of attack by a superior force, to retreat rapidly to camp. This the majority of them were enabled to do . . . Two battalions of the enemy's infantry pushed rapidly forward on both sides of the road towards the camp (Kenly had his camp north of Front Royal), and through it to the two bridges in my rear which crossed the main branch (South Fork) and North Fork of the Shenandoah, while at the same time a heavy column of infantry and cavalry crossed the railroad, and moved as if to turn my left flank . . . a battery of artillery was also got into position and opened on us, and heavy clouds of dust indicated the rapid approach of large additional numbers.'[1]

Before this the Confederates had swept through the town; and to isolate Kenly from Banks at Strasburg, Ashby's cavalry from Jackson's own division had left the Front Royal–Luray road eight miles short of Front Royal, crossed the South Fork of the Shenandoah at McKoy's Ford, and moved north-west to cut the railway and road linking Strasburg and Front Royal.

Kenly was not strong enough to hold the Confederates. Setting fire to his camp he retreated northwards beyond both the bridges, and set up a rear-guard position on Guard Hill covering the bridge over North Fork with guns on the far bank. He tried to set the bridge on fire, but this he was prevented from doing by the Louisiana infantry, who 'rushed recklessly forward, darted into the flames and extinguished the burning brands.'[2] The Confederate cavalry did not face the northern bridge, but were not long in discovering a practicable ford to get round it. The river was soon alive with horsemen; and, forcing their way through the swirling waters, four squadrons, accompanied by Jackson, gained the further bank, and formed up rapidly for the pursuit. The enemy had already retired, and the dust of the retreating column was receding fast down the road to Winchester.

At Cedarville, three miles from the last rearguard position at Guard Hill, Kenly made another stand. Here the Federal Cavalry, who had arrived from Strasburg to help, were pressed back through the Federal infantry, with some of Ewell's horsemen under Colonel Flournoy in close pursuit. The leading Confederate squadron, jammed between the fences on the road, was halted by a Federal volley at close range; but the supporting squadrons jumped the fences into the neighbouring fields and struck the crowded mass of Federal infantry with revolver and sword so that they fell back in disorder. One of Kenly's guns was surrounded, and the gunners cut to pieces; the other was soon abandoned, and with the appearance of yet more Confederate squadrons, Kenly's whole force dispersed in flight. 'Through the woods and orchards

[1] O.R., XII, i, 556.   [2] Henderson, i, 318.

the chase went on. Escape was impossible. Hundreds laid down their arms; and 250 Virginian horsemen resolutely handled and charging at exactly the right moment, had the honour of bringing in as many as 600 Federals.'[1] The enemy lost in addition 32 killed and 122 wounded. The Confederate casualties were 11 killed and 15 wounded.

Jackson played an important part in this Confederate cavalry victory. He gave the first order to charge. 'His quick eye estimated aright the discouragement of the enemy . . . infusing his own spirit into his men, he struck the hesitating foe at the decisive moment.'[2] He was well pleased with the way Colonel Flournoy's cavalry responded. He declared afterwards that he had never, in all his experience of warfare, seen so gallant and effective a charge of cavalry.

The attack on Front Royal had begun at one o'clock, but it was not until four that Banks realised that it was more than a cavalry raid. Even then it was hard to persuade him that his line of retreat was threatened and he must abandon Strasburg. When, however, the Federals did move, by sending some troops away by a safer route west of the turnpike to Winchester, and by benefiting from the delay which Jackson gave them, they managed to escape the full force of the Confederate turning movement put into operation after the defeat of Kenly.

Jackson struck the main turnpike from Strasburg to Winchester in two places, Middletown five miles north of Strasburg and Newtown six miles nearer Winchester. But the Federals carried out their retreat with skill. Colonel Gordon was sent with a regiment to cover Middletown until the army had passed through. His force, supported by cavalry and a small infantry detachment, did the job so well that the Confederates were kept clear of the turnpike until after 10 a.m., and the main body of the army, with Banks himself, reached Winchester safely.

Banks' rearguard and wagons, however, were less fortunate. When Ewell's cavalry under General Steuart reached Newtown about 11.30 a.m. they found a convoy of wagons strung out along the Valley turnpike, and threw the convoy into such confusion that several wagons were upset and captured before the Federal cavalry and infantry following them could drive the Confederate cavalry off. Next, at Middletown further south, nearly an hour later, Ashby's cavalry from Jackson's division, supported by the Louisiana brigade and some guns from Ewell's emerged from the forests to find the town's main street jammed with Banks' rearguard cavalry moving northwards. Penned in the narrow streets, the Federal squadrons found themselves struck by a cannonade from the Confederate guns and volleys from Taylor's *Tigers*,

[1] Henderson, i, 320.   [2] Dabney, ii, 95.

while those in the front who were making a desperate attempt to gallop on to Winchester, were headed off by a charge from Ashby's horsemen. Jackson witnessed this encounter and described it thus:

In a few moments the turnpike, which had just before teemed with life, presented a most appalling spectacle of carnage and destruction. The road was literally obstructed with the mingled and confused mass of struggling and dying horses and riders. [1]

Taylor was on the spot as well. He relates:

The gentle *Tigers* were looting right merrily, diving in and out of wagons with the activity of rabbits in a warren; but this occupation was abandoned on my approach, and in a moment they were in line, looking as solemn and virtuous as deacons at a funeral. Prisoners and spoil were promptly secured. The Federal horse was from New England, a section in which horsemanship was an unknown art, and some of the riders were strapped to their steeds. Ordered to dismount, they explained their condition, and were given time to unbuckle. Many breastplates and other protective devices were seen here, and later at Winchester. I saw a poor fellow dead on the turnpike, pierced through breastplate and body by a rifle ball. Iron-clad men are of small account before modern weapons. [2]

After the skirmish at Middletown, Jackson sent Ashby's force to pursue the Federal army towards Winchester, and a message was sent to Ewell to move forward on the road from Front Royal. Along the turnpike between Middletown and Newtown were a large number of wagons loaded with stores and abandoned by the Federals. This was too much for Ashby's half-starved troopers; and so many left their ranks to pillage the wagons loaded with sutler stores that Ashby had to give up the pursuit. Jackson writes: 'The artillery, which pushed on with energy to the vicinity of Newtown, found itself, from this discreditable conduct, without a proper support from either infantry or cavalry. This relaxation of the pursuit was unfortunate, as the enemy was encouraged by it to bring up, about two hours later, four pieces of artillery, which were planted upon the northern skirt of Newtown and opened upon our batteries. This fire was replied to by Capt. Poague's two rifled guns with skill and accuracy. When I overtook the advance it was thus held in check by the enemy's artillery.' [3]

Colonel Gordon about this time countermarched two Federal infantry regiments and a few more guns, and resisted the Confederates so strongly that they were held up until dusk.

When darkness came Jackson pressed forward after the retreating enemy; but his march was skilfully impeded by the Federal rearguard who pounced on the van of the Confederates at point after point. Jackson with the various

[1] O.R., XII, i, 703.   [2] Taylor, 55.   [3] O.R., XII, i, 704.

79

regiments of the Stonewall Brigade repelled each ambuscade in turn; 'but the impatient energy of the Confederate leader could not make his progress other than slow.'[1]

So important did Jackson deem it to occupy before dawn the heights overlooking Winchester, that the advance continued through the night. Douglas, Jackson's youngest staff officer, described this march, and how Jackson's resolve to press on regardless, finally weakened.

Whenever the column stopped for a minute, the sleepy officers and men would throw themselves on the ground. And thus, skirmishing and halting, marching while sleeping, the night wore away, and within a few hours of daylight we halted within two miles of Winchester. Jackson, Ashby and the staff halted and fastened their horses to the fence. The General and Ashby to keep awake were walking, separately, up and down the pike, passing each other like silent sentinels, absorbed in their own thoughts. At this hour one of the brigade commanders, Colonel Samuel Fulkerson, an excellent officer and a great favourite with the General, came up. He represented the sad condition of his men, so exhausted that each time the brigade halted and moved on a large percentage of them were left asleep in fence corners. He suggested that it would be better to wait until daylight. The General listened patiently to this reasonable suggestion and then replied: 'Colonel, I do not believe you can feel more for your men than I do. This is very hard on them, but by this night march I hope to save many valuable lives. I want to get possession of the hills of Winchester before daylight.' Then after a moment's reflection he continued: 'Colonel, you may rest your command for two hours. I will go with my brigade.' But the General changed his mind, and when dawn came the command had not moved since his interview with Colonel Fulkerson. General Banks had taken possession of the range of hills referred to by the General and was prepared to fight.[2]

General Taylor, who also rode with Jackson through the darkness, says that Major Harman, the chief quartermaster, rode up during the night and reported that the wagons were 'left behind impeded by a bad road in the Luray Valley. "The ammunition wagons?" queries Jackson sternly. "All right, sir. They were in advance and I doubled teams on them and brought them through." "Ah!" a tone of relief. To give countenance to the quartermaster, if such can be given on a dark night, I remarked jocosely, "Never mind the wagons. There are quantities of stores in Winchester and the General had invited me to breakfast there tomorrow." Jackson took this seriously, and reached out to touch me on the arm. Without physical wants himself, he forgot that others were differently constituted, and paid little heed to the commissariat, but woe to the man who failed to bring up ammunition!'[3]

Banks' position before Winchester was manned by Gordon's brigade

[1] Allan, 133.   [2] Douglas, 64.   [3] Taylor, 56.

guarding the turnpike from Strasburg, and Donnelly's brigade on the Front Royal road, both with their forces placed along a broken ridge lined in many places with stout stone walls. Still, strong as was the Federal position, there was little chance of holding it. Banks was outnumbered by two to one.

Jackson's plan was to hold Gordon in position until Ewell came up along the Front Royal road and attacked Donnelly. Then he proposed to send a column to turn Gordon's right.

The battle began with the advance of the Stonewall Brigade against Gordon's pickets, and these were quickly driven back. There followed an artillery duel in which the Confederate gunners suffered heavily, but finally silenced the Federal guns opposite the Stonewall Brigade. Meanwhile Ewell had come into action on Gordon's left, employing a small turning movement of his own to take the enemy in the flank. This was the sign for Jackson to bring forward his brigades from the reserve to start their major turning movement on Gordon's right flank. Taylor's Louisianians played a large part in this. To speed the movement of Taylor's Brigade, which was already moving forward from its reserve position, Jackson rode in the direction of Taylor's advance. Past the Virginians of the Stonewall Brigade he rode. Inquiringly they looked at him. As they had been told not to cheer, they did not greet him in the usual manner but took off their hats in silent salute. Soon Jackson found the Louisiana brigadier, who was riding ahead of his troops. One question and one sentence covered orders. 'Jackson, impassive as ever, pointed to the ridge (on the left) and said, "You must carry it."'[1]

Jackson waited a few minutes until the columns arrived, and then rode on with Taylor, under fire from the Federals. As some men fell, the Louisianians began to duck. Taylor writes: 'This annoyed me no little, as it was child's play to the work immediately in hand. Forgetting Jackson's presence, I ripped out, "What the hell are you dodging for? If there is any more of this you will be halted under fire for an hour." The sharp tones of a familiar voice produced the desired effect, and the men looked as if they had swallowed ramrods; but I shall never forget the reproachful surprise expressed in Jackson's face. He placed his hand on my shoulder, said in a gentle voice, "I am afraid you are a wicked fellow," turned and rode back to the pike.'[2]

Looking over the brow of the hill, Jackson waited while the Louisiana Tigers slipped round to a point opposite the end of a shattered and abandoned stone wall from which the Federals had earlier been enfilading the Confederate gunners. Then, about 7.30,[3] when Taylor emerged, there was staged such a spectacle as the Army of the Valley never witnessed before:

---

[1] Taylor, 57.   [2] *Ibid.*, 58.   [3] Freeman, LL, i, 402.

'The enemy poured grape and musketry into Taylor's line as soon as it came in sight. General Taylor rode in front of his brigade, drawn sword in hand, occasionally turning his horse, at other times merely turning in his saddle to see that his line was up. They marched up the hill in perfect order, not firing a shot! About half way to the Yankees he gave in a loud and commanding voice, that I am sure the Yankees heard, the order to charge; and over the stone wall they went!' [1]

Soon the other brigades could be seen advancing. Much of the Confederate army was now pouring over the ridges. Jackson watching it all could restrain himself no longer. Turning to his staff officers he said: 'Order forward the whole line, the battle's won.' Winder's men came sweeping past, and as they did so the General cried out, 'Very good! Now let's holler!' 'That is the very language the Professor used. He raised his old grey cap, his staff took up the cheer, and soon from the advancing line rose and swelled a deafening roar.' [2] Then a panic seized the Federals and the retreat became a rout through the streets of Winchester.

The operations about Front Royal show Jackson at his best as a general. His puzzling manoeuvres before the attack on Front Royal, when he had marched Taylor's Louisianians to join the force on the turnpike, and then suddenly switched back eastwards across the Massanuttons, deceived Banks completely. The attack on Front Royal was skilfully planned and well executed. The river obstacles in the rear of Kenly's camp were boldly circumvented, and the links with Banks at Strasburg, from which place help could come to Kenly, were severed by Ashby's cavalry. Flournoy's squadrons crossed the Shenandoah's South Fork at McCoy's Ford with Ashby, but keeping close to the west bank were able to come back and join in the battle at Front Royal, with good effect. Leading the van in person Jackson pressed forward Flournoy's horsemen in a vigorous pursuit, ending in their splendid cavalry victory at Cedarville.

Jackson's movements westward from Front Royal on Banks' line of retreat to Winchester were not completely successful although they achieved considerable results. As can be seen from the map (facing p. 96), only part of Banks' force kept to the turnpike. A proportion took a safer westerly route. Jackson thought Banks might even move eastward through Front Royal. He kept protective forces in that neighbourhood so long that when his westerly flank attack at last struck the turnpike it encountered only Banks' wagons and rearguard. Jackson then tried to carry out a forced march by night to Winchester after the retreating Federals. But even his driving personality

[1] Worsham, 87.   [2] Douglas, 66.

The Operations about Front Royal and Winchester : Chain of Command[1]

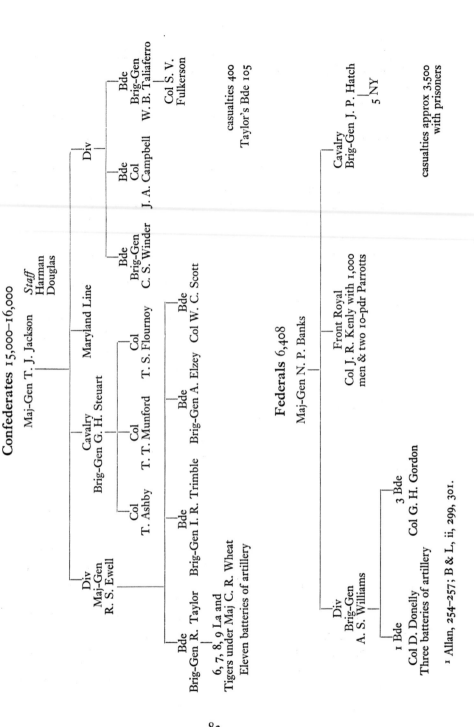

Confederates 15,000–16,000

Maj-Gen T. J. Jackson

Staff
Harman
Douglas

Div
Maj-Gen R. S. Ewell

Bde
Brig-Gen R. Taylor
6, 7, 8, 9 La and
Tigers under Maj C. R. Wheat
Eleven batteries of artillery

Bde
Brig-Gen I. R. Trimble

Cavalry
Brig-Gen G. H. Steuart

Col T. Ashby

Col T. T. Munford

Bde
Brig-Gen A. Elzey

Col T. S. Flournoy

Bde
Col W. C. Scott

Maryland Line

Div

Bde
Brig-Gen C. S. Winder

Bde
Col J. A. Campbell

Bde
Brig-Gen W. B. Taliaferro

Col S. V. Fulkerson

casualties 400
Taylor's Bde 105

Federals 6,408

Maj-Gen N. P. Banks

Div
Brig-Gen A. S. Williams

1 Bde
Col D. Donelly
Three batteries of artillery

3 Bde
Col G. H. Gordon

Front Royal
Col J. R. Kenly with 1,000
men & two 10-pdr Parrotts

Cavalry
Brig-Gen J. P. Hatch

5 NY

casualties approx 3,500
with prisoners

[1] Allan, 254–257; B & L, ii, 299, 301.

83

failed to keep the Confederate column moving. It faltered short of his objective, necessitating a formal daylight assault on the Federals in a strong position guarding Winchester. Jackson conducted this battle with great skill, executing two turning movements successfully, and using his guns to neutralise the Federal artillery. The pursuit, however, failed as it had done after M'Dowell. Ashby's cavalry, busy plundering, were not available; the other arms were too worn out to go further.

At this stage Jackson's impatience was almost uncontrollable. His staff was despatched in all directions to urge forward the remainder of the batteries and fetch the cavalry. 'We must press them to the Potomac. Forward to the Potomac,' he cried. When he received Jackson's message, General Steuart who commanded Flournoy's and Munford's regiments, refused to obey the instruction until it had been referred to his immediate commander Ewell. The time spent in locating Ewell for this purpose therefore delayed the cavalry's arrival; and an opportunity for an immediate and vigorous pursuit was lost.

Nevertheless, Banks was driven back across the Potomac, and 3,000 prisoners, 10,000 stands of much-needed small arms, several guns and a vast quantity of stores were now in Jackson's hands. About 1,500 Federal soldiers were killed or wounded for a total loss of 400 Confederates, killed, wounded or missing. And this was not all. General McDowell, starting to meet McClellan in the attack on Richmond, was once more halted in the Fredericksburg area; and 20,000 men of his command, including Shields' division in the van, were detached and sent north-west to the Valley. The Valley operations were thus achieving the strategic results the Confederate cause desired.

CROSS KEYS–PORT REPUBLIC

A feature of the Valley campaign was the sudden change of fortune of each side. The Federal higher command reacted very quickly to Banks' discomfiture. He had scarcely been driven across the Potomac before Frémont was ordered to strike at Jackson's flank from the Mountain District, and Shields, on the other flank, was sent across the Blue Ridge by McDowell. Jackson soon faced being cut off by a skilful Federal pincer movement of serious dimensions.[1] He was forced to withdraw, and all the strategic gains of the Front Royal operations appeared lost. But in his withdrawal Jackson showed all the skill he had done in the previous advance.

[1] The Stonewall Brigade were as far north as Harper's Ferry.

In his retreat south down the turnpike before Frémont, with Shields on his flank advancing towards Luray along the South Fork of the Shenandoah, the topography, and particularly the bridges over the swollen rivers, were used skilfully for his advantage.

To prevent Shields from joining Frémont across the Massanuttons through the Newmarket Gap, Jackson sent his troopers to burn White House and Columbia bridges. The fords were impassable owing to the swollen state of the river, so the destruction of these bridges removed Shields' only access to the Newmarket Gap. Jackson also destroyed the bridge at Conrad's Store, and Shields was foiled once more when he reached that town. To increase the Federal General's embarrassment 'heavy and incessant rain-storms submerged the Virginia roads. He was ahead of his supplies; much hampered by the mud; and the South Fork of the Shenandoah, cutting him off from Frémont, rolled a volume of rushing water which it was impossible to bridge without long delay.'[1]

Meanwhile, west of the Massanuttons, the rivers were also used to impede Frémont's pursuit, now developing with unusual vigour. South of Mount Jackson the North Fork of the Shenandoah is a deep and turbulent river; and on 4 June the bridge which took the turnpike over it was destroyed by Ashby's cavalry. 'Under a deluge of rain the Federals attempted to launch their pontoons; but the boats were swept away by the rising flood, and it was not till the morning that the bridge was made. The Confederates had thus gained twenty-four hours respite.'[2]

By spirited encounters with Frémont's vanguard Ashby and his cavalry played a large part in slowing up the Federal advance; but near Harrisonburg, rallying his supporting infantry on foot when his horse had been killed under him, he was shot through the heart and fell dead, a severe loss to the Confederate cause.

Jackson was making for Port Republic, a town nestling between the two arms of the South Fork of the Shenandoah. There was a bridge to reach it over the northern arm, North River, and fords to cross over the southern one, South River. North River was also joined by the stream Mill Creek which flowed directly across the road from Harrisonburg to Port Republic near Cross Keys.

Jackson chose the south side of this stream for a position for Ewell's division to stop and give battle to Frémont. Meanwhile he drew up the main body of the Valley Army just north of North River at Port Republic. He kept the cavalry out reconnoitring in the direction of Harrisonburg, and towards Conrad's Store on both sides of the river. He sent Major Hotchkiss to a signal

[1] Henderson, i, 360.   [2] Ibid., i, 361.

station on Peaked Mountain at the end of the Massanutton chain to observe both columns of the advancing enemy. He established his wagon line, with wagons containing the reserve ammunition and a drove of cattle, on the Staunton road west of Port Republic; and he made his own headquarters at Dr Kemper's house there, with only Carrington's battery and its small escort and a company of partially disabled Virginians under Captain Moore in the town itself.

Then, just as the battle of Cross Keys was beginning, and Jackson was preparing to ride out to the battlefield, dramatic events took place at Port Republic.

There was distant firing, a sudden commotion in the streets, and a breathless messenger reported that not only had the troopers on picket been surprised and scattered, but that the enemy with one field piece—and another behind—were fording South River and entering the town. Caught outside his headquarters, Jackson managed to mount and gallop off over North River bridge; but several of his staff were captured by Colonel Carroll's Federal troops, and the wagon train with its teamsters and camp followers was thrown into great confusion. Some of the wagons made off there and then on the road to Staunton. The few troops present in Port Republic kept their heads and did their best to check the invaders. A gun from Carrington's battery raked the main street of the village and a part of the Federal force was stopped by Captain Moore's company. It was Jackson himself, however, who restored the situation. Some Federals, in spite of the efforts of the headquarters guards, managed to approach the bridge over North River. Although the cavalry would not try a charge over the bridge, a Federal gun was placed in a position to cover it. This in no way deterred Jackson. He sent over Douglas to General Taliaferro's Brigade, which had already been placed under arms, for the first regiment he could get 'to bring it quickly and take that piece!'[1] Douglas met Fulkerson with the 37th Va Regt and brought it along with one of Captain Poague's guns. Jackson posted Poague's gun in a wheatfield overlooking and commanding both the bridge and the country beyond the Shenandoah River.[2] Poague writes: 'I was surprised to see a gun posted at the farther end of the bridge. For I had just come from army headquarters, and, although I had met a cavalryman who told me the enemy were advancing up the river, still I did not think it possible they could have gotten any guns into the place in so short a time. It thereupon occurred to me that the gun at the bridge might be one of Carrington's who was on that side and whose men had new uniform something like those we saw at the bridge. Upon suggesting this to the General, he reflected a moment, and then riding a few

---

[1] Douglas, 93.   [2] O.R., XII, i, 762.

paces to the left and front of our piece, he called in a tone loud enough to be heard by them, "Bring that gun up here", but getting no reply, he raised himself in his stirrups and in a most authoritative and seemingly angry tone shouted, "Bring that gun here, I say." At this they began to move the trail of the gun so as to bring it to bear on us, which when the General perceived, he quickly turned to the officer in charge of my gun, and said in his sharp, quick way, "Let 'em have it." The words had scarcely left his lips when Lieut Brown, who had his piece charged and aimed, sent a shot right among them, so disconcerting them that theirs in reply went far above us.'[1]

Fulkerson now took over. He rushed his men with a yell across the bridge, poured a volley at the enemy gunners, who fled, captured the piece; and then proceeded to clear the town.

When Fulkerson charged across the bridge, Moore also assumed the offensive, and 'did much to speed Carroll's retreat'.[2] By this time three batteries, including Poague's, supported by the Stonewall Brigade had taken up their position on the hill beyond the bridge and poured a volley after the retreating Carroll, galloping off to rejoin Shields who was advancing on the south bank of the river from Conrad's Store.

Frémont's attack on Ewell's force at Cross Keys, which followed the skirmish at Port Republic, was a half-hearted affair. Of his 24 regiments he employed only five of Blenker's Germans; and these he directed on the Confederate right which was ably secured by Trimble's brigade occupying a good defensive position. Trimble's troops were strung out among the oak trees on a flat-topped ridge, and looked across a wide meadow towards another line of woods from which the Federals would have to emerge. The Federal skirmishers drove back the Confederate pickets across the meadow; but when they were 60 paces from the oak trees, the Confederate main line rose to their feet to meet them. There was a sheet of flame followed by a resounding crash through the woods, and the German regiments fell back in confusion leaving their dead and wounded.

When the Federals showed no inclination to repeat their performance, Trimble, more skilful than his enemies, 'sent a regiment against their left to which a convenient ravine gave access, while the troops among the oaks held back,'[3] until the Confederate flank attack was fully developed. This unexpected movement completely surprised Blenker. Then, when the Confederates were reinforced by a further six regiments, there was a general advance of all Trimble's men; and the Federals were pushed back to their reserve line of guns over a mile behind Trimble's first position. In the other

[1] Allan, note 98, 267. [2] Douglas, 93. [3] Henderson, i, 374.

sectors of the Cross Keys front the battle had consisted of little more than an artillery duel. In the centre, Blenker's skirmishers were driven off by a bayonet charge; 'on the Federal right, Milroy and Schenck, the two generals who had withstood Jackson so stubbornly at M'Dowell, advanced on their own initiative through the woods. They had driven in the Confederate skirmishers, and had induced Ewell to strengthen that portion of the line from his reserve, when they were recalled by Frémont, alarmed by Trimble's vigorous attack, to defend the main position.'[1]

Jackson left the conduct of the battle of Cross Keys to Ewell; and Ewell won a victory for him there. The losses were slight on both sides, 684 Federals against 288 Confederates; but the Confederate victory caused Frémont to cower on the defensive, and in that way it achieved all that Jackson had desired. He now turned to deal with the enemy advancing towards him from Conrad's Store. Leaving a small force to contain Frémont, he issued orders for the bulk of his army to move against Shields whose leading brigades under Tyler were now about two miles east of Port Republic.

Imboden—whom we met at First Bull Run—commanded a mule battery at Port Republic. He was ordered to report to Jackson on the night before the battle. He writes: 'I reached Port Republic an hour before daybreak of June 9th, and sought the house occupied by Jackson; but not wishing to disturb him so early, I asked the sentinel what room was occupied by "Sandy" Pendleton, Jackson's adjutant-general. "Upstairs on the right", he replied.

Supposing he meant our right as we faced the house, I went up, softly entered the door, and discovered General Jackson lying on his face across the bed, fully dressed, with sword, sash, and boots all on. The low-burnt tallow candle on the table shed a dim light, yet enough by which to recognise him. He turned over, sat up on the bed, and called out, "Who is that?"

He checked my apology with "That is all right. It's time to be up. I am glad to see you. Were the men all up as you came through the camp?"

"Yes, General, and cooking."

"That's right. We move at daybreak. Sit down. I want to talk to you."

I had learned never to ask him questions about his plans, for he would never answer such to anyone. I therefore waited for him to speak first. He referred very feelingly to Ashby's death, and spoke of it as a irreparable loss. When he paused I said, "General, you made a glorious winding-up of your four weeks' work yesterday."

He replied, "Yes, God blessed our army again yesterday, and I hope with his protection and blessing we shall do still better to-day."[2]

[1] Henderson, i, 375.   [2] *Ibid.*, 377, 378.

Then seating himself, for the first time in all my intercourse with him, he outlined the day's proposed operations. I remember perfectly his conversation. He said: "Charley Winder (commanding his old Stonewall Brigade) will cross the river at daybreak and attack Shields on the Lewis farm. I will support him with all the other troops as fast as they can be put in line. General 'Dick' Taylor will move through the woods on the side of the mountain with his Louisiana brigade, and rush upon their left flank by the time the action becomes general. By 10 o'clock we shall get them on the run, and I'll now tell you what I want with you. Send the 12-pounder Parrott to Poague and let your mounted men report to the cavalry. I want you in person to take your mountain howitzers to the field, in some safe position in rear of the line, keeping everything packed on the mules, ready at any moment to take to the mountain-side. Three miles below Lewis's there is a defile on the Luray road. Shields may rally and make a stand there. If he does, I can't reach him with the field-batteries on account of the woods. You can carry your 12-pounder howitzers on the mules up the mountain-side, and at some good place unpack and shell the enemy out of the defile, and the cavalry will do the rest." [1]

In fact, as will be seen when the battle is described, the mule-battery was not very effective as the mules got out of hand when frightened by the shelling; but this extract does show Jackson in the unusual role of putting his subordinates well 'in the picture'. It was the same with the commander of the rearguard left to watch Frémont. Ewell was first summoned to headquarters, and then Patton, whose brigade (with Trimble's) was to have the task of holding Frémont.

'I found him at 2 a.m.,' says Patton, 'actively engaged in making his dispositions for battle. He immediately proceeded to give me particular instructions as to the management of the men in covering the rear, saying: "I wish you to throw out all your men, if necessary, as skirmishers, and to make a great show, so as to cause the enemy to think the whole army are behind you. Hold your position as well as you can, then fall back when obliged; take a new position, hold it in the same way, and I will be back to join you in the morning."'

Colonel Patton commented that he was doubtful about holding back Frémont for long with such a small force in country giving no great advantage for defence. He asked Jackson how long he was expected to hold the enemy in check. Jackson replied, 'By the blessing of Providence, I hope to be back by ten o'clock.' [2]

This showed that Jackson intended to defeat Shields in the five hours

[1] B & L, ii, 293.   [2] S.H.S.P., vol IX, 372.

between dawn and ten o'clock; and then return on the same day and defeat Frémont. He boldly planned to fight two major battles on one day. Because the Battle of Port Republic dragged on so long, and eventually drew in all his forces, he was not able to do so.

In all the operations about Port Republic the bridges over the various parts of the Shenandoah played a dominant part. By destroying bridges in his retreat, Jackson kept his two adversaries apart. He left the bridge over North River intact so that he could turn after beating Shields and rout Frémont; taking thereby a dangerous risk; for Frémont might have used it to join Shields. Finally, it was the partial failure of the bridge he constructed over South River to supplement the fords which caused the frustration of his plans for a double battle.

Having completed his dispositions, Jackson arranged for the feeding of his troops by ordering the wagons from the train to be sent over North River bridge 'for the purpose of issuing food to them'[1] before they started at dawn to cross both arms of the South Shenandoah and meet Shields. Then, 'awaiting the rising of the moon, which occurred about midnight, he collected his pioneers, and caused them, under his own eye, to construct a foot-bridge across the fords of the South River, by which he designed to pass his infantry down toward Lewiston. This structure was hastily made by placing wagons, without their bodies, longitudinally across the stream. The axles formed the cross-beams for the support of the floor; and the latter was composed of long boards borrowed from a neighbouring saw-mill, laid loosely from one to another.'[2]

It was intended that the flooring should occupy the whole breadth between the wheels of the wagons, giving passage to several men abreast. Unfortunately, in the middle of the stream, the wagons were not level with each other; and in one place where a drop of two feet occurred, only one of the longitudinal planks was firmly fixed at both ends. The other four or five planks were so whippy that as the men began to pass over them, several were thrown into the water. The ones who followed refused to trust themselves to any except the one solid plank; and thus the column was converted, at this point, into a single file. This meant that each brigade was slow to get across, and that Jackson's attack went in piecemeal. Although he eventually won the battle, he could not get his force concentrated until late in the day; he suffered many casualties in his early attacks owing to the insufficient numbers he could engage, and at ten o'clock, when he should have been finished with Shields, and according to his plan, have been on his way back to Cross Keys, many of his troops had not even crossed the temporary bridge.

[1] Dabney, ii, 153.   [2] Ibid., 153.

On the day of the battle, before 5 a.m., the Stonewall Brigade was assembled in Port Republic and was immediately ordered to advance. On the plain beyond, still dark in the shadow of the mountains, where the cavalry formed the outposts, the fire of the pickets, which had been incessant throughout the night, was increasing in intensity. The Federals were making ready for battle.

Jackson left Dabney to superintend the passage of the river and rode with the leading brigade. About a mile and a half along the Luray road the first pickets were encountered. They were quickly driven back to the main Federal position.

Their army had found a good defensive position at Lewiston, the group of dwellings around General Lewis' house. There is a level tract between the Shenandoah and the forests on the terraces which girdle the mountain base. This had on it fields of clover and wheat, divided by the zigzag wooden fences of the country. Near the edge of the forest stood General Lewis' house surrounded by large barns, and stables, and orchards. A country road leading from the house to Lewis Mill on the Shenandoah ran between steep banks strongly fenced. This provided excellent cover for the Federal riflemen to start with; but as they soon counter-attacked, they did not make much use of it. Two streams flowed from the wooded terraces flanking Blue Ridge across the Federal position. The further one had cut a deep ravine in its upper course above General Lewis' house; and on the northern rim of the ravine, in a clearing made for charcoal burning, a seven-gun battery had been placed. This battery dominated the whole area, and enfiladed Winder's advancing forces consisting of the Stonewall Brigade, with one regiment from Taylor's Louisianians, who were the next brigade to cross the bridge, the 31st and 52nd Va regiments, and Poague's and Penter's batteries. With the ravine in front and surrounded by a dense and almost impenetrable thicket composed of trees and laurel bushes, it was very difficult to approach. It was to become the key to the whole position.

Jackson decided that it was necessary to silence this hostile battery beyond the ravine. Poague's battery attempted this, but found it beyond their range; and Jackson sent Carpenter's battery and two regiments from the Stonewall Brigade under Colonel Allen up on to the wooded terrace to deal with it.

Allen made his way with great difficulty through the tangled thickets until he reached the Federal battery; but Carpenter could not get his guns through. Allen's infantry, unable to make any headway on their own, and subjected to a heavy fire of musketry and canister, were soon thrown into confusion and forced to retire.

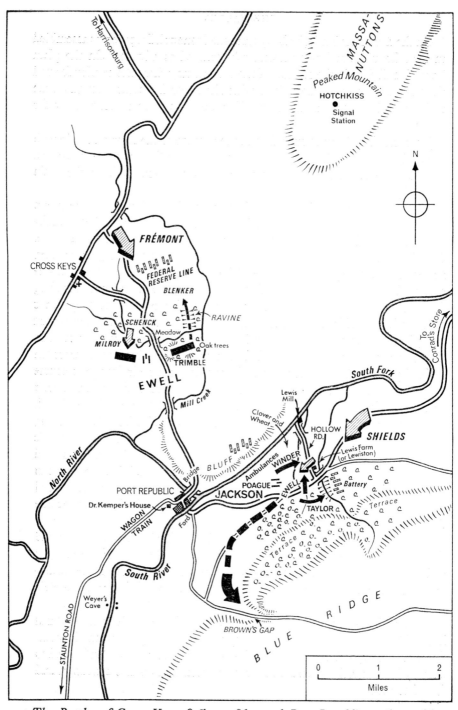

To Harrisonburg

MASSA-NUTTONS

Peaked Mountain

HOTCHKISS
● Signal
Station

N

FRÉMONT

CROSS KEYS

FEDERAL
RESERVE LINE

BLENKER

RAVINE

SCHENCK

Meadow

MILROY

Oak trees

TRIMBLE

EWELL

Mill Creek

South Fork

Lewis
Mill

Clover and
Wheat

HOLLOW
RD.

SHIELDS

To Contrad's Store

North River

BLUFF

Bridge

Ambulances

WINDER

Lewis Farm
(or Lewiston)

PORT REPUBLIC

POAGUE

EWELL

Battery

JACKSON

Dr. Kemper's House

Ford

TAYLOR

Terrace

WAGON
TRAIN

Terrace

South River

Terrace

STAUNTON ROAD

Weyer's
Cave

BLUE   RIDGE

BROWN'S GAP

0   1   2

Miles

5 The Battles of Cross Keys, 8 June 1862, and Port Republic, 9 June 1862

Receiving some of the reinforcements which Jackson was hurrying forward as fast as possible, Winder, meanwhile, tried an attack on the Federals nearer the Shenandoah, ordering three Virginian regiments to advance and carry the enemy's position along the hollow road with the bayonet. The staunch Federal Ohio troops, however, repelled every effort to drive them from the shelter of their hollow road and the buildings around General Lewis' farm. It was Winder's men who wavered and broke, so that, in spite of further reinforcements, Winder and his supporting troops were forced to retreat in confusion, past Poague's battery, one of the pieces of which was lost.

The first respite for the Confederates came through the action of Ewell. The Federal centre had advanced so far that they offered themselves for a flank attack. Ewell took two regiments south of the road into the woods and waited in a strong position with the wood behind him ready to pounce. The Federals had swung round towards the river as if to cut off and surround Winder's men against it. The sudden assault of Ewell's two regiments caught them unawares, and they wheeled south again to meet the menace to their flank and rear. After a furious conflict they were forced back by the Confederates with heavy loss.

The final defeat of Tyler's brigade was brought about by Taylor's men reinforced by Ewell. Jackson was still determined to silence the troublesome battery; and when the rest of the Louisianians arrived, Taylor was sent with them on another detour along the wooded terrace to capture the guns and at the same time take the Federals in the flank.

'Jackson was on the road, a little in advance of his line, where the fire was hottest, with reins on his horse's neck, seemingly in prayer.' Taylor writes:[1] 'Attracted by my approach, he said, in his usual voice, "Delightful excitement." I replied that it was pleasant to learn he was enjoying himself, but thought he might have an indigestion of such fun if the battery was not silenced. He summoned a young officer from his staff, and pointed up the mountain. The head of my approaching column was turned short up the slope, and speedily came to a path running parallel with the river. We took this path, the guide leading the way. From him I learned that the plateau occupied by the battery had been used for a charcoal kiln, and the path we were following, made by the burners in hauling wood, came upon the gorge opposite the battery.' Thanks to the path Taylor seems to have got through the woods fairly quickly. He seized and lost the battery several times before, with the help of Ewell, when the Federals were massing to throw him out again, he finally captured it. He writes: 'At that instant, crashing through the undergrowth, came Ewell, outriding staff and escort. He produced the effect

[1] Taylor, 74.

93

of a re-enforcement, and was welcomed with cheers. The line before us halted and threw forward skirmishers. A moment later, a shell came shrieking along it, loud Confederate cheers reached our delighted ears, and Jackson, freed from his toils rushed up like a whirlwind, the enemy in rapid retreat. We turned the captured guns on them as they passed, Ewell serving as a gunner.'[1] The attacks from two sides at once had proved too much for the Federals.

Meanwhile Jackson realised that the battle was taking so much time that it would be impossible to fight Frémont as well as Shields on that day. He therefore recalled Patton's brigade, and Trimble's which was supporting it, from Cross Keys, ordering them to burn the bridge over North River behind them.

The brigade of General Taliaferro, which had been left to occupy Port Republic, was also hurried to the front to help with the final volleys on the Federals, who were sent in full retreat to Conrad's Store with the Confederate cavalry on their heels. The Federal flight never became a rout; but prisoners were taken. 'Nearly half of an Ohio regiment were separated from their comrades by General Taliaferro, and surrendered in a body; and the pursuit was continued eight miles farther by the cavalry, who gathered, as spoils of war, small arms and vehicles, with many prisoners.'[2]

As the evening approached, General Jackson recalled his jaded men from the pursuit, and led them by a side way from Lewiston towards the mouth of Brown's Gap. When they passed the field of battle, Frémont's guns opened on them from the bluff north of the river; but they were out of range, and Frémont only succeeded in shelling some of the ambulances which were collecting the dead and wounded near the river.[3] The Confederates were outraged at this; but the Federals later denied any intent to fire on ambulances.

Frémont started to try to bridge the Shenandoah to get at Jackson; but changed his mind, and pursued by Confederate cavalry retreated back to Harrisonburg, and from there to Mount Jackson. Thus the result of the main battle at Port Republic was that both Frémont and Shields retreated northwards.

As it was Jackson's army, the Saturday following the battle was proclaimed by him as a day of thanksgiving and prayers. 'The next day a general communion was observed in the 3rd Virginia brigade, at which the Lord's Supper was dispersed, in the woods, to a great company of Christian soldiers from all the army. At this solemnity the General was present as a worshipper, and modestly participated with his men in the sacred feast.'[4]

[1] Taylor, 75, 76.   [2] Dabney, ii, 160.
[3] Allan, 206; O.R., XII, i, 716.   [4] Dabney, ii, 166.

In a letter to his wife Jackson writes: 'Our God has thrown His shield over me in the various apparent dangers to which I have been exposed. This evening we have religious services in the army, for the purpose of rendering thanks to the Most High for the victories with which He has crowned our arms.'[1]

With the end of the battle at Port Republic Jackson's famous Valley Campaign came to an end. Before it, following his part in the Confederate victory at the battle of First Bull Run, Jackson had been considered only a good executive officer, obeying orders explicitly, and exacting the same obedience from his subordinates; possessing energy without limit, and a will that stiffened with opposition. Lee was later to say of him: 'Such an executive officer the sun never shone on. I have but to show him my design, and, I know that, if it can be done, it will be done.'

But the Valley Campaign proved that he also possessed other qualities. In all but name, supreme commander of the Valley forces, he displayed strategic and tactical skill of the highest order in his handling of them. The campaign just ended was Jackson's masterpiece. The more it is studied and its difficulties comprehended, the greater it appears. The battle of M'Dowell was fought on 8 May, the battle of Port Republic on 9 June. In this month Jackson and his little army made their name. In that time he had defeated four separate armies. He had relieved Staunton of Milroy and Schenck, had driven Banks beyond the borders of Virginia, had held General McDowell with 35,000 troops from going to join McClellan, had defeated Banks, Frémont, and Shields in turn, had broken into pieces their triple combination, and had driven the Federal Administration in Washington to the verge of nervous prostration. In 30 days his army had marched nearly 400 miles, skirmishing almost daily, fought five battles, defeated four armies, two of which were completely routed, captured about 20 pieces of artillery, some 4,000 prisoners, an immense quantity of stores of all kinds, and had done all this with a loss of less than 1,000 killed, wounded and missing. Surely a more brilliant record cannot be found!

[1] Mrs Jackson, 283.

Confederates 13,000
Maj-Gen T. J. Jackson   *Staff*
                           Douglas
                           Dabney

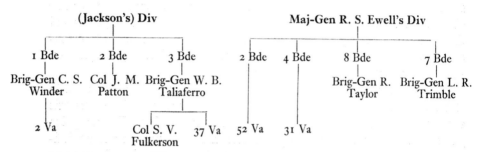

| (Jackson's) Div | | | Maj-Gen R. S. Ewell's Div | | | |

There were also Capt Moore's invalids

The artillery was under Col S. Crutchfield and included Capt J. Carpenter's battery, Capt W. T. Poague's battery with Lieut Brown, and Capt J. D. Imboden's mule battery. Brig-Gen T. Ashby commanding the cavalry was killed.

casualties 1,150

Federals 21,000

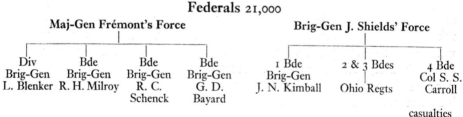

casualties
Frémont 684
Shields 1,018

[1] B & L, ii, 300, 301.

Rom

eld

MT.

NEW

sonburg

CRO
KEY

STAUNTO

Jackson's Battles in the Pattern of the War

When Abraham Lincoln was elected President of the United States in 1860 civil war became inevitable, for Lincoln believed that the fathers of the republic desired the abolition of slavery. There had long been friction between the states following an industrial economy in the north and those with a plantation economy in the south. They had different views about free trade and protection; and the South wished to retain slavery which the North wanted to abolish. The South not only believed that slavery was an economic necessity for their plantations but that they had the right to decide such matters for themselves. This involved the doctrine of States' Rights. The South interpreted the Constitution in a different way from the North. They considered they could decide most matters in their state assemblies, and even break away from the Union if they wished. The North thought the Union indissoluble and the Federal Government supreme. Unwilling to submit to the dictates of the Union Government, some of the Southern States did break away, including Jackson's Virginia, and the war was fought to bring them back into the Union.

The South won many victories in Virginia against the North until the death of Jackson in the Battle of Chancellorsville in 1863. Chancellorsville seems to end a run of success for the South. Without Jackson as his right hand man, Lee's once sure touch appears to fail. 'The death of the Southern Confederacy dates from Chancellorsville,' wrote Thomas L. Rosser, a surviving Confederate general, in 1907.[1] This, however, presents a somewhat misleading picture. There were at least three main theatres of operations of war: in Virginia, in the Mississippi region, and on the sea. In both the west

[1] See Assessment.

and at sea the North were in the ascendant from the start: Grant pushed steadily down the Mississippi; and the Federal navy blockaded the coastline, hampered the South's import of weapons of war from Europe, restricted the vital export of Southern cotton overseas and almost strangled the South economically.

In the Mississippi region General Grant proceeded down the great river greatly aided in his military operations by Federal gunboats on the river itself. By July 1863, only two months after Chancellorsville, the river had been almost closed to the Confederates, only the river ports of Vicksburg and Port Hudson remaining in their hands. This was a great strategic achievement for the Federals as the Southern States were almost cut in two, and the Confederates could no longer easily draw food and materials from the west for their military operations in Virginia. Only Vicksburg remained guarding the vital central route across the river.

As has been said, this was July 1863, only two months after the death of Jackson at Chancellorsville. Then two decisive battles were fought. Two battles lost by the South. Vicksburg in the west, which was captured by Grant; and Gettysburg in the east, where, without Jackson, Lee was defeated by General Meade. But Jackson's presence would not have made any difference to the result of the battle for Vicksburg; and from it emerged not only the selection by President Lincoln of Grant to command the Federal armies in the east, but also Grant's able lieutenant Sherman's march through Georgia to the sea, to split once again the area of the Confederacy, and to threaten a junction with Grant who was pushing down slowly but remorselessly on Richmond. All in all, the final result of the war does not appear to have depended on Jackson's death.

But what place did he and his forces have in the pattern of the war up to May 1863?

In the first two years of the war in Virginia Jackson and the men under him played an important part. Their engagements are impressive in numbers alone, including:

> Falling Waters   2 July 1861
> First Bull Run   21 July 1861
> Romney Expedition   10 January 1862
> Kernstown   23 March 1862
> M'Dowell   8 May 1862
> Front Royal and Winchester   23–25 May 1862
> Cross Keys and Port Republic   8–9 June 1862
> Mechanicsville   26 June 1862

Gaines' Mill   27 June 1862
Frayser's Farm and Malvern Hill, 30 June–1 July 1862
Cedar Run   9 August 1862
Second Bull Run Campaign   17 August–1 September 1862
Maryland Campaign   16–17 September 1862
Fredericksburg   13 December 1862
Chancellorsville   1–3 May 1863

President Lincoln's aim on the Virginian front was for his armies to drive down south from Washington to capture the Southern capital Richmond only 100 miles away. But he found it extremely difficult to select a general capable of carrying out his plans, and after every failure he chose a new leader. McDowell, McClellan, Pope, Burnside and Hooker were the successive Federal commanders in the major attacks on Richmond. Even in the defensive campaign in Maryland, between the assaults into the South of Pope and Burnside, the Northern generals were little more successful. Lincoln said of them, 'You are acting like old women trying to shoo a flock of geese across a creek.'

So far in this book Jackson's part at First Bull Run, at Falling Waters and in the Valley campaign have been described—and in that order although Falling Waters took place before Bull Run. These three are all connected with the Shenandoah Valley which, as was explained on page 14, was both the 'breadbasket of the Confederacy' and a covered approach leading towards the rear of Washington. At Falling Waters, Jackson's first battle of the war, he was trying in a small rearguard action to hold back the Federal force under General Patterson advancing from Maryland into the Valley: helping to retain the Valley as a Confederate breadbasket in fact. At First Bull Run, Jackson's brigade as part of General Johnston's force moved across from the Valley to reinforce General Beauregard who was being attacked by General McDowell near Manassas in the first 'On to Richmond' thrust by Lincoln. This reinforcement from the Valley was a major contribution to the Confederate success at Bull Run, made all the more valuable by the personal staunchness of Jackson.

The Valley campaign proper starts with the Romney expedition. Here the part played by Jackson's force in the pattern of war was the protection and extension of the area of the fertile Shenandoah Valley to provide agricultural resources to supply the Confederate armies.

In the rest of the Valley campaign Jackson's force was used, by design or otherwise, as a flank threat to Washington which diverted the attention of the Federals and thereby hampered Lincoln's next main attack on Richmond.

Of the battles yet to be described, the first embrace the series of engagements around Richmond. In these Seven Days' Battles Jackson's force is moved right across Virginia to play a more direct rôle against Lincoln's attack under McClellan. By coming in on the northern flank unheralded, he managed to contribute something to the Southern cause; even though, as will be seen, his operations were less successful than they had been in the Valley.

Next came Cedar Run and Second Bull Run which were battles and campaigns fought by Jackson—the first on his own, the second under General Lee—to hold Lincoln's next thrust on Richmond under General Pope; and highly successful they were. A feature of the Second Bull Run campaign was Jackson's famous flank march through Thoroughfare Gap round Pope's rear.

The two campaigns above were so successful that Lee considered the time ripe to invade the North itself: to replenish his armies from enemy sources, and to threaten Washington or northern towns even further afield. In the Maryland campaign which followed from this decision, Jackson first captured for Lee, Harper's Ferry, a fortified camp left in the Confederate rear after their armies had crossed the River Potomac. Jackson followed his success at Harper's Ferry by joining Lee at Sharpsburg and playing a valuable part in resisting a strong Federal attack on the Confederate left near Dunker Church.

Under Lee at Fredericksburg, Jackson's corps, on the Confederate right this time, held Burnside's first attack from across the Rappahannock.

Chancellorsville was an extension and continuation of the first battle at Fredericksburg to the west of the town. Under Lee again, and sadly for the last time, Jackson carried out his next famous flank march which was to confuse Lincoln's new commander Hooker so successfully as to cause him to withdraw his armies back across the Rappahannock.

Richmond—the Seven Days' Battles

After the battle of Port Republic the stay of Jackson's armies at the mouth of Brown's Gap was spoilt by bad weather. When, however, he marched them to the far side of South River, near Weyer's Cave, they enjoyed a period of relaxation in perfect weather conditions.

Jackson had suggested to the authorities at Richmond that, if reinforced, he could carry the war across the Potomac and threaten Washington more directly than he had done by his Valley manoeuvres. General Lee, President Davis' adviser, favoured this offensive plan in principle; but he would not commit himself. After Port Republic Lee despatched reinforcements to Jackson in the shape of the brigades of Whiting, [1] Hood and Lawton, consisting of 7,000 men; but he had still not made any decision as to Jackson's rôle.

On 17 June, however, Lee wrote to Jackson as follows:

From your account of the position of the enemy, I think it would be difficult for you to engage him in time to unite with this army in the battle of Richmond. Frémont and Shields are apparently retrograding, their troops shaken and disorganised, and some time will be required to set them again in the field. If this is so, the sooner you unite with this army the better. McClellan is being strengthened ... there is much sickness in the ranks but his reinforcements by far exceed his losses. The present, therefore, seems to be favourable for a junction of your army and this. If you agree with me, the sooner you can make arrangements to do so the better. In moving your troops you could let it be understood that it was to pursue the enemy in your front. Dispose those to hold the Valley, so as to deceive the enemy, keeping your cavalry well on their front, and at the proper time suddenly descending on Pamunkey (Richmond). To be efficacious the movement must be

[1] Whiting was put in command of the division.

secret. Let me know the force you can bring, and be careful to guard from friends and foes your purpose and your intention of leaving the Valley. The country is full of spies, and our plans are immediately carried to the enemy. [1]

Thus was brought into being a move the secrecy of which was so far developed by Jackson as to reach the nature of the ridiculous, especially in his interpretation of the sentence in Lee's letter telling him to guard his purpose from his friends.

In the Port Republic operation Jackson seems to have briefed his subordinates very adequately. Patton, for example, was instructed by Jackson how to carry out his task north of the Shenandoah when the main force marched against Shields. Ewell, Winder, Taylor, Allen, Imboden and his mule battery, all seemed to have been told clearly what was expected of them. In the move to Richmond, however, Jackson divulged nothing, even to his senior commanders, and his rules on secrecy for the men of his army bordered on the absurd.

A ready-made bluff had already been created by the movement of Whiting, Hood and Lawton to the Valley. On the way to the Valley their brigades met Federal prisoners proceeding in the reverse direction to the military prisons at Richmond, where their officers would be paroled, and thus at liberty to take information of the Valley reinforcements to Washington. This provided an opportunity of assuring that wrong information reached the Federals; and Jackson also created successful cavalry screens which stopped the knowledge of what was really happening seeping across, either up the Valley, or ahead of the army as it made its slow passage across Virginia to Richmond. In more personal aspects, however, Jackson appears to have carried secrecy too far.

When Whiting, who had been his brilliant senior at West Point, rode to Port Republic ahead of his division to ask for orders, Jackson merely told him to go back the 20 miles to Staunton, where a despatch would be sent to him next day. Whiting was furious. He declared that Jackson had treated him outrageously. Imboden asked: 'How is that possible, General, for he is very polite to everyone?' Imboden describes the incident:

Whiting replied, 'Oh! hang him, he was polite enough. But he didn't say a word about his plans. I finally asked him for orders, telling him what troops I had. He simply told me to go back to Staunton, and he would send me orders to-morrow. I haven't the slightest idea what they will be. I believe he hasn't any more sense than my horse.'

Seeing his frame of mind, and being a guest in my house, I said little. Just after breakfast, next morning, a courier arrived with a terse order to embark his troops on the railroad and move to Gordonsville at once, where he would receive further

[1] O.R., XII, iii, 913.

orders. This brought a new explosion of wrath. 'Didn't I tell you he was a fool, and doesn't this prove it? Why, I just came through Gordonsville day before yesterday.'

However he obeyed the order, and when he reached Gordonsville he found Jackson there; and his little Valley army coming after him; a few days later McClellan was astounded to learn that Jackson was on his right flank on the Chickahominy. Shortly after the Seven-Days Battles around Richmond, I met Whiting again, and he then said: 'I didn't know Jackson when I was at your home. I have found out now what his plans were, and they were worthy of Napoleon. But I still think he ought to have told me his plans; for if he had died, McClellan would have captured Richmond. I wouldn't have known what he was driving at, and might have made a mess of it. But I take back all I said about his being a fool.'[1]

Another illustration of the lengths to which secrecy was taken at this stage is found in an incident occurring on the march to Richmond. One of Hood's Texans left the ranks on the march, and was climbing a fence to go for a cherry tree near at hand when Jackson rode by and saw him.

'Where are you going?' asked the general.

'I don't know,' replied the soldier.

'To what command do you belong?'

'I don't know.'

'Well, what state are you from?'

'I don't know.'

'What is the meaning of all this?' asked Jackson of another.

'Well,' was the reply, 'Old Stonewall and General Hood gave orders yesterday that we were not to know anything until after the next fight.'[2]

Jackson laughed and rode on.

MECHANICSVILLE

By the time Jackson reached the neighbourhood of Richmond, McClellan's armies had made their way up the peninsula between the York and James rivers; they had fought the battle of Seven Pines south of the Chickahominy, and entrenched near Richmond—one signpost, just within their lines bearing the legend: to Richmond $4\frac{1}{2}$ miles. But McClellan's main force was south of the Chickahominy. Only General Porter's Vth Corps was to the north; and the Chickahominy's wooded swampy banks made contact between the two parts of the Federal army very difficult.

This offered General Lee an opportunity to attack McClellan's isolated north corps in detail, and relieve Richmond by 'lifting the young Napoleon

[1] B & L, ii, 296, 297.   [2] J. E. Cooke, 205.

from his entrenchments to the east of that city'.[1] Lee decided to leave only Magruder's and Huger's divisions to watch the eastern entrenchments, and move the rest of his army to attack Porter's Vth Corps north of the Chickahominy. It was to join in this attack that Jackson was brought from the Valley.

Directly McClellan realised that he was not going to get the support of McDowell's army in his assault on Richmond he became worried about his right wing. Without McDowell's presence at Fredericksburg, and the promise of his further advance south, McClellan's north flank was completely in the air. The Confederate cavalry leader Stuart had demonstrated this by his famous march round McClellan's army. Then, without McDowell, there was little need to maintain a dangerous line of supply along the exposed railway to White House and York River. Instead, he now considered moving his base to a new and easily defended position on the James River to the south. To do this 'he secured by careful examination full information of the roads, and the character of the country over which he would be obliged to move ... and as early as 18 June sent vessels loaded with supplies to the James River.'[2]

Apprehension about Jackson's possible participation in the battle for Richmond seems to have been present in the minds of the Federal commanders at an early stage. Porter writes: 'We did not fear the results of such an attack if made by the forces from Richmond alone; but if in addition we were attacked by Jackson's forces, suspicions of whose approach was already aroused, we felt we should be in peril.'[3]

On 24 June more definite news of Jackson was received. General McClellan telegraphed Porter that a deserter had informed him that Jackson was in the immediate vicinity, ready to unite with Lee. But they could obtain from Washington at that time no further confirmation of their suspicions, nor any information of the fact that Jackson had left the Valley. McClellan was just as much in the dark about the movement of the bulk of Lee's forces northwards. In fact, the result of fighting on 25 June in the entrenchments east of Richmond was to convince the corps commanders engaged that there had been no reduction of forces on their front, to take part in any movement on the Federal right flank.

This was the situation preliminary to the furious Seven Days' Battles in which Lee sought the destruction of McClellan's exposed right wing, and by drawing him from his entrenchments, the raising of the siege of Richmond; while McClellan strove to preserve the safety of his right wing, and to gain sufficient time to enable him to effect a change of base to the James.

---

[1] O.R., XI, ii, 623.   [2] B & L, ii, 325.   [3] *Ibid.*, 326.

16 *The Seven Days' Battles around Richmond: The Battle of Frayser's Farm (Glendale, 30 June 1862. Federal troops under General Kearney fighting in th woods. Kearney was killed at the Battle of Chantilly after Second Bull Ru: From a drawing by Alfred R. Waud (1828-1891)*

18 *Federal gunboats from the James River firing at the Confederates attacking
Malvern Hill 'damaged friends almost as much as the enemy'. From a drawing
by Alfred R. Waud (1828–1891)*

19 *The Battle of Malvern Hill, 1 July 1862*
*A Federal gun fires over its own troops at the Confederates charging Malvern
Hill. From a drawing by Alfred R. Waud (1828–1891)*

In the battles around Richmond from 26 June to 2 July 1862, Jackson dominated the scene. On 26 June vast clouds of dust to the north indicated his presence to the Federals. These dust clouds, however, were far distant, and Porter believed that the felled trees blocking the tracks, and the cavalry patrols delaying Jackson, would prevent him attacking that day. Porter proved correct; but it made no difference. The mere passive presence of Jackson at Hundley's Corner at the end of the day was sufficient to cause the Federals to retreat to another position further east at Gaines' Mill, although they had had much the best of the bloody encounter east of Mechanicsville along Beaver Dam Creek.

Porter's men were well forward covering Meadow Bridge and Mechanics-ville Bridge. Lee's plan was for Branch's Carolina brigade of A. P. Hill's Light Division to cross the Chickahominy at Winston Bridge, which was clear of Federals, and advance eastwards close to the river clearing Meadow Bridge. A. P. Hill's other brigades were then to cross Meadow Bridge and sweep down to clear Mechanicsville Bridge for the crossing by D. H. Hill's division, followed by Longstreet's division. Meanwhile Jackson was to play an important part in the operation. Moving down from the north to Hundley's Corner, he was to place his forces in the rear of Mechanicsville.

Jackson's crossing of the Virginia Central railway to Fredericksburg from Richmond, was the signal for Branch to start. When the advance developed, Jackson was to turn the north flank of the Federal advanced forces. Thus 'to the four divisions of Generals A. P. Hill, D. H. Hill, Jackson and Longstreet was entrusted the task of turning the right flank of the Yankee army.'[1]

As far as Jackson was concerned everything went wrong. He was late getting across the railway start line, and thus delayed Branch. He was out of communication with his colleagues for most of the time; and when he reached Hundley's Corner five hours late at the end of the day, he decided, in spite of the noise of battle in the south-west, to bivouac there. Instead of moving to the sound of guns, as expected, he waited until next day.

After their skirmishers had fallen back from the bridges, the Federal advanced troops from McCall's Third Division held a position along Beaver Dam Creek, a stream joining the Chickahominy from the north, a mile east of Mechanicsville (see Map facing p. 112). 'The position selected on the Beaver Dam Creek was naturally a strong one, the left resting on the Chickahominy and the right extending to thick woods beyond the upper Mechanicsville

[1] O.R., XI, ii, 623; Henderson, ii, 26, note I, states: Jackson's division—so called in Lee's order—really consisted of 3 divisions: Whitings, Jackson's (Winder) & Ewell's. D. H. Hill's division was also attached to Jackson.

road, which were occupied.'[1] The stream was waist deep and bordered by swamps. Along it McCall put in position six 10-pounder Parrotts and ten 12-pounder guns. Where necessary, fields of fire were cleared of trees, and the felled trunks used to block tracks; but the approaches generally were over open plain exposed to a murderous fire of all arms.

It was expected that Jackson would be in the position assigned to him by early dawn, and all A. P. Hill's preparations were made with the view to moving early. Branch, however, did not hear from Jackson until about 10 a.m., when he immediately crossed the river, and proceeded to carry out his rôle. He was delayed by the Federal skirmishers and advanced but slowly.

A. P. Hill says: 'Three o'clock having arrived, and no intelligence from Jackson or Branch, I determined to cross at once rather than hazard the failure of the whole plan by longer deferring it.'[2] With the help of only Ripley's brigade from D. H. Hill's division, A. P. Hill tried to storm the strong Federal position alone. Apparently unaware, or regardless, of the great danger in their front, A. P. Hill's troops moved on with animation and confidence, as if going to parade, or engaging in a sham battle. Suddenly, when half way down the bank of the valley, McCall's men opened up rapid volleys of artillery and infantry fire, which strewed the road and hill-side with hundreds of dead and wounded, and drove the main body of the survivors back in rapid flight to and beyond Mechanicsville. In the extreme north a small Confederate force secured a foothold on the east bank, but had to retire under cover of darkness. Later in the afternoon, greatly strengthened, the Confederates renewed the attack with spirit and energy, some reaching the borders of the stream; but only to be repulsed with terrible slaughter. Night put an end to the conflict.

It had been a victory for the Federals. Yet, as has been stated, because of Jackson's position in their rear they retreated afterwards. Porter writes: 'General McClellan had joined me on the battle-field at an early hour in the afternoon. While we discussed plans for the immediate future, influenced in our deliberations by the gratifying results of the day, numerous and unvarying accounts from our outposts and scouts warned us of the danger impending on the arrival of Jackson, and necessitated a decision as to which side of the Chickahominy should be held in force. He left me later at night with the expectation of receiving information at his own headquarters from the tenor of which he would be enabled to decide whether I should hold my present position or withdraw to a well selected and more advantageous one east of Gaines' Mill, where I could protect the bridges across the Chickahominy,

---

[1] O.R., XI, ii, 623.   [2] *Ibid.*, 835.

over which I must retire if compelled to leave the left bank.'[1] At 3 a.m. Porter was ordered to withdraw.

It is obvious that Mechanicsville was not a success for Jackson, or his staff, or the men of the Army of the Valley. Jackson had found the approach march wearying and difficult, and his men had not responded in their customary manner to his demands for early starts and fast marches. 'The Army of the Valley had been marching and fighting since early spring and were worn out,' says Douglas,[2] to explain this. Douglas also lays the blame for their partial failure on lack of knowledge of the country and poor staff work. In spite of two good guides familiar with the country like Major Whiting and Dabney's brother, Jackson seemed lost in a country unknown to him without his skilled topographer and mapmaker, Hotchkiss, who had been left behind to map in the Valley. Then, the Rev Major Dabney, who had sufficed as chief of staff in the Valley, was not equal to conducting the complicated movements of Jackson's corps among the forests and swamps of the Chickahominy. 'While he did his duty faithfully, he could not be of service to the General in such an emergency; and as for training a staff to its duties, he knew nothing about it. He resigned within two weeks because of ill health. One thing is certain, no one on the march that day with Jackson saw any let-up in his unceasing push.'[3]

Porter, too, made it difficult for Jackson to keep to his timetable. The felled trees blocking the routes to Hundley's Corner, and the constant encounters with determined Federal cavalry rearguards, were probably enough to explain Jackson's slowness. His failure to march to the sound of the guns, however, remains inexplicable. Certainly the other generals thought Jackson should have entered the fight. Longstreet says: 'Jackson came up, marched by the fight without giving attention, and went into camp at Hundley's Corner.'[4] Trimble, who was so keen to fight and did so well at Cross Keys, comments: 'Before sundown the firing was not more than 2 miles distant, and in my opinion we should have marched to the support of General Hill that evening.'[5]

GAINES' MILL

The Federals' new position south of Gaines' Mill was another very strong one. Porter was reinforced by 9,000 men under General Slocum and placed his

[1] B & L, ii, 331. [2] Douglas, 106. [3] Ibid., 106.
[4] Longstreet, 124. [5] O.R., XI, ii, 614.

forces around the perimeter of a low plateau east of Powhite Creek and north of Alexander and Grapevine Bridges, by which they could be reinforced by McClellan, or, if need be, retire across the Chickahominy. The plateau itself was surrounded by marshy, wooded, sluggish creeks. These in places cut deep channels forming further obstacles; and only the north-east by McGehee's Hill was clear of obstructions.

Three roads approached the Gaines' Mill position, two direct from Mechanicsville, running parallel to the Chickahominy, and the third from the direction of Old Cold Harbour towards McGehee's Hill. A. P. Hill's and Longstreet's divisions followed the first two, and Jackson was again sent round the flank, to approach from Old Cold Harbour.

The Confederate task to storm Porter's position was a formidable one. 'The wooded ridge which encircled the position (beyond Powhite Creek, but on the Confederate side of the other encircling creeks) afforded scant room for artillery, and it was thus impracticable to prepare the attack by a preliminary bombardment. The ground over which the infantry must advance was completely swept by fire, and the centre and left were defended by three tiers of riflemen, the first sheltered by the steep banks of the creeks, the second halfway up the bluff, covered by breastwork, the third on the crest, occupying a line of shelter-trenches; and the riflemen were supported by a dozen batteries of rifled guns.'[1] There were also Federal heavy guns sweeping the north bank of the river from the other side.

As at Mechanicsville, the Confederate attack failed in combination; and Jackson appears to have been partly responsible for this. His divisions found the route to Old Cold Harbour blocked by felled timber, and defended staunchly by Federal sharpshooters. They also took the wrong road on one occasion, and lost time thereby. 'General Jackson had selected young men of the vicinage, found in a company of cavalry near him, for guides. When he asked them the road to Cold Harbour, his habitual reticence, in this instance too stringent, withheld all explanation of his strategic designs. They therefore naturally pointed him to the direct and larger road as the route to Cold Harbour. After marching for a mile and a half, the booming of cannon in his front caught his ear and he demanded sharply of the guide near him, "Where is the firing?" The reply was, that it was in the direction of Gaines' Mill. "Does this road lead there?" he asked. The guide told him that it led by Gaines' Mill to Cold Harbour. "But," exclaimed he, "I do not wish to go to Gaines' Mill. I wish to go to Cold Harbour leaving that place on my right." "Then," said the guide, "the left-hand road was the one which should have been taken; and had you let me know what you desired, I could have directed

---

[1] Henderson, ii, 27, 28.

you aright at first." Nothing now remained but to reverse the column, and return to the proper track. It was manifest that an hour of precious time must be lost in doing this, while the accelerated firing told that the battle was thickening in the front, and every heart trembled with the anxious fear lest the irreparable hour should be lost by the delay. But Jackson bore the same calm and assured countenance, and when this fear was suggested to him, he replied, "No, let us trust that the providence of our God will so overrule it, that no mischief shall result." Nor was he mistaken in his confidence; for the time thus allowed to General D. H. Hill enabled him to reach the desired point of meeting north of Cold Harbour, just in front of Jackson, and brought them into precise conjunction.'[1]

Because of the delay, then, D. H. Hill's division got ahead of Jackson's divisions; and when A. P. Hill's division came into action, the only support forthcoming from the north, for some considerable time, was from one of D. H. Hill's batteries.

It appeared to be a repetition of what happened at Mechanicsville with A. P. Hill's division going in on its own. This time, however, it was by design. Lee, the overall Confederate commander in the battle, felt convinced that McClellan, when attacked, would move off north to guard his communications with White House and York River. He did not believe that McClellan would bring Porter back across the Chickahominy; he had heard nothing of the building up of Federal stores to the south, and the creation of a new base on the James River. He thus ordered Jackson to draw up his troops so as to meet such a contingency, waiting to catch the Federals driven back by Hill as they retreated north. 'For a time, therefore, General Jackson held his troops back in the margin of the woods looking towards the highway, and along the line of their march, in the hope that the enemy, retreating before Generals A. P. Hill and Longstreet would expose their flank to a crushing blow from him.'[2]

Lee was wrong in his estimate of the Federal reaction to Jackson's position at Old Cold Harbour. He thought that, as at Mechanicsville, when they found Jackson threatening their northern flank, they would lose no time in retreating and this time north towards their base on York River. Stuart and the Confederate cavalry were also sent off towards the north on the same errand of interrupting a Federal retreat in that direction. In fact, the Federals did no such thing.

When the battle of Gaines' Mill developed, Jackson played a dominant part in its outcome, for his troops made a valuable contribution to the Confederate victory there.

[1] Dabney, ii, 181, 182.　　　　[2] *Ibid.*, 183.

A. P. Hill's division approached from New Cold Harbour, and attacking Porter's position from the north-west, was engaged for a long while on its own. He writes: 'My division was thus engaged full two hours before assistance was received. We failed to carry the enemy lines, but we paved the way for the successful attacks afterward, and in which attacks it was necessary to employ the whole of our army that side of the Chickahominy. About four o'clock reinforcements came up on my right from General Longstreet and later Jackson's men on my left and centre, and my division was relieved of the weight of the contest. It was then continued on more equal terms, and finally the extreme left of the enemy's line was most gallantly carried by Hood's brigade (from Whiting's division temporarily attached to Jackson's corps). At seven o'clock the general-in-chief (Lee) in person gave me an order to advance my whole line and to communicate this order as far as I could to all commanders of troops. This was done, and a general advance being made, the enemy was swept from the field, and the pursuit only stopped by nightfall and the exhaustion of our troops.'[1]

This describes the battle of Gaines' Mill in the barest outline; but the details of it are much more difficult to unravel, and the appraisement of Jackson's part the hardest task of all.

The full employment of all the Confederate divisions, which was soon shown as necessary to break into Porter's strong position behind the swamps, was only slowly achieved by Lee. Jackson's corps, except for D. H. Hill's division, was slow to reach its position at Old Cold Harbour. When it did arrive, even D. H. Hill's division was held back on the policy of Jackson forming a line and cutting off the retreat of Porter's men when they had been flushed out of their position by A. P. Hill. D. H. Hill says: 'Jackson posted my division in the woods to the left of the road and facing toward the firing at Gaines' Mill in order to intercept the forces that Longstreet and A. P. Hill might drive in that direction.'[2] Longstreet, meanwhile, closer to the Chickahominy, was held back to await Jackson's corps' entry into the battle. The parts of the defences facing Longstreet were the strongest of the whole Federal perimeter. In front stretched open country enfiladed by Federal guns from south of the river. Between him and the enemy was a well-nigh impenetrable swamp.

Eventually Jackson gave up waiting for the Federals to be driven into his arms. He says: 'But it soon became apparent, from the direction and sound of the firing that General A. P. Hill was hard pressed, and I ordered a general advance of my entire corps, which commenced with General D. H. Hill upon

[1] O.R., XI, ii, 837.　　　　[2] O.R., XI, ii, 624; B & L, ii, 355.

the left, and extended to the right.'[1] Jackson's corps, however, even then only entered the fray piecemeal; some of his divisions were delayed by bad staff work.

To go back to the arrival of the rest of Jackson's divisions at Old Cold Harbour, following D. H. Hill's division which got there first: when the column had to be reversed on the Gaines' Mill road, Ewell's division in the rear took instead the lead, and left Whiting and Winder far behind. Ewell was met by one of Lee's staff and directed off to support the left of A. P. Hill's division, covering the road from New Cold Harbour into the centre of the enemy's position past Porter's headquarters at Watt's house. Before long Ewell's troops were thrown forward towards the swamp which lay between them and the Federals. They found some of Hill's men in bad shape, straggling off to the rear. Trimble writes: 'Here we met two regiments retiring from the field in confusion, who cried out, "You need not go in; we are whipped; you can't do anything!" Some of our men said, "Get out of our way; we will show you how to do it!"'[2] Telling his men to use only the bayonet, Trimble led them gallantly down the slope to the swamp, cheering them on with, 'Charge, men; charge!' In this way Trimble drove back Morell's troops from their forward positions; but with serious losses, including Colonel Seymour commanding the Louisianians in the place of Taylor, who was ill, and Rob Wheat commanding the Tigers. Both these officers were killed, and the Louisianians became demoralised.

Whiting's division was also diverted later to A. P. Hill's sector; but it took a lot of time and energy to get him there. When Jackson learned that Ewell's division was now engaged, he sent the only staff officer at hand, Major Harman, to tell Whiting and Winder, still on the road leading to Old Cold Harbour, to move across and fill in the gap between Ewell and D. H. Hill on the Confederate left. Major Harman knew all about horses and wagons and little about military terms.[3] Harman gave General Whiting a muddled version of Jackson's order. Believing himself to have been snubbed by Jackson earlier, when he had mistaken D. H. Hill's column for a force of the enemy, Whiting was in a bad humour. He took little trouble to find out Jackson's real meaning, with the result that neither Whiting's nor Winder's divisions got on the move until Major Dabney, discovering nothing happening, and checking up on the delay, reached Whiting and repeated Jackson's orders.

'General,' he began, 'has Major Harman delivered you General Jackson's instructions?'

---

[1] O.R., XI, ii, 553.　　　[2] *Ibid.*, 615.　　　[3] Freeman, LL, i, 527.

'Yes,' answered Whiting, in tones that Dabney regarded as surly, 'that man has been here with a medley of nonsense.'

'Did he tell you it was the General's wish you should engage the enemy immediately?'

Dabney then went on to explain carefully what Jackson wished. Whiting was disposed to argue, but eventually got his division moving. Then he ran into General Lee, from whom he was prepared to accept orders. In his own report Whiting says: 'I met several aides from different generals, all desiring assistance, and informing me that the troops of both General D. H. and A. P. Hill were hard pressed. Advancing, I shortly met the commander-in-chief, who indicated a direction a little to my right.' [1]

Eventually Whiting's men took up a position on the right of all Jackson's men. Led by Hood's brigade, they passed through the men of A. P. Hill's shattered line where many were 'skulking from the front in a shameful manner,' [2] and were the first to pierce the Federal defences. It was Hood's Fourth Texas Regiment which achieved this. Jackson writes:

On my extreme right General Whiting advanced his division through the same dense forest and swamp (surrounding almost the whole Federal position), emerging from the wood near the public road and at the head of the deep ravine which covered the enemy left. Advancing thence through a number of retreating and dis-ordered regiments he came within range of the enemy's fire, who, concealed in an open wood protected by breastworks, poured a destructive fire for a quarter of a mile into his advancing line, under which many brave officers and men fell. Dashing on with unfaltering step in the face of those murderous discharges of canister and musketry, General Hood and Colonel Law at the heads of their respective brigades, rushed to the charge with a yell. Moving down a precipitous ravine, leaping ditch and stream, clambering up a difficult ascent, and exposed to an incessant and deadly fire from the entrenchments, these brave and determined men pushed forward, driving the enemy from his well-selected and fortified position. In this charge, in which upward of 1000 men fell killed and wounded before the fire of the enemy, and in which fourteen pieces of artillery and nearly a regiment were captured, the Fourth Texas, under the lead of General Hood, was the first to pierce these strong-holds and seize the guns. [3]

Meanwhile, on the extreme Confederate left, D. H. Hill's men and Winder's Stonewall Brigade were piercing the position held by Sykes' regulars. Hill's infantry, having skilfully outflanked and captured a battery on their left which enfiladed them, made a bold and dashing charge, in which the troops of Winder joined, and the enemy yielded the field in disorder, 'I have always believed that this was the first break in the Federal line,' writes Hill. [4] It

[1] O.R., XI, ii, 563.   [2] *Ibid.*, 563.   [3] *Ibid.*, 555, 556.
[4] B & L, ii, 355.

disposed of Sykes' division of regulars who had fought stubbornly the whole day. An observer with Porter's and Slocum's forces, the Comte de Paris, says of Syke's retreat: 'Fearfully reduced as they were, they care less for the losses they have sustained than for the mortification of yielding to volunteers.'

The break-throughs in the north-west by the Texans along the New Cold Harbour—Watt's house road, and in the north which disposed of Sykes' regulars, heralded the beginning of the end. Longstreet moved north and supported Whiting's assault, and helped in driving the Federals from their last position. 'Many of our men continued the pursuit beyond in a rather straggling condition,'[1] he writes. There followed one of the strangest episodes of the battle. Some of Cook's 5th US Cavalry were covering their artillery who were limbering up to retreat. Seeing Longstreet's straggling advance, they attempted a charge. Maddened by the shot and shell their horses stampeded through the artillery lines and stampeded the artillery horses in their turn, 'carrying off with sudden fright the limbers of our artillery, just prepared to pour their irresistible fire into a pursuing foe. With no infantry to support, and with apparent disaster before them, such of the remainder of these guns as could be moved were carried from the field; some deliberately, others in haste.'[2] The Federal artillery had been the mainstay of Porter's defence. Previous to the final break-through he had posted artillery in large force just in rear of his centre and left. To this unfortunate cavalry charge, Porter attributes his final defeat.

What had been Jackson's part in the battle? He had brought his corps into the battle, albeit a little tardily. Some of his divisions had been diverted by Lee and others out of his arranged pattern, but passing through A. P. Hill's shattered troops they had turned the tide in the west and broken through Sykes' regulars in the north. Jackson is described as riding around on his gaunt sorrel sucking the inevitable piece of lemon, his face crimson, his eyes burning, exalted as usual by the conflict. His right hand sometimes lay open and flat on his thigh, 'but now and then was raised in the air as was his habit— a gesture which the troops learned to believe was as significant as the extended arms of Aaron. But the lemon was not abandoned.'[3] To each divisional commander he sent the same message, 'Tell them this affair must hang in suspense no longer; sweep the field with the bayonet!'[4]

As at Mechanicsville the battle ended when darkness fell. D. H. Hill halted his division which was advancing on the road leading to the bridge over which the Federals were escaping. He writes: 'It was now quite dark, and I took the responsibility of halting all the troops on our left. General

[1] O.R., XI, ii, 758. [2] B & L, ii, 340. [3] Douglas, 109.
[4] Dabney, ii, 195.

Winder thought that we ought to pursue the enemy into the woods, on the right of the Grapevine Bridge road; but, not knowing the position of our friends, nor what Federal reserves might be awaiting us in the woods, I thought it advisable not to move on.'[1] Cheers were heard from the area of the bridges. It was clear that Federal reinforcements had arrived. Two brigades sent over by McClellan arrived in time to form a rearguard to hold the bridge and stave off a terrible disaster. Jackson was too far back at the time to carry on the fight which had been broken off by his subordinates. In any case Lee was in charge. Thus on the night of the battle the Confederates remained where the issue of the fight had found them.

Across Grapevine Bridge road the pickets of the hostile forces were in close proximity, and men of both sides, in search of water, or carrying messages, strayed within the enemy's lines. Jackson himself, it is said, came near to capture. Riding forward in the darkness, attended only by a few staff officers, he suddenly found himself in the presence of a Federal picket. Judging rightly of the enemy's morale, he set spurs to his horse, and charging into the midst, ordered them to lay down their arms; and 15 or 20 prisoners, marching to the rear, amused the troops they met on the march by loudly proclaiming that they had the honour of being captured by Stonewall Jackson. These men were not without companions. 2,830 Federals were reported either captured or missing. 4,000 had fallen on the field of battle. The Confederate casualties were even a clearer proof of the severity of the fighting. So far as can be ascertained 8,000 officers and men were killed or wounded.

FRAYSER'S FARM AND MALVERN HILL

After the defeat of the Federals at Gaines' Mill the Confederates did not know the direction in which McClellan would retreat. Possibilities were: to the north-east to White House on the York River, after recrossing the Chickahominy down river; or, eastwards back to Yorktown and Fort Monroe at the tip of the Peninsula; or, to the south to some point on the James River. The long columns of dust rising above the forests to the south of the Chickahominy suggested the last. To make sure, Stuart and the cavalry were despatched towards White House, and the Confederate army remained on the battlefield waiting for the game to bolt. Lee says: 'We were compelled to wait until his (McClellan's) purpose should be developed.'

[1] B & L, ii, 357.

In the evening of the day after the battle, signs of a general movement were reported from the entrenchments stretching from Seven Pines to the Chickahominy; and Lee concluded that McClellan was retreating to the James.

Lee's plan to intercept the Federals was another complicated one requiring the co-ordinated movements of separated columns. Magruder's and Huger's divisions were already in the entrenchments south of the Chickahominy, and these were ordered to strike directly at the enemy's flank north and south of White Oak Swamp respectively (*see* Map facing p. 112). Longstreet and A. P. Hill crossed at New Bridge and moved after Huger south of White Oak Swamp. Jackson crossed over Grapevine Bridge with strict orders from Lee, which he all too rigidly obeyed, to cross White Oak Swamp and establish himself on the Long Bridge road south of it. Jackson's route was the one used by McClellan who found it difficult to get his army away as his supply and ammunition train consisted of over 5,000 wagons, and he was encumbered with many heavy guns.

The first Confederate attack was made by Magruder on McClellan's rearguard near Savage's Station. It was easily repulsed by the Federals, as Huger failed to help, and Jackson was delayed north of the Chickahominy having to rebuild Grapevine Bridge to enable his forces to cross the river. This Confederate delay enabled McClellan to pass all his army, including the guns and wagon train, over the difficult obstacle provided by White Oak Swamp; after which he destroyed the only bridge over it behind him.

The next operation took place at Frayser's Farm where 'the enemy were strongly posted across Long Bridge road about 1 mile from its intersection with the Charles City road.'[1] Huger was held up by felled trees across his track. Jackson could not get across White Oak Swamp. He writes: 'We found the bridge destroyed and the ordinary place of crossing commanded by their batteries on the opposite side, and all approach to it barred by detachments of sharpshooters concealed in a dense wood close by . . . a heavy cannonading in front announced the engagement of General Longstreet at Frazier's (*sic*) farm and made me eager to press forward; but the marshy character of the soil, the destruction of the bridge of the marshland creek, and the strong position of the enemy for defending the passage prevented my advancing until the following morning. During the night the Federals retired. The bridge was rapidly repaired by Whiting's division, which soon after crossed over and continued the pursuit, in which it was followed by the remainder of my corps.'[2]

Colonel Munford of the 2nd Virginia Cavalry who had joined him from

[1] O.R., XI, ii, 495.　　　　　　　[2] *Ibid.*, 556, 557.

the pursuit of Frémont in the Valley, suggests that Jackson made considerable efforts to get over White Oak Swamp. Certainly he went forward with the cavalry to the broken bridge over the swamp, and accompanied by three or four members of his staff,[1] floundered across the swamp with them; but the ford was miry and deep, and impracticable for either artillery or infantry, and they had to retire. He also sent a brigade to force a passage at Brackett's Ford, a mile up stream. Every road and track, however, was obstructed by trees and abattis, and it was found that a major passage there was impracticable, although two companies did get over the creek and drive back some enemy pickets. 'Having ascertained that the enemy was present in great strength on the further bank, that every road was obstructed, and that there was no means of carrying his artillery over the creek, or favourable ground on which his infantry could act, Jackson gave up all hope of aiding Longstreet.'[2]

Longstreet and other fellow generals of Jackson were critical of his inaction. The Federal General Franklin considers that had Jackson attacked in the neighbourhood of both Brackett's Ford and White Oak Bridge simultaneously, Longstreet's battle at Frayser's Farm might have ended differently. 'In fact, it is likely that we should have been defeated on that day had General Jackson done what his great reputation seems to make it imperative that he should have done.'[3] Longstreet even considers that Jackson had plenty of time to march around the head of White Oak Swamp to join him; for General Wright of Huger's division, he says, 'marched his brigade from the head of the swamp to Jackson's line at the bridge, and returned making several halts and crossings to reconnoitre,'[4] in a short period of time. Jackson's principles, however, would not permit this. He demanded of his subordinates implicit, blind obedience and did not allow his orders to be questioned by them. He obeyed his superiors in the same fashion. Lee's orders told him to follow the route he took. He was not prepared, without further instructions from Lee, to depart from them.

During the night which followed the battle at Frayser's Farm, the whole Federal army fell back eight miles to Malvern Hill—a strong defensive position on a plateau, rising to a height of 150 feet above the surrounding forests. 'On either flank the plateau was somewhat guarded by ravines and tangled marshlands, while the front approach was over ascending slopes so broken as to make advancing artillery combat slow and hazardous.'[5] Lee was unwell at this stage and asked Longstreet to reconnoitre the Malvern Hill position

[1] Dr McGuire's testimony; he was one of them.
[2] Henderson, ii, 53. [3] B & L, ii, 381. [4] Longstreet, 150, 151.
[5] *Ibid.*, 141.

for him. Longstreet went to a hill to the west, as high as the plateau where Porter's men were drawn up, from which he got a fair view of the Federal position on Malvern and Crew Hills and the open country in front of Jackson's advancing forces from the north. While Longstreet was making his reconnaissance a dead calm reigned. Jackson's batteries were still out of range, but were marching quietly to their gun positions. Porter had decided not to waste ammunition until his enemy were in range; but the large number of his guns were apparent; and these seemed to Longstreet, viewing from afar, to be about 'eighty on his front, besides the siege battery in rear'.[1] Longstreet considered that the open space in front of Jackson's advance offered scope for his 100 guns to bombard the Federals. This fire, combined with cross-fire from 40 Confederate guns on the hill in the west, would shatter the enemy defences sufficiently to allow a Confederate infantry assault to be attempted with a good chance of success. Longstreet reported his findings to Lee and then returned to his command.

Jackson expressed himself opposed to a frontal attack, preferring to turn the enemy's flank;[2] but Lee adopted Longstreet's plan, with disastrous results.

It was not until four o'clock that the Confederate line of battle was formed. Jackson's corps with Whiting's and D. H. Hill's divisions led the attack from the north. In the north-west came Huger's division; and in the west and south-west Magruder's and Holmes' divisions. Longstreet's and A. P. Hill's divisions were in reserve (*see* Map facing p. 112)

The Confederate assault was ruined by the failure of enough of Jackson's guns to get into position. 'The obstacles presented by the woods and swamp made it impracticable to bring up sufficient artillery to oppose successfully the extraordinary force of that arm employed by the enemy.'[3] When some of Jackson's guns got through and unlimbered for action, the concentrated fire of the Federal guns knocked them to pieces. The Confederate batteries on the west fared even worse. When the first guns finally opened, 'Porter shifted his aim from his proper front, which Jackson failed to combat, and put in the fire of forty guns against the eight-gun battery of our right. The gun-boat batteries (from the James) also came into that practice, but it was found they damaged friends almost as much as the enemy, and they were ordered to discontinue. Jackson's cross-fire, feeble at best and at long range, was finally drawn off by other batteries far on the enemy's right, so that the eight guns were soon piled in a heterogeneous mass of caissons, guns, limbers and horses. Some other batteries got into action at the same point, eight or ten guns at a time, but suffered like disaster.'[4]

[1] Longstreet, 142, 143.   [2] Henderson, ii, 61.   [3] O.R., XI, ii, 496.
[4] Longstreet, 144.

Then real catastrophe occurred for the Confederates. As the artillery bombardment had obviously failed, Lee assumed that his commanders would realise that his original plan of attack was now abandoned. This assumption proved wrong. Lee took Longstreet round to reconnoitre a possible turning movement on the Federal eastern flank. Finding it feasible, he had just ordered Longstreet's and A. P. Hill's divisions to march in that direction when the battle began. Unfortunately, through some mistake on the part of Lee's staff, the order to attack which had already been issued was not rescinded. The signal for the advance, when the batteries had raked the Federal lines, was a charge with a yell[1] by Armistead's brigade of Huger's division, Armistead being in a position, it was thought, to see the result of the bombardment. Believing that he heard this appointed signal, General D. H. Hill sent his force forward, and Jackson sent in three brigades of the Stonewall Brigade as reinforcements. Magruder's division also came into action; but the Confederate assaults were made piecemeal, and the Federals easily drove them back with great slaughter. 'The Federals disposed in several lines were in overwhelming strength. Their batteries were free to concentrate on the advancing infantry. Their riflemen, posted in the intervals between the artillery masses, swept the long slopes with a grazing fire, while fence, bank, and ravine gave shelter from the Confederate bullets.'[2] The Confederates 'were repulsed at all points with fearful slaughter, losing six thousand men and accomplishing nothing'.[3] The Confederate troops were demoralised by this. Trimble writes that he found, next morning, the whole army in the utmost disorder: thousands of straggling men asking every passer-by for their regiments; ambulances, wagons and artillery obstructing every road; and altogether, in a drenching rain, presenting a scene of the most woeful and disheartening confusion.[4] McClellan's army, however, in spite of Porter's victory at Malvern Hill, was in no better shape; and he writes that his men were completely exhausted and worn out. 'If possible,' he says, 'I shall return tonight to Harrison's Bar (Landing) where the gunboats can render more aid in covering our position.'[5] The condition to which McClellan was reduced seems to have been realised by Jackson, and this shows his ability to appreciate a situation. The crushing defeat of his own troops failed to disturb his judgment. While others stated that McClellan was likely to attack in the morning, and that the Confederate army was in no condition to resist him, Jackson was positive that McClellan would clear out. He proved correct. On 2 July it was discovered that the Federals had withdrawn during the night, leaving the ground covered with dead and wounded. Harassed, and closely

[1] O.R., XI, ii, 677.   [2] Henderson, ii, 63.   [3] B & L, ii, 403.
[4] O.R., XI, ii, 619.   [5] O.R., XI, iii, 282.

followed by the Confederate cavalry, they succeeded in reaching the James. There, they had the protection of Herring Creek, encircling Harrison's Landing, and the support of their gunboats. Little further Confederate action was taken; and on 8 July, directing the cavalry to watch McClellan, General Lee fell back on Richmond.

In a way, both sides had achieved their aim. Richmond was relieved, for McClellan's army was later withdrawn to reinforce the Federal force on the Rappahannock; but McClellan had also managed with considerable skill to change his base from the York River to the James, a difficult operation of war with the Confederates on his flank and in his rear.

Jackson's part in the Seven Days' Battles did not match up to the reputation he had gained in the Valley. Longstreet writes: 'The Seven-Days' Fighting, although a decided Confederate victory, was a succession of mishaps. If Jackson had arrived on the 26th—the day of his own selection—the Federals would have been driven from Mechanicsville without a battle. His delay there, caused by obstructions placed on his road by the enemy, was the first mishap. He was too late in entering the fight at Gaines' Mill, and the destruction of Grapevine Bridge (and White Gap Bridge) kept him from reaching Frayser's farm until the day after that battle . . . Jackson was a very skilful man against such men as Shields, Banks and Frémont, but when pitted against the best of the Federal commanders he did not appear so well.'[1]

[1] B & L, ii, 404, 405.

Seven Days' Battles: Chain of Command [1]

Confederates
Gen R. E. Lee

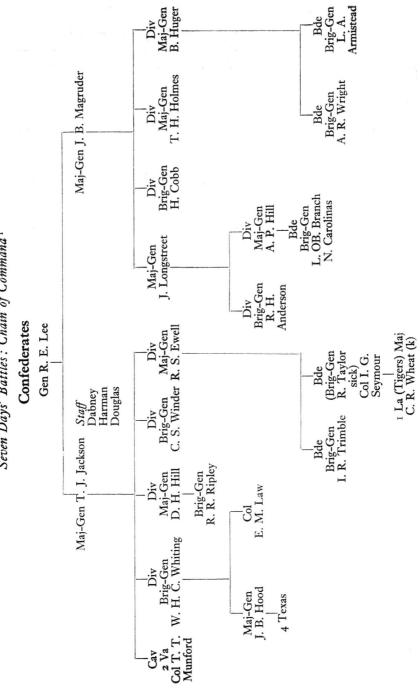

casualties 20,135

[1] B & L, ii, 313–317.

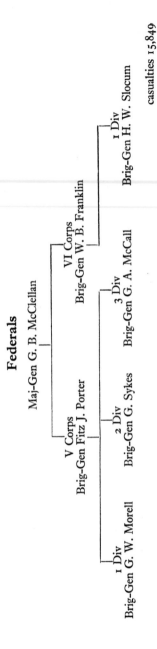

Federals

Maj-Gen G. B. McClellan

V Corps
Brig-Gen Fitz J. Porter

VI Corps
Brig-Gen W. B. Franklin

1 Div
Brig-Gen G. W. Morell

2 Div
Brig-Gen G. Sykes

3 Div
Brig-Gen G. A. McCall

1 Div
Brig-Gen H. W. Slocum

casualties 15,849

Cedar Run

On 26 June 1862, the armies of the Union were reorganised. To divert forces from Lee's army facing McClellan at Harrison's Landing in the east, the scattered armies of McDowell, Sigel and Banks to the north were consolidated for attack, as the Army of Virginia, and placed under the command of General John Pope, who had been successful in operations in the West, particularly in capturing Island No 10 on the Mississippi.

Pope almost immediately alienated many of his new command by a bombastic address in which he implied that the troops in the East were not as good fighters as those he had commanded in the West. 'I have come to you,' he said, 'from the West, where we have always seen the backs of our enemies —from an army whose business it has been to seek the adversary, and beat him when found, whose policy has been attack and not defence . . . I presume that I have been called here to pursue the same system, and to lead you against the enemy. It is my purpose to do so and that right speedily . . . Meantime, I desire you to dismiss from your minds certain phrases, which I am sorry to find much in vogue amongst you. I hear constantly of taking strong positions and holding them—of lines of retreat and bases of supplies. Let us discard such ideas . . . Let us study the probable line of retreat of our opponents, and leave our own to take care of themselves. Let us look before and not behind. Success and glory are in the advance. Disaster and shame lurk in the rear.'[1]

Pope also stated when asked where his headquarters would be, 'In the saddle.' Lee, it is said, commented, chuckling, when he heard of this remark, 'He has his headquarters where his hindquarters ought to be!'

[1] O.R., XII, iii, 474.

To the Confederates, however, Pope was particularly obnoxious because he introduced elements of total warfare. He ordered his troops to live off the country; and he announced that bushwhackers were to be shot as traitors. On 23 July Pope's generals were instructed to arrest every Virginian within the limits of their commands, to administer the oath of allegiance to the Union, and to expel from their homes all those who refused to take it. This order was preceded by one directing the arrest of five prominent citizens, to be held as hostages to suffer death in the event of any soldiers being shot by bushwhackers.[1] The Confederate Government retaliated by declaring that Pope and his officers were not entitled to be considered as soldiers. If captured they were to be imprisoned so long as their orders remained unrepealed; and in the event of any unarmed Confederate citizens being tried and shot, an equal number of Federal prisoners were to be hanged.[2] These retaliatory measures—and a general diversion owing to the extensions of the war—improved the position considerably; but the operations north of Gordonsville, where Jackson with two divisions had been despatched to guard the Virginia Central Railway, were watched with considerable interest in the South. 'This new general,' it was said to Jackson about Pope—now based on Sperryville—'claims your attention.' 'And, please God, he shall have it,' was the reply. Nevertheless, with all his peculiar characteristics Pope was no despicable foe. The Federal cavalry under him were now employed with a boldness which had not hitherto been seen; and even General Banks was spurred to activity!

Jackson had drawn back his cavalry, and moved his infantry south of Gordonsville. His main object was to defend the important Virginia Central Railway which linked Richmond with the Shenandoah Valley through Gordonsville to Charlottesville and Staunton (*see* Map facing p. 96). Pope, however, appeared confident of cutting the rail link. 'Within ten days,' he reported, 'unless the enemy is heavily reinforced from Richmond, I shall be in possession of Gordonsville and Charlottesville!'

Meanwhile Lee had decided to reinforce Jackson. This is shown in his letter to Jackson dated 27 July, 1862: 'I have received your despatch of the 26th instant. I will send A. P. Hill's division and the 2nd Brigade of Louisiana volunteers to you . . . I want Pope to be suppressed . . . A. P. Hill you will, I think, find a good officer, with whom you can consult, and by advising with your division commanders as to your movements, much trouble will be saved you in arranging details, and they can act more intelligently.'[3] Then Lee told him to hide his troops as much as possible until he could strike a blow at

---

[1] Backwoodsmen—in this case guerrillas.   [2] Henderson, ii, 82.
[3] *Ibid.*, 80.

Pope, and be prepared to return to Richmond when done, if necessary. Lee said he would endeavour to keep General McClellan quiet.

Lee, in this letter, seems to be asking Jackson to try to keep his subordinate officers better informed. Jackson, however, remained as reticent as ever during the Cedar Run operation which was to follow, and with unfortunate results.

For that encounter Jackson and his corps were in better shape than they had been for the Seven Days' Battles. The Confederate regiments, as a rule, were very weak. The losses of the Seven Days', of Winchester, of Cross Keys and of Port Republic had not yet been replaced. Companies had dwindled down to sections. Brigades were no stronger than full battalions, and the colonel was happy who could muster 200 muskets. But the waste of the campaign was not altogether an evil. The weak and sickly had been weeded out. The faint-hearted had disappeared, and if many of the bravest had fallen before Richmond, those who remained were hardy and experienced soldiers. The army that lay around Gordonsville was the best yet that Jackson had commanded. The horses, which had become useless in the Peninsula, had soon regained condition on the rich pastures at the foot of the south-west mountains. Nearly every man had seen service. The officers were no longer novices. The troops had implicit confidence in their leaders, and their morale was high. They had not yet tasted defeat. Whenever they had met the enemy he had abandoned the field of battle. With such troops much might be risked, and if the staff was not yet thoroughly trained, the district in which they were now operating was far less intricate than the Peninsula. There were also many in the Confederate ranks who were familiar with the country; and the quick pencil of Captain Hotchkiss, Jackson's trusted engineer, who had rejoined from the Valley, was once more at his disposal. [1]

An interesting strategic situation now developed in the centre of Virginia. Pope's three corps were moving south towards Culpeper Court House: Banks' Corps followed by Sigel's from the north, McDowell's Corps, with Rickett's division leading and followed by a division of Burnside's corps from the north-east and east.

When Jackson was informed about this, he saw at once a chance of moving first to Culpeper Court House, and defeating each of Pope's corps in detail before they concentrated. Thus he advanced northwards. He was by no means displeased when he learned who was in command of the Federal advance. 'Banks is in front of me,' he said to Dr Hunter McGuire, his medical director. 'He is always ready for a fight'; and then laughing, he added as if to himself, 'and he generally gets whipped.'

[1] Henderson, ii, 86, 87.

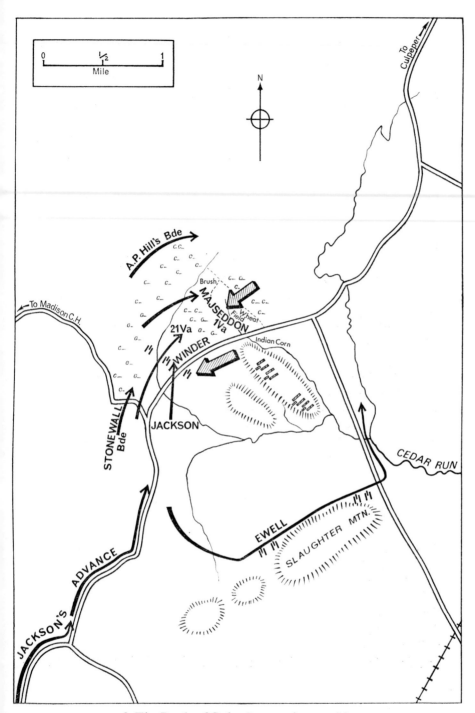

8 The Battle of Cedar Run, 9 August 1862

On 7 August, starting late in the afternoon, the Confederates marched eight miles by a country track, and halted at Orange Court House. So far so good; but Culpeper was still 20 miles distant; and two rivers, the Rapidan and Robertson, both defended by Federal cavalry, barred the road.

On the next day everything went wrong. Jackson altered his order of march, and sent Ewell by another route towards Culpeper. A. P. Hill received no clear orders as to the new march instructions and, offended by Jackson's reticence and the inefficiency of his staff, made little effort to get his column out of the difficulties in which they found themselves. These were created by the crossing of Ewell's and Hill's lines of march; and Hill's advance was delayed for many hours by Ewell's ambulances and wagons. The result was that instead of marching 20 miles, Ewell's division covered eight and Hill's only two. [1]

On 9 August the Confederate advance began at an early hour. Hill, anxious to redeem his shortcomings, marched before daylight, and soon caught up the rear of Winder who was behind Ewell in the long column on the Culpeper road.

Shortly before noon, Ewell's advanced troops came upon Federal cavalry, with their guns behind them, on a low ridge with Indian corn on its slopes beyond the south fork of Cedar Run which crossed under the Culpeper road. After a brief reconnaissance, Jackson made his plan. A large force of artillery was ordered to come into action on either side of the advanced guard. Ewell was told to carry out a turning movement round the east flank of the Federals across the slopes of Slaughter Mountain; [2] a hill dominating the whole position, on which guns were also placed. Finally, Winder was ordered to attack on the left, and A. P. Hill to form the reserve.

These movements took time. The Confederate column, 20,000 infantry and 15 batteries, occupied about seven miles of the road and took over two hours to deploy.

The preliminary bombardment proceeded according to plan; but Ewell was delayed by the cross-fire of his own guns on Slaughter Mountain; and, early in the engagement, Winder was mortally wounded by a shell near the Culpeper road.

Then, before the Confederates' thrusts developed, Banks attacked. The Federal assault came in the centre, and on the west of the Culpeper road beyond the fork to Madison Court House (*see* Map p. 125).

The north-western area was forested but with a large wheatfield between two lines of woodland north-west of the road. Along the border of the wheat-

[1] O.R., XII, ii, 181.   [2] Also called Cedar Mountain.

field about 500 men of the 1st Va of Colonel Garnett's 2nd Brigade, under Major Seddon, were posted. The Stonewall Brigade, which should have been just behind them, was half a mile distant in the rear of Winder's artillery. Jackson visited the area and warned Colonel Garnett to watch out for his flank, and a courier was posted with Major Seddon with instructions to report any movements of the enemy in the thick woodland on his extreme left.[1] The Federal attack, however, was too sudden for them. Beyond the wheatfield, 1,500 Federals had formed up in the wood. First came the skirmishers making good use for cover of the shocks of wheat and bushes; then emerged the main body with fixed bayonets and colours flying. Their long line overlapping the Confederates, they moved across the 300 yards of open wheatfield. Major Seddon reports: 'At about 5.45 o'clock a large brigade of the enemy emerged from the woods beyond the wheat-field, and advanced against our lines in fine order at a double-quick. A (Indian) corn field on the right (of the road) and a brush field on the left of the wheat-field prevented me from seeing either wing of the enemy, which seemed to extend indefinitely in both directions. By order, the battalion fired as the enemy came within 150 yards of our position, with very little effect. By this time the enemy were close upon our front and had closed in upon our left flank. Seeing this the battalion gave way, and retreated rapidly in great confusion . . . All the officers of the battalion strove most gallantly to hold the men to their position, and made most heroic endeavours to rally them after they had broken.'[2]

Chaos and confusion reigned on the Confederate left for a time. By Jackson's orders, Winder's batteries were at once withdrawn, and not a gun was lost. The infantry of the left and centre, however, did not escape so lightly. Every regimental commander in Garnett's 2nd Brigade was either killed or wounded, and the other brigades were driven back and broken. Some regiments attempted to change front, others retreated in disorder. Men were captured and recaptured, and blue and grey mingled in close conflict amid the smoke. Then, while the Federals were unsupported, the Stonewall Brigade entered the fray. Breaking into the mêlée on the left of the Culpeper road, these five staunch regiments, undismayed by the disaster, opened a heavy fire. The Federals stopped and drew together to meet the Virginians, and just at that moment, Jackson rode up and turned the tide of the battle in the favour of the Confederates. He sent off orders to Ewell to attack from Slaughter Mountain, and for A. P. Hill to enter the battle with the reserves. Then he galloped forward, unattended by either staff-officer or orderly, and found himself in the midst of his own men, his soldiers of the Valley, no longer presenting their usual stubborn front but an ungovernable

[1] O.R., XII, ii, 200.   [2] Ibid., 205.

mob, breaking rapidly to the rear, and on the very verge of panic. Drawing his sword for the first time in the war, his voice pealed high above the din; the troops caught the familiar accents, instinct with resolution, and the presence of their general acted as a spell. 'Rally, men,' he shouted, 'and follow me!' The 21st Va were the first to respond. With a wild yell their remnant rushed to the front. Then the officers of other regiments, inspired by the example of their commander, bore their colours forward, and the men, catching the enthusiasm of the moment, followed in the path of the 21st. The Federals recoiled. [1]

By this time two brigades from A. P. Hill's reserve division were moving round the Federal right, and Ewell's brigades, clear at last of the line of fire of their own guns, were turning the Federal east flank. Outflanked on both right and left, the Federals began to retreat, the cavalry making charges to ease the pressure on their infantry. As darkness fell the Confederates crossed Cedar Run and swept up the slope beyond.

Jackson pushed forward through the night under a full moon. At this moment Pope himself arrived on the scene; but surprised by a salvo from Jackson's guns, was constrained to do what he said he had never done in the West, turn his back on the enemy and seek a safer position. Jackson did not persevere. On 10 August he withdrew to his old position on Cedar Run. He now realised that it was not just Banks' division but the bulk of Pope's army which lay before him. Regretfully he returned to his old camps near Gordonsville.

Cedar Run provides many illustrations of Jackson's virtues and failing as a general. The early move on Culpeper to defeat Pope's corps in detail showed his strategic wisdom. His reticence on the march there, in spite of Lee's hints to be more forthcoming with his divisional commanders, and the consequent trouble with Hill, illustrates one of his failings. His tactical plan for the attack appears to be very sound; but the failure to brief all his commanders of the whole plan brought trouble. Winder's successor appears to have been in the dark after Winder was killed, and this added to the confusion on the left. Jackson's personal leadership at the crisis of the battle shows him at his very best, and it is incidents like this which have made him so renowned. Cedar Run even shows Jackson displaying a rare sense of fun. Douglas, his youngest staff officer, and then bearing the grandiose title of inspector-general, was sent by Jackson to General Ewell with an order to move forward and attack. After remaining a little while to explain to him the situation on the left, which was now hotly engaged and needed Ewell's cooperation, Douglas started to return over the field by which he had come.

[1] Henderson, ii, 95.

When he had gone half way, he found himself in a dilemma. The enemy's skirmishers had cut him off. Not knowing the country, he concluded he had better return to Ewell, but some of the enemy's pickets or skirmishers had cut off his retreat there as well. A line of them was also coming up from the front. Towards the rear he saw no Federals at all; only a repulsive fence, which seemed grown up with bushes and impassable for his horse. Scattering shots falling and whizzing about him warned him to be up and doing. Having no choice, he made a rush for the fence; his horse urged with the spur and apparently frantic with fright, did not hesitate, but making a desperate leap he landed on the other side and threw a shower of ploughed dirt into the air. After the battle, when they were riding to the rear, and the staff were guying him about the 'big jump' he had told them of, to the General's quiet amusement, he persuaded them to go a little out of their way to see evidence of it. The General consented, and when he had looked at the place, he turned in the saddle and said: 'Gentlemen, the evidence is conclusive—that—Douglas was badly scared!' Then, with what was almost a chuckle, he ambled off to headquarters.

Jackson was to say that this battle was the most successful he fought, but in his report to Lee he offered the usual, modest 'God blessed our arms with another victory.'[1]

[1] Burke Davis, 282.

Cedar Run : Chain of Command[1]

Confederates 20,000

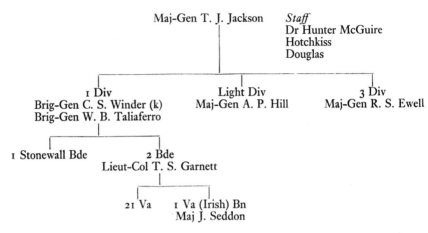

Maj-Gen T. J. Jackson   *Staff*
Dr Hunter McGuire
Hotchkiss
Douglas

1 Div
Brig-Gen C. S. Winder (k)
Brig-Gen W. B. Taliaferro

Light Div
Maj-Gen A. P. Hill

3 Div
Maj-Gen R. S. Ewell

1 Stonewall Bde

2 Bde
Lieut-Col T. S. Garnett

21 Va   1 Va (Irish) Bn
Maj J. Seddon

casualties 1,365

Federals 17,900 not all engaged

Army of Virginia

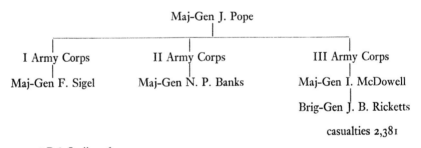

Maj-Gen J. Pope

I Army Corps

Maj-Gen F. Sigel

II Army Corps

Maj-Gen N. P. Banks

III Army Corps

Maj-Gen I. McDowell

Brig-Gen J. B. Ricketts

casualties 2,381

[1] B & L, ii, 496.

130

The Second Battle of Bull Run

After the battle at Cedar Run the Federal army camped in the neighbourhood of Culpeper Court House north of the battlefield; and the Confederates fell back behind the Rapidan. The Confederates had now been greatly reinforced; Longstreet's corps had joined Jackson's corps; and the army was under the command of Lee. The senior commanders went to the top of Clark's Mountain on the south bank of the Rapidan to reconnoitre the enemy position; Longstreet says: 'With General Lee I proceeded to the mountain, and, climbing to its summit, we raised our glasses and turned them to the north. There, between the two rivers,[1] clustering around Culpeper Court House, and perhaps fifteen miles away, we saw the flags of Pope's army floating placidly above the tops of the trees. From the summit of the mountain we beheld the enemy occupying ground so weak as to invite attack. Realising the situation, General Lee determined on speedy work, and gave orders that his army should cross the Rapidan on the 18th and give battle.'[2]

Lee decided to cross the river secretly and pass behind Pope's east flank, thereby placing his army between Pope and Washington. This plan, however, came to nothing. During a preliminary cavalry reconnaissance Stuart was nearly caught by a Federal patrol, and only escaped by making his horse leap a gate out of the garden of his temporary billet. Unfortunately he left behind, not only his famous plumed hat, but his despatchbox containing, among other papers, a letter from Lee disclosing that Jackson had been strongly reinforced. Then the cavalry who were to form the van of the Confederates were late in getting into position, and supplies for the other troops took a couple of days to assemble, so that Lee's army did not move until the 20th

[1] Rapidan and Rappahannock.   [2] B & L, ii, 515.

August, instead of the 18th. This delay saved Pope. By the time Lee's forces were ready to start, the Federals, warned of a probable attack, and given time to get away, pulled back rapidly behind the formidable barrier of the Rappahannock. The next phase of the operation took the form of a river war, with the opposing forces facing each other on either side of the Rappahannock. To begin with the Confederates sought a crossing; and Longstreet's corps probed in the south by Kelly's Ford; while Jackson's corps moved north and attempted to get across at Sulphur (Warrenton) Springs. Pope, meanwhile, moved up and down the river disputing the attempts to cross. All that seemed necessary was to guard the fords, and most of the advantage lay with the defence. Pope seemed likely to be able to hold Lee off until reinforced by McClellan, who had now left the Peninsula and was disembarking his troops at Aquia Creek and Alexandria near Washington.

Then came two exploits, one by Jackson's men and the other by Stuart and the cavalry, which firmly convinced Pope that there would be no further serious attempt to turn his right flank.

When Jackson reached the ruined bridge and ford at Sulphur Springs, it seemed to offer a crossing place, and only a few of the enemy's cavalry could be seen in the neighbourhood. Ordered to cross, the 13th Georgia dashed through the ford and occupied some cottages on the far bank, while Early's brigade, also of Ewell's division, with two batteries crossed by an old milldam, a mile below, and took the ridge beyond. The next morning the pioneers were ordered to repair the bridge. The bridge had been burned and torn down, and General Jackson went to work to rebuild it. He set the example in his own person, until he was completely drenched by the falling rain and covered with mud from head to foot; and his example had the desired effect on his troops, who, wading in water up to their waists without murmuring, lifted heavy logs and replaced fallen timbers until the work seemed to progress by magic.[1] Early's troops had now taken up a position behind a creek up river. Here at nightfall the Federal cavalry attacked them, but were easily beaten back. Then, while Longstreet's corps demonstrated against Pope down river to occupy his attention, Jackson passed over another brigade. At dawn on the 24th, however, as the Federals were reported to be advancing in force, Jackson withdrew all his forces again to his own side of the river. On the face of it, the operation appears futile; but it produced indirect advantage for the Confederates.

Stuart with 1,500 cavalry and two guns moved north through Jeffersonton, crossed the Rappahannock at Waterloo Bridge and Hart's Mill, a few miles

[1] Douglas, 133.

20 *The Battle of Cedar Run, 9 August 1862*

The Federal attack in the wheatfield area. The Federals in foreground 'with fixed bayonets and colours flying', attacking Major Seddon's men. From a drawing by Edwin Forbes (1839–1894)

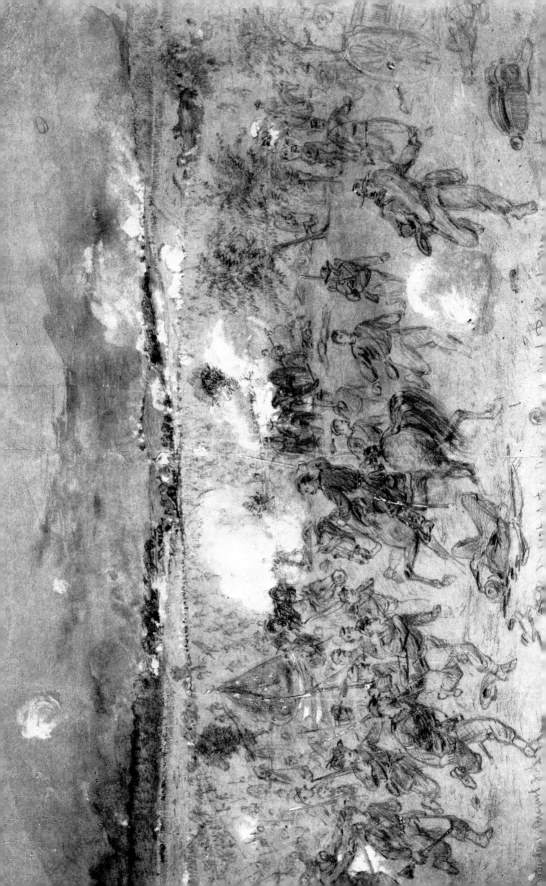

below, and took the direct road to Warrenton. He says: 'From this point I directed my march ... with a view to destroy the railroad bridge near Catlett's Station, and the telegraph line, and thus cut the enemy's line of communication. I had not proceeded far before a terrific storm set in which was a serious obstacle to the progress of artillery, and gave indications of continuing for a sufficient time to render the streams on my return impassable ... we soon found ourselves in the midst of the enemy's encampments, but the darkest night I ever knew. Fortunately we captured at this moment, so critical, a negro who had known me in Beverley, and, who, recognising me, informed me of the location of Pope's staff, baggage, and horses, and offered to guide to the spot.'[1] Stuart's cavalry found the railway bridge too difficult to destroy; but having dealt with the telegraph and set the camp ablaze, they returned the way they had come with 300 prisoners, including many officers, Pope's despatch book giving his strength and dispositions, and Pope's hat, his military cloak, and one of his uniform coats. Stuart was delighted with these. He hoped to trade them for his plumed hat.

But the importance of both Jackson's crossing and Stuart's raid lay in the fact that they both withdrew after making them. Pope fully believed both attempts had failed, and the Confederates had been twice repulsed. He thought Lee's army would not try again on this flank.

Before the battle of Second Bull Run Jackson had to make new appointments, and most important was a new commander for the Stonewall Division in place of Winder who had been killed at Cedar Run. The possibilities were Taliaferro, his senior brigadier but one of the troublemakers of the Romney days, and Starke, a Virginian by birth who had lived in New Orleans, a tough fighter commanding one of the Louisiana brigades. The qualifications of Starke, and Taliaferro—the latter eventually preferred—were probably studied by Jackson more closely than his letters and his reported conversation indicated. He was never indifferent to brigade and regimental command, but he did not balk at giving battle because his subordinates were inexperienced. His reliance primarily was upon discipline, upon himself, upon God; not upon the eminence of his officers.[2]

There were at this time also problems of administration and discipline. His quartermaster and commissary services were not working well. The troops were ill fed.[3] Officers were not uniformly setting the example they should in discipline, which was very bad as regards straggling. To discourage this weakening of his army when every bullet counted, Jackson staged a dramatic warning. Three deserters who had been caught, court-martialled and

[1] O.R., XII, ii, 731.   [2] Freeman, LL, ii, 66.
[3] Hotchkiss, MS Diary, 74, 75.

The Battle of Second Bull Run (Manassas), 30 August 1862. From a drawing by Alfred R. Waud (1828–1891). A Federal Battery firing canister at point-blank range tries to check General Longstreet's charge against the Federal left wing while a mounted officer attempts to rally his fleeing men

condemned, were prepared for execution. Blindfolded, they were placed by the side of open graves, and the whole of Jackson's Division (Taliaferro) to which they belonged, were paraded to see the three men fall before the firing firing squad, and then marched by in file to view the dead bodies and observe how they had been riddled.[1]

On 24 August Lee had a conference at Jeffersonton. What occurred at this council of war was never made public although Douglas says that Longstreet and Stuart were there as well as Jackson, and relates that he overheard Jackson saying, 'I will be moving within an hour.'[2] Dr Hunter McGuire says: 'The day before we started to march round Pope's army, I saw Lee and Jackson conferring together. Jackson—for him—was very much excited, drawing with the toe of his boot in the sand, and gesticulating in a much more earnest way than he was in the habit of doing. General Lee was simply listening, and after Jackson had got through, he nodded his head, as if acceding to some proposal. I believe, from what occurred afterwards, that Jackson suggested the movement as it was made, but I have no further proof than the incident I have just mentioned.'[3]

In any case the responsibility was Lee's; and it was a very bold plan that he adopted. Jackson was to march northwards, crossing the Rappahannock's westerly tributary, Hedgeman's Creek, but keeping to the west of Carter's Run from the north (see Map facing p. 144). Reaching Salem, Jackson was to turn and pass through the Bull Run Mountains at Thoroughfare Gap and move on eastwards to cut near Manassas the railway which formed Pope's line of supply.

On the evening of 24 August Jackson began his preparations for the most famous of his marches. The order of march was Ewell's division followed by A. P. Hill's Light Division, then Taliaferro's division. This seems to have been arranged because Jackson was still worried about Hill. Ewell was a fast, sure man on the road. If Hill followed him and kept Ewell's pace, there could be none of the tardiness that Jackson charged against the so-called Light Division. Should Hill fall behind, despite Ewell, then the Stonewall Division, under Taliaferro, could close on Hill and press him on.[4]

Three days' cooked rations were carried in the haversacks, and a herd of cattle together with the green corn standing in the fields were relied upon for subsistence until requisition could be made on the Federal magazines. The troops marched light. Knapsacks were left behind. Tin cans and a few frying-pans formed the only camp equipment.

[1] Moore, 99, 100.　　　　　　　[2] Douglas, 135.
[3] Henderson, ii, 123, 124.　　　　[4] Freeman, LL, ii, 84.

The divisions forded Hedgeman's Creek at Hinson's Mill. One of Jackson's Foot-Cavalry writes:

I recall a sumptuous banquet of 'middling' bacon and 'collards' which I was fortunate to obtain during the delay at Hinson's Mill where we forded the river, and the still more dainty fare of tea and biscuits, the bounty of some good maiden ladies—the only episodes of the march which stand out with distinction. It was far into the night when the column stopped, and the weary men dropped beside their stacked muskets and were instantly asleep, without so much as unrolling a blanket. A few hours of much-needed repose, and they were shaken up again long before 'crack of day', and limped on in the darkness only half-awake. There was no mood for speech, nor breath to spare if there had been, only the shuffling tramp of the marching feet, the steady rumble of wheels, the creak and rattle and clank of harness and accoutrement, with an occasional order, uttered under the breath and always the same: 'Close up! close up, men!'[1]

This was Jackson's cry on the march, and passed on and repeated by his officers.

When Jackson stood to watch his army go by, the men of Ewell's division saw their general and were about to give a cheer; but he raised his hand to stop them, and the word went down the column, 'Don't shout, boys, the Yankees will hear us!' Then, when his own Stonewall regiments passed, he could not restrain them; and was heralded by a particularly wild rebel yell. 'It is no use,' said Jackson, turning to his staff, 'you see I can't stop them'; and then, with pride, half to himself, 'who could fail to win battles with such men as these?'[2]

Every precaution was taken to conceal the march from the enemy. The roads in the direction of the Federals were watched by cavalry, and so far as possible the column was directed through woods and valleys; and sometimes, took to the fields. Another soldier of the Foot-Cavalry tells of crossing at Hinson's Mill and thence going 'several miles right through the country, over ditches and fences, through woods until we came to a public road'.[3]

Passing through Thoroughfare Gap the troops looked down on the open country to the east. At Hay Market and Gainesville came the first encounters with the Federals in the shape of a dozen or so troopers more like stragglers than a patrol. Colonel Munford 2nd Va Cavalry, says: 'on the evening of the 26th the advanced guard captured 12 or 15 Yankees ... they seemed entirely ignorant of any movement of our army, and we pressed on to Bristoe Station.'[4] Douglas, who needed a fresh horse and another pistol from the

[1] B & L, ii, 532, 533.   [2] Dabney, ii, 266.
[3] Worsham, 118.   [4] O.R., XII, ii, 747.

Federals, received permission to join Munford in the attack on Bristoe Station. He writes:

A charge was made upon the place, the Federal guard of cavalry was put to flight with a few prisoners and I got a horse and a pair of pistols. Instantly a train of cars, loaded with stores, came dashing past. The dismounted cavalry poured an ineffective volley into it, but it rushed on its way and bore the alert to Manassas Junction. In a few minutes more the advance of the infantry, their weariness forgotten in the excitement, came up at double-time, and were more successful in their attempt to stop two trains which came steaming into the station about the same time. They had no stores of any value and were subsequently burnt. It was after nine o'clock at night when we got entire control of Bristoe Station; yet, before midnight General Jackson sent General Stuart with some cavalry and General Trimble with his brigade to take possession of Manassas Junction, the great depot of supplies. The work was quickly and well done; before daylight Trimble took the works at Manassas with little loss. [1]

On the morning of the 27th, leaving Ewell at Bristoe Station, Jackson moved the rest of his command to Manassas Junction. Near Bristoe Station the railway crossed over Broad Run, and the stream formed a good defensive position behind which Ewell might have made his stand. He preferred otherwise and went to meet Pope. Pope's leading force under General Hooker was near at hand and staged an attack in the afternoon. Although this was repulsed by Ewell, he crossed back over Broad Run, burnt the bridge to delay Hooker, and joined Jackson at Manassas.

Manassas was a main Federal commissary depot, and stores of all sorts were found there in abundance. The cavalrymen had helped themselves liberally to horses upon their arrival, [2] but Trimble held a stern hand on the actions of his two regiments of the vanguard. Instead of being allowed to plunder, they were ordered to guard the captured stores. The Stonewall Brigade, which reached Manassas soon after daylight, likewise was restrained, was kept under arms, and was ordered out to positions around the junction to guard against a possible Federal attack. A. P. Hill's men were less controlled. Trimble complains: 'It was with extreme mortification that in reporting to General A. P. Hill for orders about ten o'clock, I witnessed an indiscrimate plunder on the public stores, cars, and sutlers' houses by the army which had just arrived, in which General Hill's division was conspicuous, setting at defiance the guards I had placed on the stores.' [3]

With the Federals on his heels, Jackson soon came to the conclusion that it was impossible to take away a tithe of the stores; and when an issue of rations had been made, the bakery set working, and the liquor barrels staved

---

[1] Douglas, 137, 138. [2] O.R., XII, ii, 721. [3] Ibid.

in or placed under guard, the regiments were let loose on the magazines. 'Orders were issued for us to take four days' rations with us,' says Worsham. 'It was hard to decide what to take, some filled their haversacks with cakes, some with candy, others oranges, lemons and canned goods. I know one who took nothing but French mustard, filled his haversack and was so greedy that he put one more bottle in his pocket. This was his four days' rations, and it turned out to be the best thing taken, because he traded it for meat and bread, and it lasted him until we reached Frederick City. (Antietam campaign). All good times have an end, and, as night approached, preparations were made to burn everything that we could not carry; and not long after sunset the stores were set on fire, our division, taking up our march as soon as the fires got well under way.'[1]

The first part of Jackson's mission had now been performed. He had cut the line of supply of the Federal army, wrecked its depôt, and assured its withdrawal from the Rappahannock. Now he had to keep his foe perplexed until he was joined by Longstreet.

Before Pope reached Manassas Junction, Jackson marched his brigades away. The subsequent manoeuvres of the Confederate divisions and of Pope's many scattered corps are complicated, and the reasons for their comlex movements difficult to explain.

Jackson got his divisions into a tangle from the lack of clarity of his orders to his commanders, and the inefficiency of the guides he supplied to lead them away from Manassas. Taliaferro's division marched north from Manassas, through Newmarket, skirted the west of the First Bull Run position, crossed Young's Branch and the Warrenton-Centreville turnpike, and took up a position on Groveton Ridge,[2] south of Sudley Springs and north of Groveton, a house or two on the turnpike at the cross road. A. P. Hill's division was probably meant to move to the same place, and Ewell's as well. But guides were provided who did not know where to go.[3] A. P. Hill crossed Bull Run at Blackburn's Ford and proceeded to Centreville; and Ewell, following behind him, also crossed at Blackburn's Ford. Ewell, realising his mistake, then marched upstream along the left bank of Bull Run, crossed back at Stone Bridge, and took up a position in the centre of Groveton Ridge alongside Taliaferro. A. P. Hill eventually left Centreville and marched westwards up the turnpike to join the others, taking the most easterly position.

Unwittingly, Jackson had completely mystified and misled Pope, who now had no idea where Jackson's forces were. His own corps were marching on

[1] Worsham, 121, 122.
[2] Sudley Mountain and Stony Ridge are other names for it.
[3] Freeman, LL, ii, 104.

Manassas junction from the west and south-west; Sigel's and McDowell's from Gainesville; Reno's and Heintzelman's from Greenwich in the west (it was Hooker from Heintzelman's corps who turned Ewell out of Bristoe Station), and Porter's and Banks' from Warrenton (*see* Map facing p. 144). McDowell's corps and Porter's corps were difficult to control. When McDowell reached Gainesville, he sent back Ricketts' division to stop Longstreet coming through Thoroughfare Gap, despatched King's division straight along the turnpike towards Stone Bridge, and then proceeded to Manassas without letting Pope know where he, or his divisions, had gone. Porter disobeyed Pope's order to join the battle from Manassas, moving only as far as Dawkins Branch. A second and more peremptory order brought in Porter opposite Jackson's right; but by doing this Longstreet was allowed freedom to turn Pope's left. Porter was court-martialled by Pope and dismissed the service for his actions at Second Bull Run.[1]

When Pope heard of the Confederate presence at Centreville, he ordered Reno's and Heintzelman's corps to march there; but by the time they arrived, A. P. Hill had left. As far as Pope was concerned he had lost his prey. He had no idea now where Jackson's forces had gone.

Jackson had drawn up his forces on Groveton Ridge. This was a good position on the flank of Pope's march from the Rappahannock towards Manassas Junction and Centreville. It was also near Thoroughfare Gap through which Longstreet's corps was coming in support.

There now occurred a chance encounter west of Groveton which led to the great battle called Second Bull Run.

Jackson's outposts to the west of Groveton reported that a Federal column was advancing eastwards from Gainesville. He decided to move Taliaferro's division to intercept it, with two of Ewell's brigades in support; but when these forces reached Browner House, a mile west of the Groveton crossroads, it was realised that the Federals had no knowledge of Jackson's presence at Groveton, and were, in Jackson's words, 'leaving the road and inclining toward Manassas Junction'.[2] Towards sunset on the same day, however, another blue column, compact and well closed, came marching up the turnpike from Gainesville, this time keeping to the road and marching straight for Stone Bridge. Jackson rode forward to reconnoitre, boldy exposing himself to the enemy while doing so. The Federals paid little attention to the lone horseman on the ridge to the north, and marched stolidly on. Jackson found it impossible to resist the temptation to attack such unwary prey. Galloping back to

[1] Much later in the war Porter was reinstated.
[2] O.R., XII, ii, 644, 645.

Taliaferro's men lying in the woods north of the turnpike about Browner's House, he called to their officers, 'Bring up your men, gentlemen!' Soon throughout the woods, from the charging Confederates pushing their way in and out of the undergrowth, sounded the Rebel Yell, on this occasion, 'a hoarse roar like that from cages of wild animals at the scent of blood'.[1] As a background to the Yell came the booming of Confederate batteries firing at the unsuspecting column over the heads of their own infantry. The massacre and destruction of the Federals seemed imminent. But it was not to be. The victims were King's division of McDowell's corps, tough fighters from Indiana and Wisconsin. When attacked, they gave as good as they got.

For once Jackson had ignored flanking movements and staged a simple head-on assault. It was far from successful, and proved to be one of the costliest battles Jackson ever fought. Although King pulled back to Gaines-ville, and later to Manassas Junction, and left Jackson in possession of the battlefield, Confederate casualties were high. Among the distinguished Con-federate fallen were: Ewell, who later lost his leg from his wound; and Taliaferro, who stayed out the day, but had to hand over his command after-wards to Starke, who thus got the Jackson Division after all.

From the battle at Groveton, Pope had at last discovered the position of the Confederates. Although, with Ricketts' division watching Thoroughfare Gap, he should have known that Longstreet's approach was imminent, he planned to concentrate 25,000 men east of Jackson and a similar number comprising McDowell's and Sigel's corps west of him to 'crush Jackson before Longstreet could by any possibility reach the scene of action'.[2]

Pope's plan was sound enough; it was the execution of it which went sadly wrong. McDowell's corps was too strung out to be concentrated on the west; and his corps, and Sigel's, and Reynolds' division which was originally with them, though all destined for an attack on the west flank, swung in and came up on the centre; Ricketts' division made the feeblest of attempts to hold Longstreet, and also came back for a centre attack. Meanwhile, Porter, destined for the east flank, moved a short stage to a position where he could have held Longstreet, and then when ordered to join the fight from the west, refused to move. As has been stated, when he eventually came into the fight, he also joined the centre.

As the battle opened, and vigorous artillery exchanges were begun, some Confederates looking towards the distant Bull Run Mountains in their rear, saw a long cloud of dust and wondered hopefully if it were caused by the feet

[1] Blackford, 172, 173.   [2] O.R., XII, ii, 38.

of the regiments of Longstreet's column. General Starke, now commanding the Jackson Division, sent off a horseman to find out. Soon the courier came galloping back. 'It's Longstreet,' he cried, even before he reached his general; and a great cry that Longstreet had come was taken up by men all down the line. [1] Longstreet had brushed aside Bufold's cavalry at Thoroughfare Gap, and outmanoeuvred Ricketts' division by sending some of his brigade through Hopewell Gap to the north. Ricketts withdrew and joined King's division at Gainesville. They both later moved on Bristoe and Manassas Junction, without telling Pope who was out of touch with their commander McDowell.

The battle began with a foray against Jackson's wagon train, which was repelled by the cavalry supported by the horse artillery. Then came two attacks on Ewell's front. After one of these, a Confederate officer was taking his company to task for shooting down a very brave Federal major who had been leading his men on horseback. So brave a man should have been captured not killed, he said. Jackson overheard this and said: 'No captain, the men are right; kill the brave ones; they lead on the others.' This was always Jackson's view. He had said the same to Ewell at Port Republic when Ewell wanted to spare a gallant foe.

The next Federal attacks were on A. P. Hill's part of the line. Although much of Jackson's position occupied an unfinished railway cutting, and was potentially strong, trees on both sides allowed covered approaches for attackers, and this nearly proved disastrous for Hill. By midday the heavy attacks on Hill were becoming almost continuous. Federals, making use of the cover of the trees, were assembling in the railway cut itself, and had started forcing their way between two of Hill's brigades on the northern side of the cut. About this time Hill sent a message to Jackson by Douglas, who happened to be there. He said that he was being pressed very hard and might not be able to hold on. Jackson received this news grimly. He sent back Douglas with the stern message, 'Tell him if they attack him again he must beat them!' Then moving over towards the left flank he met Hill in person, and told him, 'General, your men have done nobly; if you are attacked again, you will beat the enemy back.'

A rattle of musketry broke along Hill's front. 'Here it comes,' he said and galloped off, Jackson calling after him, 'I'll expect you to beat them.'

It was a desperate struggle on the left; but Hill's men did manage to hold on. Reinforced by Early of Ewell's division, they staged a successful counterattack which cleared the Federals from the railway cutting, and drove them back to the position from which they had launched their first attack. General

[1] Worsham, 130, 131.

22 *The Battle of Antietam (Sharpsburg), 17 September 1862.*
*'Bloody Lane', where Jackson's brother-in-law General D. H. Hill resisted
staunchly and suffered many casualties. 'The dead lay so thick in the lane that
a man could have walked its length without touching the ground'*

23 *Ruins at Manassas Junction after Jackson's raid of 17 August 1862*

24 *The Battle of Antietam (Sharpsburg), 17 September 1862, showing Dunker Church in front of West Wood and a Confederate battery firing at Sumner's Federal troops. From a painting by James Hope (1818–1892)*

25 *Federal pickets watching the Confederate Army crossing the Potomac into Maryland on a bright moonlight night. From a drawing by Alfred R. Waud (1828–1891)*

Hill sent a message to Jackson: 'General Hill presents his compliments and says the attack of the enemy has been repulsed.'

Jackson's face broke into one of his rare smiles as he answered: 'Tell him I knew he would do it.'[1] By sunset, it seemed that the worst was over. For the time being, the gallant Union Troops had had enough. 'When the sun went down their dead were heaped in front of the incomplete railway, and we sighed with relief, for Longstreet could be seen coming into position on our right.'[2] The Confederate casualties were also very heavy, and included the brave Trimble, badly wounded by a Belgian explosive bullet. Dr Hunter McGuire expressed concern at the losses. 'General,' he said, 'this day has been won by nothing but stark and stern fighting.'

'No', answered Jackson, 'it has been won by nothing but the blessing and protection of Providence.'[3]

For the second day of the battle of Bull Run, Longstreet's corps was formed up on the right of Jackson's; and Lee assumed command of all the Confederate forces with his headquarters just south of the turnpike behind Longstreet's corps, which was placed diagonally across the turnpike just west of Groveton, forming an angle with Jackson's line (*see* Map p. 142). This folding round by Longstreet produced significant tactical advantages. It was the battle-winning factor at Second Bull Run.

The morning of 30 August was hot, silent and dry. Where the scorched grass caught, it burned briskly and sent white smoke across the blue sky.[4] The Federals appeared strangely passive. Jackson, riding over to the Stonewall Brigade on his extreme right to view the scene, saw some Union troops moving south among the woods. This he interpreted as a withdrawal.

'It looks as if there will be no fight to-day,' he commented to Colonel Baylor commanding the Brigade, 'but keep your men ready for action.'[5]

Jackson was completely wrong. In mid-afternoon, at a drowsy time of day when all was nods and yawns among the waiting Confederates, the storm broke. A rain of shot and shell struck Jackson's right.

An officer rode up and reported that Colonel Baylor had been shot down and that his successor in command wanted help.

Jackson did not catch the names. 'What Brigade, sir?' he asked.

'The Stonewall Brigade.'

Promising quick reinforcement, Jackson added, 'Go back, give my compliments to them, and tell the Stonewall Brigade to maintain her reputation.'

[1] Douglas, 140.   [2] Chamberlayne, 100, 101.
[3] Dabney, ii, 281.   [4] Moore, 117.
[5] Freeman, LL, ii, 122.

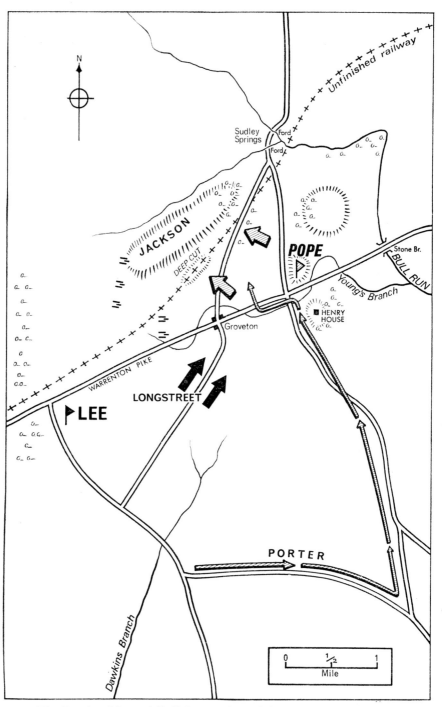

9 *The Battle of Second Bull Run or Second Manassas, 30 August 1862*

The pressure on Jackson's corps now reached its maximum. Porter's men made a particularly savage assault on the railway-cutting in front of Colonel Johnson's brigade of Jackson's old division, in the section known as Deep Cut. Johnson writes: 'Before the railway cut the fight was most obstinate. I saw a Federal flag hold its position for half an hour within ten yards of a flag of one of our regiments in the cut, and go down six or eight times; and after the fight a hundred men were lying twenty yards from the cut, some of them within two feet of it. The men fought until their ammunition was exhausted and then threw stones. An officer killed one with a stone, and I saw the man after the fight with his skull fractured.'[1]

Jackson usually relied on his own forces. This time the odds seemed so great that he was constrained to ask General Lee for help from Longstreet to bolster the line.[2]

Lee ordered Longstreet to send Jackson a division as support. Wisely as it proved, Longstreet decided to disregard the letter of the order from Lee. Instead of despatching a division, he brought up his artillery to a ridge facing the Federal left flank, and raked with his guns the long blue lines moving up on Jackson's position. The result was all that Longstreet had expected. Deep rents were torn in the enemy ranks, their colours went down one after another; their charge was turned into a retreat, and they soon broke. Longstreet gave the order for the general advance of his corps. They moved forward pivoting on their left and swept over by Chinn House, Bald Hill, Henry House, the familiar site of First Bull Run. Jackson also ordered his thin line to advance. The Federals, admitting defeat, streamed over Stone Bridge to occupy a defence position at Centreville.

Riding back after the battle, Jackson noticed a disabled soldier trying to climb up the railway embankment where the fight had been so hot. He rode up to the soldier and asked him if he were wounded. 'Yes, General; but have we whipped them?'[3] Jackson replied in the affirmative and dismounting approached the soldier who told him he belonged to the Stonewall Brigade and had been wounded four times. An examination showed that this last wound was a deep one in the flesh of the thigh. Jackson told a member of his staff to get the man carried to a more comfortable place, and get Dr McGuire to help him if he could.[4]

The last phase of the Second Battle of Bull Run comes as an anticlimax. Reynolds' division, Sykes' regulars and other available troops made a stand

[1] B & L, ii, note 508 under a picture of Deep Cut.
[2] O.R., XII, ii, 647.
[3] Douglas, 144.
[4] See chapter 'Assessment.'

on Henry Hill, poignant with memories of the previous year. Holding back repeated Confederate assaults, they made possible the retreat of the rest of Pope's army over Stone Bridge to the strong defences of the Centreville plateau, where 10,000 fresh troops of Franklin's corps had arrived from Washington on 29 August.

Considering the Centreville position as unfavourable for a direct attack, Lee sent Jackson's corps, followed later by Longstreet's, by Sudley Springs, Pleasant Valley, and the Little River turnpike, in an effort to turn the Federal right. The movement, however, was anticipated by Pope, who moved Stevens' and Kearney's divisions to check it. In a sharp contest in a rainstorm at Chantilly on 1 September 1862, Stevens and Kearney were killed; but Jackson was repulsed. During the next four days Pope retired to the defences of Washington.

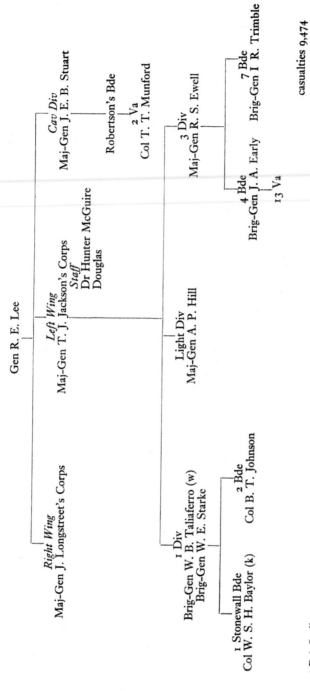

Second Bull Run : Chain of Command [1]

Confederates 49,000

Army of Northern Virginia

Gen R. E. Lee

Right Wing
Maj-Gen J. Longstreet's Corps

Left Wing
Maj-Gen T. J. Jackson's Corps
Staff
Dr Hunter McGuire
Douglas

Cav Div
Maj-Gen J. E. B. Stuart

Robertson's Bde

2 Va
Col T. T. Munford

3 Div
Maj-Gen R. S. Ewell

4 Bde
Brig-Gen J. A. Early

13 Va

7 Bde
Brig-Gen I R. Trimble

casualties 9,474

Light Div
Maj-Gen A. P. Hill

1 Div
Brig-Gen W. B. Taliaferro (w)
Brig-Gen W. E. Starke

2 Bde
Col B. T. Johnson

1 Stonewall Bde
Col W. S. H. Baylor (k)

[1] B & L, ii, 499, 500.

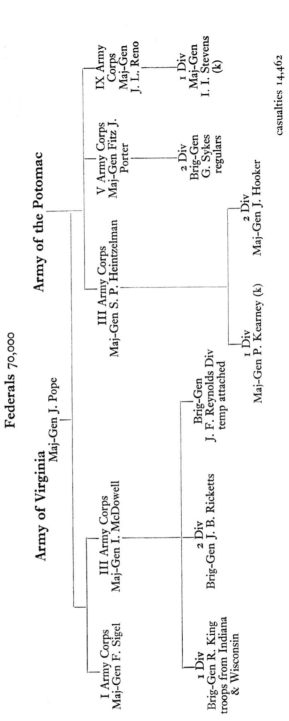

Second Bull Run: Chain of Command [1]

Federals 70,000

Army of Virginia
Maj-Gen J. Pope

Army of the Potomac

I Army Corps
Maj-Gen F. Sigel

1 Div
Brig-Gen R. King
troops from Indiana
& Wisconsin

III Army Corps
Maj-Gen I. McDowell

2 Div
Brig-Gen J. B. Ricketts

Brig-Gen
J. F. Reynolds Div
temp attached

III Army Corps
Maj-Gen S. P. Heintzelman

1 Div
Maj-Gen P. Kearney (k)

2 Div
Maj-Gen J. Hooker

V Army Corps
Maj-Gen Fitz J. Porter

2 Div
Brig-Gen
G. Sykes
regulars

IX Army Corps
Maj-Gen
J. L. Reno

1 Div
Maj-Gen
I. I. Stevens
(k)

casualties 14,462

[1] B & L, ii, 499, 500.

146

Maryland Campaign

After the Confederate victory at the Second Battle of Bull Run, Lee decided, with the approval of President Jefferson Davis, to cross the Potomac and enter Maryland. Parts of Maryland were sympathetic, and it was thought that the presence of a Southern army there might induce Maryland to ally herself with the South. Lee also hoped to recruit men for his armies, and obtain supplies of food and clothing. By moving north, Lee thought that he could draw the Federals away from Richmond, and keep their armies north of the Potomac.

Lee's plan included the movement of his line of supply westward to the Shenandoah Valley; he intended to have as his ultimate objective the penetration of Pennsylvania, and hoped to cut the railway to the west at Harrisonburg, and, if all went well, to turn his attack to Philadelphia, Baltimore, or Washington, as might seem best for the South's interests. [1]

Lee's army, with D. H. Hill's division as advanced guard, and screened by Stuart's cavalry, crossed the Potomac between 4 and 7 of September by the fords in the vicinity of Leesburg, [2] and then camped near Frederick City.

To an inexperienced eye the Confederates little resembled a conquering army. The men were dirty, unkempt ruffians, and several of the leading officers were incapacitated or under arrest.

Lee had tripped when his horse was frightened while he was about to mount, and had broken a bone in one hand and sprained the other. He rode

[1] B & L, ii, 605.
[2] O.R., XIX, i, 952: Jackson had some difficulty in getting his wagons across the Potomac; see Appendix.

into Maryland in an ambulance. Longstreet had rubbed a raw blister on one heel and entered in a carpet slipper. The day after Jackson crossed, he too had an accident that laid him out and caused him to travel by ambulance as well. He had been presented by one enthusiastic citizen with a gigantic grey mare. She appeared a little heavy and awkward for a war horse, but Jackson's favourite charger, Little Sorrel, [1] had been temporarily stolen, and the present seemed a timely one. The next morning, however, when he mounted his new steed and touched her with his spur, the undisciplined beast reared straight in the air, and standing erect for a moment, threw herself backward, horse and rider rolling on the ground. The general was stunned and severely bruised and lay on the ground for some time before he could be removed. [2]

In addition to these mishaps, there were serious conflicts in the higher command. Fortunately Brigadier General Garnett, who had been awaiting charges since Kernstown, and had nearly faced a court-martial at Cedar Run before the battle intervened, was given command in another corps by the kindly Lee. Hood, however, was under arrest [3] for refusing to relinquish some ambulances his men had captured, and A. P. Hill had been relieved of his command by Jackson.

On the night before the march into Maryland, Jackson had given strict orders for his divisions to start at dawn. When he rode forward Hill's division was not moving because the men of the leading brigade were filling their canteens. Hill was absent and Jackson got the brigades started. Feeling the division had made a bad beginning, he kept his eye on the column; and not long afterwards he found men straggling badly and Hill riding at the head, paying no attention. Jackson had strict instructions for his troops to halt every hour. Hill, however, paid no heed and did not call a halt. Jackson stopped one of Hill's brigadiers, and, through him, halted the column. Hill then came back and demanded of the brigadier his reason for halting.

The brigadier replied, 'By General Jackson's order, sir.'

Hill turned to Jackson who was sitting silent on his horse. With some statement that if Jackson was to give the orders, he was superfluous, Hill unbuckled his sword and offered it to Jackson. [4]

'Consider yourself under arrest for neglect of duty,' Jackson answered, and subsequently directed Branch to take command of the division.

Jackson showed similar sternness in his attitude to straggling, which on the way to Maryland reached appalling proportions. Thousands of men fell

[1] See Note on Jackson's horses, p. 156.
[2] B & L, ii, 620.
[3] Hood was put under arrest by General Evans, his temporary commander.
[4] Freeman, LL, ii, 148.

behind or disappeared, and Jackson met this characteristically. His order was that men who left the ranks were to be shot without argument.[1] The Federals, of course, had the same problem. Halleck writes to McClellan: 'Straggling is the great curse of the army, and must be checked by severe measures . . . I think, myself, that shooting them while in the act of straggling from their commands, is the only effective remedy that can be applied. If you apply the remedy you will be sustained here.'[2]

Pilfering and plundering was as rife as ever in the Maryland campaign; and there was one rare occasion when Jackson appears to have disobeyed an order of Lee's concerning it. 'Lee came across a soldier who had stolen and killed a pig which he was surreptitiously conveying to his quarters. Positive orders having been given against pillage of every kind, this flagrant disregard of his commands threw the general into an unusual passion. Though generally disinclined to capital punishment he determined to make an example of this skulking pilferer, and ordered the man to be arrested and taken back to Jackson with directions to have him shot. Jackson, on receiving the culprit, could not quite see the utility of his execution, when men were already scarce, and it struck him that it would answer the purpose quite as well to put the fellow in the front ranks of the army at the most threatened point and let the enemy perform the work assigned to him. He accordingly did so, placing him where his chance of being shot was an excellent one. The fellow, though fond of surreptitious work, was not wanting in courage, and behaved gallantly. He redeemed his credit by his bravery, and came through the thick of the fight unscathed. If a commonplace witticism be not out of order here, it may be said that, although he lost his pig he 'saved his bacon'.[3]

The reception of the Confederates in Maryland was mixed. Some of the young women were forthcoming in the extreme, but very few of the men were recruited into Lee's forces. Whittier's poem suggests that the aged Barbara Fritchie flaunted the Stars and Stripes with a ' "Shoot if you must this old grey head, but spare your country's flag," she said.' Though a much-loved legend, this is probably not strictly true. Union flags, however, were certainly waved defiantly at the Confederates in Maryland.

On Sunday, Jackson sought a church to attend, and, there being no service in the Presbyterian Church, he went to the German Reformed. As usual he fell asleep, but this time more profoundly than his wont. His head sunk upon his breast, his cap dropped from his hands to the floor; the prayers of the congregation did not disturb him, and only the choir and deep toned organ

---

[1] Jackson's MS, Letter Book, 60.
[2] B & L, ii, note, 605.
[3] Hotchkiss Papers, 69; and Long 222.

awakened him. The minister was credited with much loyalty and courage because he prayed for the President of the United States in the very presence of Stonewall Jackson. Being asleep, the general did not hear the prayer, and if he had he would doubtless have felt like replying as General Ewell did, when asked if he would permit the usual prayer for President Lincoln—'Certainly, I'm sure he needs it.' [1]

Lee thought that with the Confederate presence so far advanced as Frederick City, the Federals would evacuate Harper's Ferry; but General Halleck from Washington ordered it to hold out. Lee, therefore, made plans to assault it. He ordered McLaws with his own and Anderson's division to approach Harper's Ferry from the north and occupy the Maryland Heights on the north bank of the Potomac, overlooking the town. Walker's division was ordered to move down the Potomac and destroy the aqueduct of the Chesapeake and Ohio canal near where the Monocacy joins the Potomac, and then cross the Potomac and approach Harper's Ferry from the east to occupy the Loudoun Heights which overlook the town across the Shenandoah. [2] Jackson, meanwhile, was ordered forward to cross the Potomac at Williamsport, move down and drive out the garrison of Martinsburg into Harper's Ferry, and then to attack the town over the Bolivar Heights from the west. The three columns were told to rejoin the main army at Hagerstown after they had captured Harper's Ferry; and when they had set out, Lee left Frederick City and took the rest of the army through the passes of the long ridge of South Mountain westwards.

In giving General Walker his instructions he disclosed some of his aims. He said: 'Besides the men and material of war which we shall capture at Harper's Ferry, the position is necessary to us, not to garrison and hold, but because in the hands of the enemy it would be a break in our rear line of communication with Richmond. A few days rest at Hagerstown will be of great service to our men. Hundreds of them are barefooted, and nearly all of them are ragged.' This dependence of the Southern Army on the North for its weapons and equipment was a feature of the war. Worsham, one of Jackson's Foot Cavalry, writes:

At the commencement of the war, the Southern army was as poorly armed as any body of men ever had been. In the infantry, my own regiment as an example, one company had Springfield muskets, one had Enfield, one had Mississippi rifles, the remainder the old smooth bore flint-lock musket that had been altered to a percussion gun. The cavalry was so badly equipped that hardly a company was uniform in that particular; some had sabres, nothing more, some had double-barrel guns, some

---

[1] B & L, ii, 621.
[2] Before the attack on Harper's Ferry, A. P. Hill returned to his command.

had nothing but lances; while others had something of all. One man with a sabre, another with a pistol, another with a musket, another a shotgun, not half a dozen men in the company armed alike. The artillery was better, but the guns were mostly smooth bore, and some of the horses had wagon and plough harness. It did not take long for the army of Northern Va to arm itself with better material. When Jackson's troops marched from the Valley to Richmond to join Lee in his attack on McClellan, they had captured enough arms from the enemy to replace all that were inferior, and after the battles around Richmond all departments of Lee's army were as well armed. After that time the captures from the enemy kept us up to their standard. Our ammunition was always inferior to theirs. Towards the close of the war, nearly all equipments in the army of Northern Va were articles captured from the Yankees. All the wagons were captured, and to look at them on the march, one would not know that they belonged to the Confederacy, many of them having the name of the brigade, division and corps of the Yankee army branded on them. Nearly all the mules and horses had US branded on them; our ambulances were from the same generous provider, our tents also, many of them having the name of the company, etc., branded on them; most of the blankets were those marked US, and the rubber blankets or cloths; the very clothing that the men wore was mostly captured, and we were allowed to wear their pants, underclothing and overcoats. As for myself, I purchased only one hat, one pair of shoes, and one jacket after 1861. We captured immense quantities of provisions, and nearly all the 'hard tack' and pork issued to us was captured. [1]

There now occurred a dramatic incident which should have given all the advantages in the coming encounter to General McClellan. Copies of the order for the movement of the three columns on Harper's Ferry were sent to all the commanders. This was Lee's famous General Order No 191; and Jackson, to make sure D. H. Hill was informed, had a duplicate made and sent to him. Hill should thus have received two copies. Most of the copies arrived safely, and were carefully secured by their recipients. Longstreet is said to have chewed his up after perusal, to make sure that it did not get into the wrong hands. [2] The order sent to General D. H. Hill from general head-quarters was carefully preserved; but Jackson's copy never arrived. [3] It seems to have been mislaid and left behind in the camp at Frederick City.

When the Federals moved in there, it was found by two Federal soldiers.

Private Barton W. Mitchell and Sergeant John M. Bloss turned their gear aside and lay down on the cool grass. They lapsed into the idle talk of soldiers, discussing McClellan who had returned as their leader, or their retreat from Manassas just a few weeks before, or perhaps a recent letter from home. Mitchell had just rolled over and was about to pull his cap over his eyes, when he spotted a piece of paper

[1] Worsham, 106, 107.   [2] B & L, ii, 607.
[3] Longstreet 213; B & L, ii, 570 note: Hill says it was Lee's copy that was lost.

wrapped around what appeared to be several sticks. Upon investigation he found it to be three cigars of fine quality. This type of luxury was not easy to come by for the common soldier. While they leaned back like men of leisure and prepared to light up, they opened the paper and made a quick survey. Suddenly the cigars became insignificant. The paper they held in their hands was of obvious vital military importance. Mitchell read the names of Jackson, Longstreet and Lee, names which had been burned deeply in his memory. At once the two men rushed to their commander, Colonel Silas Colgrove. Colgrove saw immediately that he held in his hands the key to the Confederate plans. It read: 'Headquarters, Army of Northern Virginia, Special Orders 191', and it was addressed to D. H. Hill and signed, 'By the command of General R. E. Lee: R. H. Chilton, Assistant Adjutant-General.' In a matter of minutes it was in the hands of Colonel S. E. Pittman, division adjutant and once a good friend of Chilton—the two men had served in the army before 1861. Pittman quickly identified the handwriting and hastened to McClellan's tent and requested an audience. The general was in conference but summoned Pittman in. McClellan's own cautious nature put him on the defensive immediately. Was it an elaborate hoax? Pittman assured him that he recognised Chilton's signature; there could be no doubt about its authenticity. The general was overjoyed. The game was over. He now knew Lee's secret. Victory was a simple mathematical equation. McClellan was closer to Lee's separate wings than the wings were to each other. A quick drive into the centre of the separated segments would crush the Army of Northern Virginia. In jubilation he cried: 'Here is a paper with which, if I cannot whip Bobby Lee, I will be willing to go home.' A wire was sent to Lincoln, 'I have all the plans of the rebels, and will catch them in their own trap.'[1]

Although a Southern sympathiser residing at Frederick City heard about McClellan's find of the 'Lost Order,' and after a hard, hurried ride reached Lee to inform him of the bad news, the Confederates were still in a most dangerous position. Everything depended on whether Jackson and the others could capture Harper's Ferry, and rejoin Lee, in time to support him in meeting McClellan's now certain attack.

HARPER'S FERRY

The town of Harper's Ferry is situated at the junction of the Shenandoah River with the Potomac. It was quite capable of defence against Jackson's attack from the west where the Bolivar Heights ran across from one river to another; but it was completely commanded by the Loudoun Heights east of the Shenandoah, which were occupied by Walker's artillery, and by the still

---

[1] The *Herald-Mail*, Hagerstown Centennial edition, Monday 27 August 1862, article by James V. Murfin.

more lofty Maryland Heights on the other side of the Potomac, which McLaws set about seizing.

With McClellan in possession of Lee's order, everything now depended on the speed with which Harper's Ferry could be taken. Jackson started well. The Martinsburg garrison under General White was driven out, and sought refuge, as expected, with Colonel Miles' troops at Harper's Ferry. 'Jackson organised a grand hunting match driving all the Federal detachments before him, and forcing them to crowd into the blind alley of Harper's Ferry.'[1] In Martinsburg, which in the words of the song was 'back in ole Virginny', Jackson found himself being mobbed by the ladies. He gave his autograph generously, cut a button from his coat for a little girl, and then submitted patiently to an attack by the others, who soon stripped the coat of all the remaining buttons. The following day, he passed through Halltown, and drew up his forces facing the Bolivar Heights. There he had to wait for McLaws and Walker to get their guns into position on their respective heights opposite him. There were two batteries and a brigade of infantry on the Maryland Heights; but their commander did not offer much resistance to McLaws although he had his men behind breastworks and abattis. Walker occupied the Loudoun Heights even more easily. Harper's Ferry was now completely surrounded.

Jackson had difficulty in communicating with McLaws and Walker on the other side of the rivers. The messages he sent and received are recorded by his signal officer.[2] They were able to tell him when they were ready— McLaws took a long time to do this. They also informed him that the enemy had passed through the passes of South Mountain and was threatening to come down from the north to relieve Harper's Ferry. He ordered them to bombard the Bolivar ridge from the rear while he attacked it from his side. A. P. Hill's division was ordered to attack alongside the Shenandoah on the Federal left, supported by Lawton's division in the centre along the turnpike. A brigade and a battery of Jones' division was to make a noisy demonstration on the Federal right towards the Potomac, but the rest of his divison was ordered to move along the turnpike with Lawton's.

In the end Confederate artillery encircled Harper's Ferry. There were several batteries supporting Jackson's own front besides the pieces firing down on the town from the heights. Then during the night Colonel Crutchfield, Jackson's chief of artillery, 'crossed ten pieces of Ewell's (Lawton) division over the Shenandoah and established them on the right bank so as to enfilade the enemy's position on the Bolivar Heights.'[3]

[1] Comte de Paris, Henderson, ii, 215.   [2] O.R., XIX, i, 958, 959.
[3] Jackson's report, O.R., XIX, i, 954.

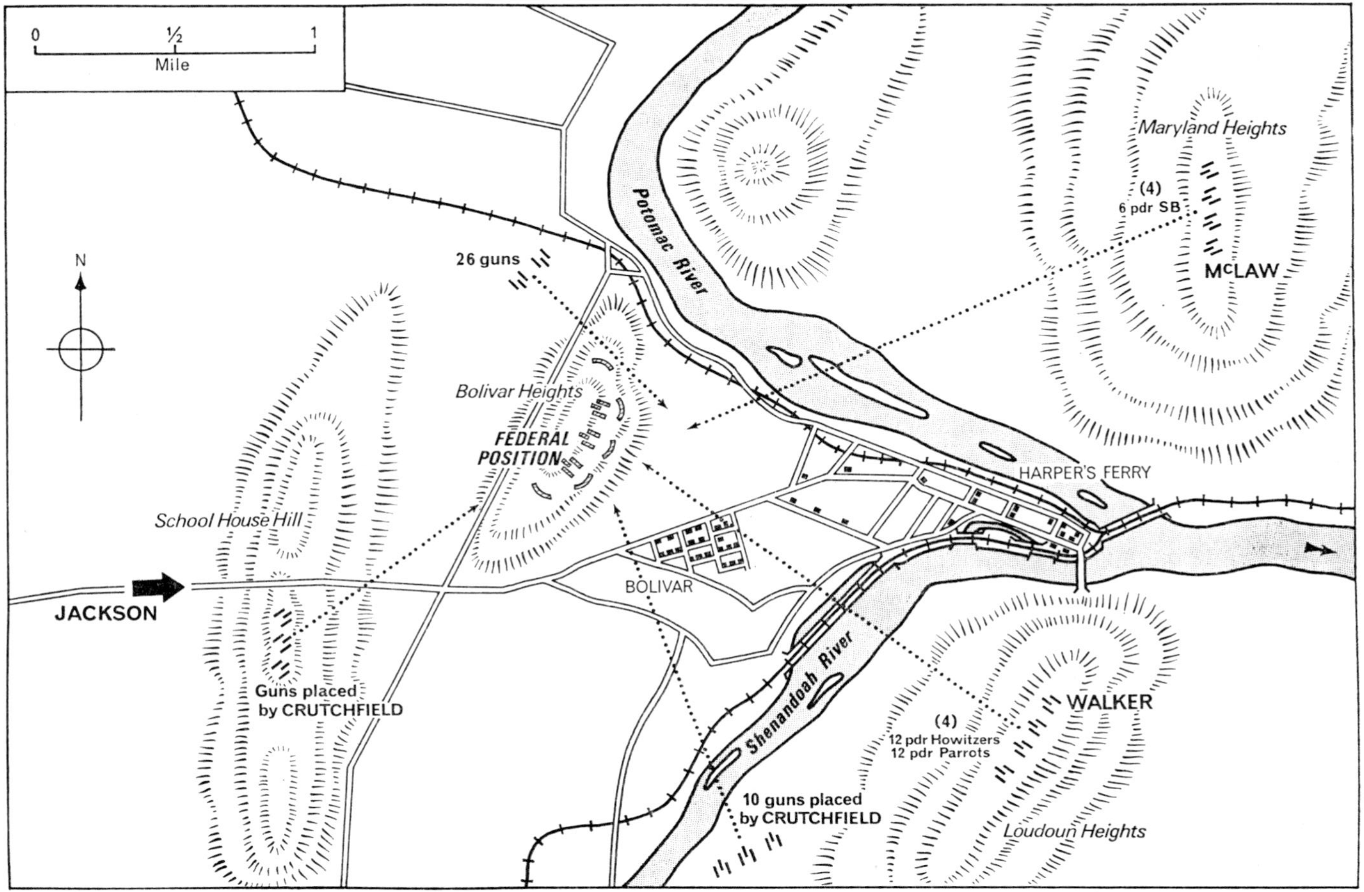

Maryland Heights

McLAW

6 pdr SB.

(4)

HARPER'S FERRY

WALKER

Loudoun Heights

12 pdr Howitzers
12 pdr Parrots

(4)

Potomac River

Shenandoah River

10 guns placed
by CRUTCHFIELD

BOLIVAR

26 guns

Bolivar Heights

FEDERAL
POSITION

School House Hill

Guns placed
by CRUTCHFIELD

½
Mile

1

0

N

JACKSON

11 The Bombardment and Capture of Harper's Ferry, 16 September 1862

The battle for Harper's Ferry lasted from the evening of 14 September until 7.30 a.m. on 15 September. No attempt was made during the Sunday evening to storm the Bolivar Heights; but the pounding received from the Confederate guns took the heart out of the defenders. From nearly every point of the compass, from the lofty heights to north and east, from Jackson's own artillery in the west and south, a ceaseless hail of shells swept the narrow neck to which the garrison was confined.

During the night, as has been mentioned, ten guns, to shoot in enfilade from the south, and complete the circle, were moved across the Shenandoah; and the Confederate infantry, along the western slopes of the Bolivar Heights, pushed forward their line nearer the hapless Federals, to be ready for their final charge, following the bombardment at dawn.

The dawn bombardment was worse than the evening one had been. 'The morning was still and clear, giving us a full view of the lines of the lofty mountains. Simultaneously the great circle of artillery opened, all firing to a common centre, while the clouds of smoke, rolling up from the tops of the various mountains, and the thunder of the guns reverberating among them, gave the idea of so many volcanoes.'[1] It became an artillery victory. Before the charge was sounded for Hill's men to advance, the white flag was hoisted. For the loss of no more than 100 men Jackson had captured Harper's Ferry with his artillery alone.

When the white flag went up, Douglas was sent forward with a single orderly to meet the approaching General Julius White and his body of staff officers, White having taken over command from Colonel Miles who had just been killed by a shell. General White told Douglas he wished to see Jackson about the surrender of his troops.

As they all made their way back to meet the Confederate commander, a Federal staff officer riding alongside Douglas told him that if Colonel Miles had not been killed they would have made more of a fight of it. Douglas was struck by the contrast in appearance between White and Jackson at their meeting. General White, he said, was mounted on a handsome black horse and his uniform, gloves and boots were immaculate; while Jackson was badly dressed and worse mounted. The interview was a short one, for General White immediately accepted Jackson's demand for unconditional surrender, and was handed over to General A. P. Hill for the latter to arrange the details of the terms.

The completeness of the victory was marred only by the escape during the night, of 1,200 Federal horsemen. They crossed the pontoon bridge, and passing swiftly up the towpath under the Maryland Heights, rode boldly

[1] Moore, 139.

beneath the muzzles of McLaws' batteries and away. Jackson had feared this might happen. 'I called the attention of Major-General McLaws, commanding on Maryland Heights, to the guarding against such an attempt,' he writes.[1] Darkness and temerity made it possible in spite of Confederate watchfulness. Yet the haul was great indeed. 12,520 prisoners, 13,000 small arms, 73 pieces of artillery and several hundred wagons. The last a real treat for Jackson the wagon hunter!

While A. P. Hill remained at Harper's Ferry to supervise the surrender, Jackson and the others, their task accomplished, hurried northwards to support Lee in a greater battle. They were directed for this, not to Hagerstown, but to Sharpsburg.

Note

LITTLE SORREL
Civil War Mount of General Thomas J. Jackson

In the Spring of 1861, while Jackson was commanding the post at Harper's Ferry, his troops seized an east-bound Baltimore & Ohio train which included a car of Western horses intended for use by the Federal Cavalry. As Jackson had no mount of his own at Harper's Ferry, he decided to buy one of these horses. He selected a large and powerful sorrel gelding.

While he was examining the animals, he saw among them a smaller, well-rounded sorrel gelding of the type long familiar in Virginia as a lady's riding horse. Historians think that Jackson, believing the war would be of short duration, decided to buy the little sorrel and take him home as a present to Mrs Jackson. Accordingly, he purchased both animals, the big sorrel and the little sorrel.

Riding the two horses soon showed that the larger gelding had a hard trot and was not an easy horse to handle. The little sorrel was what a lady's riding horse should be in temper and pace and also proved to have extraordinary endurance. Jackson retained both mounts, but chose to ride Mrs Jackson's horse almost exclusively. He gave Chaplain B. T. Lacy the use of the big sorrel.

Because the animal was intended for a lady's use, Jackson named it 'Fancy', though his attendants, to distinguish it from the larger horse called it the 'Little Sorrel'.

The horse was described as a rather small animal, not more than 15 hands high, and his colour a dark sorrel. If he had any white markings on either

[1] O.R., XIX, i, 954.

Harper's Ferry: Commander's [1]

Confederates

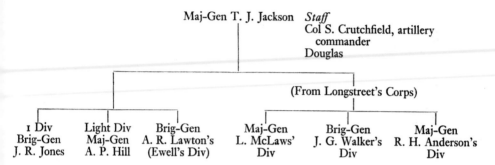

Maj-Gen T. J. Jackson   *Staff*
           Col S. Crutchfield, artillery
             commander
           Douglas

(From Longstreet's Corps)

1 Div	Light Div	Brig-Gen	Maj-Gen	Brig-Gen	Maj-Gen
Brig-Gen	Maj-Gen	A. R. Lawton's	L. McLaws'	J. G. Walker's	R. H. Anderson's
J. R. Jones	A. P. Hill	(Ewell's Div)	Div	Div	Div

casualties trifling

Federals

Col D. S. Miles—Brig-Gen J. White (from Martinsburg)

casualties 12,737—including prisoners

[1] B & L, ii, 618.

head or legs, they were small and hardly noticeable. His withers were rather high and his back somewhat hollowed as he became older.

Little Sorrel, a quiet animal with an easy canter, became known for his endurance. Jackson rode the little horse at the field of First Manassas (or Bull Run) when General Barnard E. Bee of South Carolina made the statement that gave Jackson his immortal nickname: 'Look at Jackson and his Virginians standing like a stone wall.' The Confederate general rode Little Sorrel thoughout the Valley campaign and was astride Little Sorrel the night of 2 May 1863, when he received his fatal wounds at Chancellorsville.

Following Jackson's death, Little Sorrel was sent by the Governor of Virginia to the general's family and he lived many years on the farm of Jackson's father-in-law in Lincoln County, North Carolina. Eventually he was returned to the Soldiers' Home in Richmond, Virginia, and was more than 30 years old when he died there about 1886.

Following Little Sorrel's death, both his skin and his skeleton were preserved. The mounted hide was on display for many years at the R. E. Lee Camp Museum and the skeleton was located at the Carnegie Institute Museum in Pittsburg. Both subsequently were turned over to the Virginia Military Institute where they are on display in the Institute's Preston Library.

During the winter at Moss Neck (*see* p. 183) a handsome English saddle and bridle was sent to Jackson from England by an admirer, Colonel Fremantle of the Coldstream Guards. This is the saddlery now on Little Sorrel at the VMI.

SHARPSBURG

While Jackson was capturing Harper's Ferry, McClellan advanced westwards through the passes of South Mountain; and in the vicinity of the two most vital crossings, Turner's Gap in the north and Crampton's Gap in the south, rearguard actions were fought by Lee's troops. Meanwhile, Longstreet, who had already reached Hagerstown, was called back to help.

There were two separate engagements in the battle of South Mountain. Up at Turner's Gap, two Federal corps under General Burnside fought hard to storm the heights; but it was not until midnight that D. H. Hill's position was turned by a Federal flanking movement through another defile. Then, to avoid annihilation, Hill withdrew to Sharpsburg, Lee's new concentration point for his forces behind Antietam Creek. Down at Crampton's Gap,

through which General Franklin pushed 18,000 of his troops, the Federals also managed to establish a position by nightfall on the west side of South Mountain, opposed by forces sent north by McLaws from the Maryland Heights overlooking Harper's Ferry. Fortunately for the Confederates, the Federals, believing that they were outnumbered by forces only a third of their strength, advanced no further.

With McClellan's masses approaching at a snail's pace, and the likelihood of the forces under Jackson at Harper's Ferry soon rejoining him, Lee came to perhaps the most daring of his many audacious decisions.[1] Placing his forces along the ridge running along the line of the Hagerstown turnpike through Sharpsburg, with the Antietam Creek to his front, and the Potomac to his rear, he stood fast to meet McClellan's assault.

Lee's defensive position at Sharpsburg was a good one. His flanks were reasonably secure. The right flank was protected by the Potomac and the Antietam. The left was more open; but Stuart skilfully secured, before the Federals, a dominating hill near Nicodemus Farm, and placed his guns there to command the area. Antietam Creek across Lee's front, although shallow, formed an obstacle to McClellan's advance, and, in the event, largely confined him to the bridges for his crossings; but the Potomac in Lee's rear stretched 200 yards from shore to shore and had few fords, and only one practicable for wagons. The three main features which come into the story of the battle were: Dunker Church on the Hagerstown road, and the North, East and West Woods around it; the Sunken Road, or Bloody Lane, joining the Hagerstown turnpike at right angles from the east between Dunker Church and Sharpsburg; and Lower Bridge, or Burnside Bridge, over the Antietam in the south.

Dunker Church, which was a focal point of much activity during the battle, belonged to a group who called themselves Brethren; but their associates in the neighbourhood called them Dunkers or Dunkards. The word Dunker is a corruption of the German word *tunken*, to dip. Immersion was their form of baptism. These people had given up their homes in Germany because they refused to conform. They were pacifists and would rather be killed than be a killer. It was strange that their church should be the centre of the bloodiest battle of the war!

The Confederates generally did not entrench; but around Dunker Church parallel ledges of outcropping limestone, both within West Wood and along the Hagerstown road, rising as high as a man's waist, gave good cover from shot and shell. Surrounding the fields and orchards in front of Sharpsburg were low stone walls, and in some places there were sunken roads. Fronting

[1] Dupuy & Dupuy, 160.

Burnside Bridge, the Confederates lined the banks with rifle-pits and breast-works of rails and stones. [1]

The Confederates had fair fields of fire except in the north, where they were masked to some degree by trees. On the other hand the Federals were protected by a run of low hills on the far side of Antietam Creek behind which could form up unmolested.

McClellan's plan was for the three corps of Hooker, Mansfield, and, later, Sumner, to cross Upper Bridge and attack the Confederates through the woods in the north. At the same time, Burnside's corps would attack the stone bridge in the south to pin down the Confederate's right, and as McClellan says, 'as soon as one or both of the flank movements were fully successful, to attack their centre with any reserve I might have in hand.' [2]

The battle which began on the evening of 16 September 1862, and ended in the gathering darkness of the following day, was the bloodiest single day of the war. Some historians are of opinion that it was the determining feature of the entire conflict.

About 2 p.m. on 16 September, Hooker's corps crossed Antietam Creek by Upper Bridge, and having reached the Hagerstown turnpike, faced south-wards and made contact late in the afternoon with Hood's men (*see* Map p. 162). A sharp action occurred causing Hood to draw back his skirmishers. After dark Hooker's men went into bivouac in North Wood, east of the turnpike. Hooker's evening attack had done little but warn Lee where the assault would come next morning.

At 11.30 p.m., on the same evening, the XIIth Corps under Mansfield also crossed the Antietam, followed the route taken by Hooker, and bivouacked for the night a mile and a half north of Hooker's troops. Two corps—say 18,000 or 19,000 men—were now across the creek, and menacing the Confederate left. But they were not so disposed as to act in unison; and they were not under one commander. [3]

It was not a peaceful night. The atmosphere was tense. Pickets fired at each other throughout the dark hours. One green Union regiment nearly caused a major clash in the early morning when it got excited over an accidentally dis-charged rifle. Although there was little talk among the men, each knew instinctively that the morning would bring a mighty and fierce battle. The steady rain was taken as an evil omen. [4]

Daylight was slow in coming. The rain had stopped, but a foggy mist covered the fields. The battle began again where it had left off, by another attack by Hooker's men across the cornfield between North Wood and East

[1] O.R., XIX, i, 31. [2] O.R., XIX, i, 30. [3] Ropes, ii, 358.
[4] Murfin, 15.

Wood (*see* Map p. 162). The shock fell on Ewell's division under Lawton, and Jackson's old division under Jones. Jackson's Georgians, Louisianians and Virginians, with a few Alabama regiments and two from Carolina, clashed with Hooker's men in the cornfield, and met the long blue lines with musket fire heavy enough to halt them momentarily. Then Hooker ordered up 36 of his guns and pounded the Confederates with them. The artillery fire was deadly accurate, and the carnage terrible. Bits of bodies, rifles and fence rails flew in the air, and the corn was ripped to shreds. Then came a charge and countercharge, and a hand-to-hand fight to the finish such as neither side had ever experienced. Regiments were whittled away to nothing. Divisions took ghastly losses: high on the Union side; higher still for Jackson's men who were gradually pushed back to West Wood and Dunker Church.

Then, Hood's Texans, heroes of Gaines' Mill, who had been pulled from the front line in East Wood early in the morning for a hot meal, were rushed back into the fight. The Texans were angry at the interruption of their meal, and fought with great fury. They pushed into the cornfield, or what was left of it, sending the Northerners fleeing for cover. Following after them, however, they were struck by a burst of canister from six Federal 12-pounder Napoleons which, meeting the charging Texans at point-blank range, sent them in their turn in reverse, back to West Wood, spent and exhausted.

If the corps of General Mansfield had been at hand while this action was being fought, it might have turned the scale in favour of the Federals. As it was, encamped a mile and a half away, although it started to Hooker's support at the first sound of cannon, Mansfield's men did not get into action until Hooker's troops were exhausted and retiring to the shelter of their artillery. Mansfield was soon killed, but was replaced by Brigadier-General A. S. Williams, a brave and distinguished officer, who brought the corps forward through Hooker's men so that they struck Hood's Texans and drove them back behind Dunker Church.

All McClellan's attacks were at this time striking the Confederate left, and Lee boldly moved troops from the south to reinforce his threatened flank. The next assault was also aimed at the north. This time it came from Sumner's corps which had been delayed from lack of orders from McClellan, and was impatient to play a part in the battle. Sumner, marching with his two divisions under Sedgwick and French, soon got his corps in confusion, for he led Sedgwick's division almost due westwards but allowed French's to stray off to the south (*see* Map p. 162).

This allowed the Confederates the opportunity of carrying out the first of three successful enfilade attacks which eventually won them the battle. Sedgwick's division moved westwards from Upper Bridge past East and

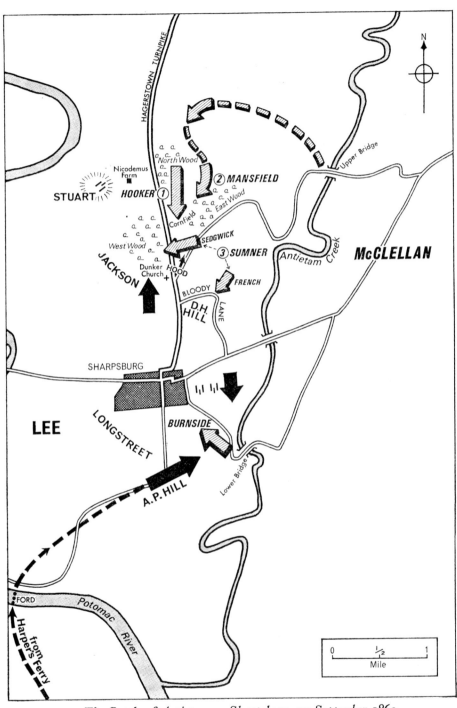

12 The Battle of Antietam or Sharpsburg, 17 September 1862

West Woods and finished up half a mile to the west of Dunker Church (*see* Map p. 162). The direction of this advance gave Jackson his opportunity. Receiving McLaws' and Walker's divisions as reinforcements from Longstreet, he punched hard with them northwards so that they caught Sedgwick's division in the flank and virtually destroyed it.

The faulty formation of the Federals, which helped to bring about their misfortune, is described by Palfrey. He says: 'Sedgwick's division emerged from the cornfield into open ground near the pike, and swept steadily forward. There were no fences at the part of the pike where they crossed to delay them. Their march was rapid and nearly directly west. There was little distance between the lines. The recollection of the survivors range from fifty feet to thirty paces. Not a regiment was in column. There was absolutely no preparation for facing to the right or left in case either of their exposed flanks should be attacked.'[1] 'After we had expended from 40 to 50 rounds at the enemy it became evident that he was moving a large force on our left, where his firing became terrific ... the attack of the enemy on the flanks was sudden and in overwhelming force. In this terrible conflict three regiments of the brigade lost nearly one-half their entire force engaged,' writes the Federal commander of the 1st Brigade.[2] The two leading brigades were so close together that they could not change front and present a line of battle to the enemy. An attempt was made by the third line to face about, but it was frustrated by the heavy fire. There could be but one issue to such a struggle. In spite of the heroic exertions of Sumner and Sedgwick and their brave subordinates, it was impossible to offer any effective resistance. The loss was terrible—over 2,200 officers and men—and it was all sustained in a very few minutes. Sedgwick himself was three times wounded and finally had to leave the field. The division fell back in more or less disorder perhaps a third of a mile to the north and reformed under the protection of the batteries.[3]

In the north the Confederates had met, and held, three powerful attacks. Meanwhile, French's division straying south from Sumner's corps had struck the Confederate centre, meeting D. H. Hill's division on the Sunken Road which became known as Bloody Lane. Much of the road was deeply rutted, eroded and washed out from heavy grain-carrying wagons. It was on this road that D. H. Hill had positioned two brigades, well entrenched behind breastworks of fence rails and out of sight. Hill says: 'The men were beginning to fall back, and efforts were made to rally them in the bed of an old road, nearly at right angles to the Hagerstown pike, and which had been their position previous to the advance. These efforts, were only partially

[1] Palfrey, 83, 84.   [2] O.R., XIX, i, 311, 312.
[3] Ropes, 365.

successful. Most of Colquitt's brigade took no further part in the action. Garland's brigade (Colonel McRae commanding) had been demoralised by the fight at South Mountain and when they thought they were being out-flanked broke and fell to the rear. Only Rodes' and Anderson's men were in the old road, and some stragglers had been gathered up and placed upon their left.'[1]

As the Federals advanced, a Confederate shell hit an entire row of beehives in the orchard north of the Sunken Road. It was touch-and-go for a while as the men ran for cover from a strange combination of bullets and bees. Then it was the holocaust of the cornfield all over again, and of longer duration: the battle over the Sunken Road lasted three and a half hours. One Federal soldier wrote that the dead lay so thick in the lane that a man could have walked its length without touching the ground. Another Federal eye-witness says: 'I was astonished to observe our troops moving along the front and passing over what appeared to be long heavy columns of the enemy without paying any attention whatever. I borrowed a glass from an officer and dis-covered this to be actually a column of the enemy's dead and wounded lying along the hollow road.' After the battle of the Sunken Road, Lee's centre was shattered; but fortunately for the Confederates, although McClellan had a reserve of 10,000 men in hand, he decided to pursue his attacks in the north and centre no further. Instead he at last managed to make the sluggish Burnside move forward in the south.

Burnside had been amazingly late starting; and his delay had enabled Lee to send reinforcements to Jackson from Longstreet's corps. Burnside had been ordered by McClellan to carry Lower Bridge—later to be called Burnside Bridge. Although Antietam Creek could be forded in many places, it was only after Burnside had charged the bridge unsuccessfully several times that he sought alternative crossings. When he did get across, however, Toombs' men of D. R. Jones' division facing him, even with their rifle-pits, and behind their breastworks of stones, found it difficult to hold the Federal assault. In the end it was the other two enfilade attacks of the three mentioned which won the day for the Confederates. First, guns were put into position south of Sharps-burg and blasted Burnside's leading brigades on the right flank; next, in the nick of time, A. P. Hill's division, its task at Harper's Ferry completed, crossed the Potomac at Boteler's Ford, and were flung straight at Burnside's left. This threw Burnside's men into confusion. Hill says: 'The enemy had already advanced in three lines, had broken through Jones' division, cap-tured McIntosh's battery, and were in the full tide of success. With a yell of

---

[1] O.R., XIX, i, 1022, 1023; see page 168 for list of A. P. Hill's brigades.

defiance, Archer charged them, retook McIntosh's guns, and drove them back pell-mell. Branch and Gregg, with their old veterans, sternly held their ground, and pouring in destructive volleys, the tide of the enemy surged back, and, breaking in confusion, passed out of sight' [1] to regroup down by the Creek, as darkness fell.

At Sharpsburg, Lee with less than 50,000 men stopped McClellan with 90,000; and some 12,500 Federals and 13,000 Confederates lay dead and wounded after the bloodiest one-day battle of the war. All that night and all the next day the opponents faced one another warily. On the night of 18 September, Lee, unmolested, withdrew unhurriedly across the Potomac.

Jackson's contribution in the Maryland campaign and the battle of Sharpsburg was a major one. Since his victories in the Valley, his fame, somewhat obscured by Mechanicsville, Gaines' Mill, Frayser's Farm and Malvern Hill, had increased by leaps and bounds; and now the swift seizure of Harper's Ferry and the defence of West Wood were added to the victory of Cedar Run, the march to Manassas Junction and the three days' battle about Groveton. Before the battle, he supported Lee in his decision to stand and fight; and during it, he handled the defensive operation in the north soundly and calmly. His calmness is illustrated by the following passage: 'Shortly before eleven o'clock his medical director, appalled by the number of wounded men sent back from the front, and assured that the day was going badly, rode to West Wood in order to discuss the advisability of transferring the field hospitals across the Potomac. Dr McGuire found Jackson sitting quietly on Little Sorrel behind the line of battle, and some peaches he had brought with him were gratefully accepted. He then made his report, and his apprehensions were not made less by the weakness of the line which held the wood. The men, in many places, were lying at intervals of several yards; for support there was but one small brigade, and over in the cornfields the overwhelming strength of the Federal masses was terribly apparent. Yet his imperturbable commander, apparently paying more attention to the peaches than to his subordinate's suggestions, replied by pointing to the enemy and saying quietly, "Dr McGuire, they have done their worst."' [2]

Jackson directed Lee's reinforcements into the fight cleverly, and by their flank attack on Sedgwick's division, the battle in the north was stabilised. In the afternoon, in obedience to instructions from Lee, he moved further north with a view to turning the Federal right; but this came to nothing. He writes: 'I found his numerous artillery so judiciously established in their front and extending so near to the Potomac, which here made a remarkable

---

[1] O.R., XIX, i, 981.　　　　　[2] Henderson, ii, 256.

bend, as will be seen by reference to the map herewith annexed, as to render it inexpedient to hazard the attempt.'[1]

Lee's opinion of his worth is shown in a letter to President Davis in which he was recommending both Longstreet and Jackson for promotion to lieutenant-general. He says of Jackson: 'My opinion of the merits of General Jackson has been greatly enhanced during this expedition. He is true, honest, and brave; has a single eye to the good of the service, and spares no exertion to accomplish his object.'[2]

[1] O.R., XIX, i, 956, 957.　　　　　　　　[2] O.R., XIX, ii, 643.

Sharpsburg : Chain of Command [1]

Federals 87,164   60,000 engaged

Maj-Gen G. B. McClellan

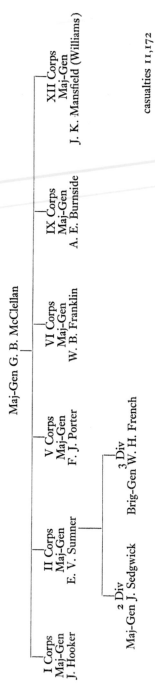

I Corps	II Corps	V Corps	VI Corps	IX Corps	XII Corps
Maj-Gen	Maj-Gen	Maj-Gen	Maj-Gen	Maj-Gen	Maj-Gen
J. Hooker	E. V. Sumner	F. J. Porter	W. B. Franklin	A. E. Burnside	J. K. Mansfield (Williams)

2 Div
Maj-Gen J. Sedgwick

3 Div
Brig-Gen W. H. French

casualties 11,172

[1] B & L, ii, 598–603 & O.R., XIX, ii, 169–180, 803–810.

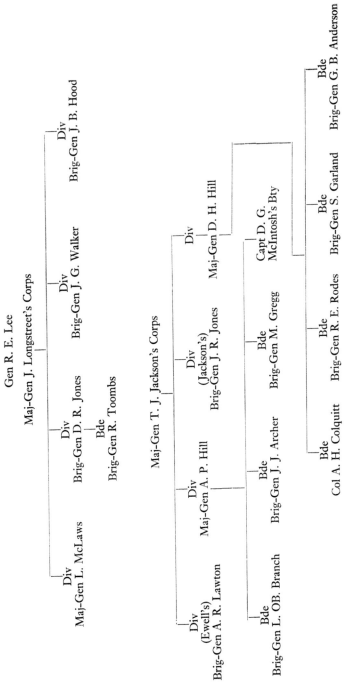

Sharpsburg : Chain of Command [1]

Confederates less than 40,000

Gen R. E. Lee

Maj-Gen J. Longstreet's Corps

Div
Maj-Gen L. McLaws

Div
Brig-Gen D. R. Jones

Bde
Brig-Gen R. Toombs

Div
Brig-Gen J. G. Walker

Div
Brig-Gen J. B. Hood

Maj-Gen T. J. Jackson's Corps

Div
(Ewell's)
Brig-Gen A. R. Lawton

Div
Maj-Gen A. P. Hill

Div
(Jackson's)
Brig-Gen J. R. Jones

Div
Maj-Gen D. H. Hill

Bde
Brig-Gen L. OB. Branch

Bde
Brig-Gen J. J. Archer

Bde
Col A. H. Colquitt

Bde
Brig-Gen M. Gregg

Bde
Brig-Gen R. E. Rodes

Capt D. G.
McIntosh's Bty

Bde
Brig-Gen S. Garland

Bde
Brig-Gen G. B. Anderson

casualties 12,410

[1] B & L, ii, 598-603 & O.R., XIX, ii, 169-180, 803-810.

168

Fredericksburg

After the Battle of Sharpsburg, some of McClellan's troops followed Lee's rearguard across the Potomac, and captured four of its guns; but Jackson ordered A. P. Hill's division back to deal with the intruders and the Federals were driven down the bluffs and across the river again. McClellan then remained north of the Potomac for about a month during which Stuart encircled McClellan's army in another of his flamboyant cavalry raids. This reconnaissance brought back useful information. Lee was provided with an accurate report by Stuart of the Federal dispositions, from which it was clear that McClellan's army was still being reinforced from Washington and that no new oversea expedition against Richmond was likely. Several hundred fine horses from the farms of Pennsylvania were also brought back by Stuart's troopers to provide remounts.

Meanwhile, north of Winchester in the Shenandoah Valley, Lee's army was recuperating. Stragglers from the march into Maryland had streamed back, and replacements from Richmond had also come in. The army now topped the 80,000 mark, and welcome supplies had arrived.

During a visit to Winchester, Jackson dined with Hunter McGuire's father, and afterwards, at the request of Miss McGuire, went to be photographed. When the photograph was about to be taken, the photographer pointed out that one of Jackson's buttons was missing. Jackson produced the button from his pocket, asked for a needle and thread, and said that to save time he would sew it on himself. He did not do it very skilfully; and the button, the third from the top on his left breast was out of line. It is however, probably the best photograph ever taken of him.

Jackson also had an opportunity of renewing his acquaintance with his old friend Dr Graham and his family at Winchester. One day he went to the manse to dinner with them, and the Graham children were allowed to stay up and play with him. They climbed all over him as usual, and he seemed overjoyed to see them, and expressed a hope of getting back to spend the winter in his old room at the manse. Only his wife Anna's presence was wanting to complete the pleasure of the evening. [1]

At this time, Major von Borcke, a German on Stuart's staff, arrived at Second Corps headquarters bringing a fine uniform coat as a present from Stuart, who had become a great admirer of Jackson. Jackson was loth to wear this garment, resplendent as it was with gold lace. He much preferred to continue in his old battleworn coat. When, however, other well-wishers completed his new outfit it was different. Trousers came from some good friends in the north of the Valley; new riding boots from the people of Staunton; and a smart hat arrived from Richmond; and he was prevailed upon to turn himself out in his new splendour for the battle at Fredericksburg, with unexpected results.

Before leaving the Valley General Lee visited Jackson's camp to try to settle the difference between Jackson and A. P. Hill, both of whom had preferred charges against each other, although as has been mentioned, A. P. Hill had been allowed to return to his command for the battles of Harper's Ferry and Sharpsburg. What transpired at Lee's meeting with his two generals has never been disclosed, but although the quarrel was temporarily settled, Jackson, at least, is known to have been soon seeking evidence for renewed charges against Hill.

During this last stay in the Valley, great interest in religion was displayed in Jackson's camp, and Jackson sometimes attended prayer meetings there. Douglas describes a visit with his general to one of these. As they approached the camp—it was after dark—Jackson was recognised, and a runner sprinted on before and gave the news. They noticed as they approached that, in many tents squads of fours were sitting around a candle in an inverted bayonet stuck in the ground as a candlestick, absorbed in games of cards. As the General approached, the light would go out, the cards would be put down in place just as they were held, and the players would crawl out and fall in behind. When Jackson reached the place of prayer, lo, the whole camp was there. Bowed heads, bent knees, hats off, silence! Stonewall Jackson was kneeling to the Lord of Hosts, in prayer for his people! When he left the soldiers followed him back through the camp before they returned to their

[1] Mrs Jackson, *Memoirs*, 258.

cards. It was from a scene like this that a well-known engraving 'Prayer in Stonewall Jackson's Camp' was probably conceived.

That evening, on reaching headquarters, Jackson was greeted at tattoo, not only with the customary rolling drums, but also by the wild and joyous *Rebel Yell*, for which the Stonewall Brigade was famous, taken up in turn by all the brigades of the encampment. The mighty roar was impressive in the extreme. When it was at its height, Jackson came out, bareheaded, from his tent, walked to the fence and leant his elbows on the topmost rail. Resting his chin upon his hand he waited in silence until the conclusion of this strange serenade. The shouts decreased, the noise became fainter and fainter, and when it had almost ceased to be audible, he lifted his head to catch the last note and its echo. When it was over he returned slowly to his tent and said as he entered, 'that was the sweetest music I ever heard.'

The scene of the war now changed to the east, where Burnside, who had replaced McClellan in command of the Federal forces, chose the direct route through Fredericksburg for the next Northern attack on Richmond. In sympathy with their foes, the Confederates moved east as well, and prepared a defensive position behind the Rappahannock at Fredericksburg to stop the Federals approaching their capital.

Jackson left the Valley during the last week in November. Passing down the Valley pike for the last time through Strasburg to Newmarket, he turned east over the Massanuttons to Luray, and then crossed the Blue Ridge and the plain of Virginia to an area south-east of Fredericksburg, receiving the good news that while he was making this march he had become the father of a little daughter Julia.

The Battle of Fredericksburg anticipated features of later wars: pontoon bridging of a river under fire, beachhead landings, street fighting, heavy and sustained artillery bombardments, the skilful use of artillery crossfire by the Confederates, communications by Beardslee's Magnetic Telegraph, and observation from balloons by the Federals.

The Confederate position was a strong one. Longstreet's corps defended the northern part of the line as far south as Deep Run; and Jackson's corps the shorter southern line from Deep Run to Massaponax Creek (*see* Map p. 173).

Longstreet's corps stretched from the Rappahannock along the Marye's Heights' ridge, including Stansbury's Hill, to Marye's Hill, a key point in the Confederate position where a sunken road bordered by a stone wall with a protective bank provided good breastworks. The right of Longstreet's position, including what came to be called Lee's Hill and Howison's Hill, was

not quite so strong; but fire from the batteries on the hills criss-crossed the plain to the east over which the Federals must advance (*see* Map p. 173).

Jackson's corps was more concentrated, occupying Prospect Hill, the short ridge running north-west from Hamilton's Crossing to Deep Run. A canal and drainage ditch lay between the Confederates and the town. Jackson had his guns on his flanks, with Pelham's guns, under Stuart, giving enfilade fire from the south in a position east of the railway. His infantry were on the edges of the woods on the hill. A coppice extended from the centre of Jackson's position between Lane's and Archer's brigades for 600 yards across the railway; and this offered a covered approach which was utilised by Meade's attacking troops during an early phase of the battle.

Burnside formed his army into three 'grand divisions', each composed of two corps. The Right Grand Division was under Sumner and this was to cross the Rappahannock by pontoon bridges opposite the town, move through the streets and storm Marye's Heights. Franklin's Grand Division was to cross just south of Deep Run and attack Jackson's position. Hooker's Grand Division in the centre was to provide general support, and a 150-gun concentration of Union artillery on Stafford Heights would cover the troops crossing the river. Burnside thus proposed to make a river crossing in the face of his enemy already established on the far side, and then assault their main position on the ridge beyond.

There was a delay for the Federals while they waited for their engineers with the pontoons to arrive from Harper's Ferry; but on the foggy morning of 13 December, following a bombardment, the attempt was made to build the pontoon bridges.

Opposite Fredericksburg difficulties soon arose. McLaws, the rest of whose division was on Marye's Hill, sent Barksdale's brigade to dig rifle pits, make barricades, and man some of the houses on the edge of the river to prevent a crossing. These were in position in time to take a severe pounding from the Federal bombardment. The roar of the cannon, the bursting shells, the falling of walls and chimneys, and the flying bricks and other material dislodged from the buildings by the iron balls and shells, adding to the fire of the infantry from both sides and the smoke from the guns and from the burning houses made a scene of indescribable confusion. Nevertheless, Barksdale's Mississippians held up the bridgebuilders who only managed to extend the pontoons a few yards towards Fredericksburg.

Meanwhile, General Franklin's engineers had completed some bridges below the mouth of Deep Run without much interference, and crossed over a portion of his division; yet because of the failure of Sumner's men in front of

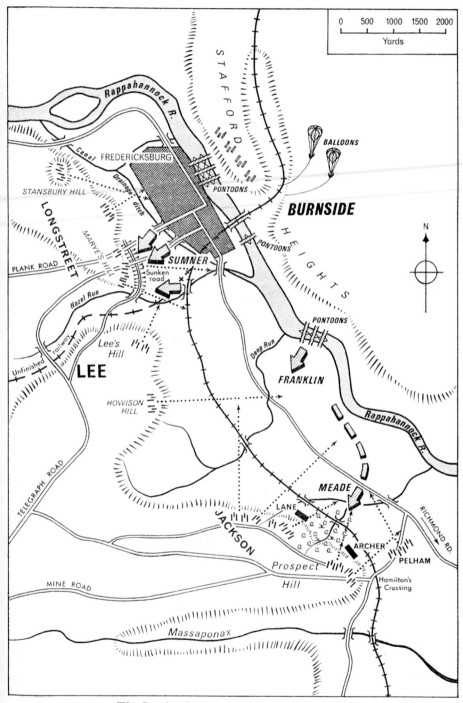

13 *The Battle of Fredericksburg, 13 December 1862*

Fredericksburg, he withdrew all but one brigade, to await the result of Sumner's new attempt.

It was Captain Weymouth's men who eventually managed it. He describes how, as follows:

On our arrival at the river at daylight, we found but a small section of the bridge laid, in consequence of the commanding position which the enemy held on the right bank of the river secreted as they were behind fences made musket-proof by piling cord-wood and other materials against them. After a fruitless attempt of eight hours duration to lay the bridge where the enemy had absolute control of the river front, the idea was abandoned, and notice was sent down to us at the river that the enemy would be shelled again from the heights, with orders to take to the pontoon-boats and cross and dislodge the enemy in order to enable the engineers to complete the bridge. [1]

And this is how it was done. The instant the artillery ceased firing they took to their boats and poled across the river under heavy musket fire. It was not easy. They were met with such resistance from Barksdale's brigade, very aptly styled by General Longstreet 'Confederate hornets', that it was nearly dusk before they gained anything of a bridgehead.

Franklin, thus was still the first to advance. As the fog lifted the Confederates on Marye's Hill saw that while on Longstreet's front no body of troops could be seen on the Fredericksburg side of the river, on Jackson's front the enemy had crossed, for their long blue lines were plainly visible. Not long afterwards, Franklin's Grand Division was seen advancing in two lines against Jackson's front, marching in most magnificent order. It looked, remarked Longstreet, as if Jackson would receive the first blow. [2]

Jackson had 30,000 men on or near Prospect Hill, and 57 of his guns in position on his flanks, with one long-range Whitworth gun just beyond Massaponax Creek; but A. P. Hill's division alone manned the whole front line.

Jackson's confidence was never greater than when, accompanied by his staff, he rode round his position. He was not, however, received quite as enthusiastically as usual by his soldiers. No customary cheer was raised as he rode by. They were used to the old stained tunic, the VMI cadet cap, and Little Sorrel; they did not recognise their beloved leader in the finery of Stuart's coat, in the new gold banded General's hat from Richmond, and mounted on another charger.

Jackson's troops were well hidden; and Burnside seems to have believed that there was little opposition to him on Prospect Hill. He ordered Franklin

[1] B & L, iii, 121.   [2] Longstreet, 307.

to seize the ridge in front of him, and to do this Meade's Pennsylvanian division was used. Meade advanced in three lines with skirmishers in front and on the flank; but no sooner had the first line crossed the Richmond road than his left was assailed by shot and shell from the guns of Captain Pelham, the 21-year-old boy commander. Pelham had his own horse artillery and a section from Captain Poague's Rockbridge Artillery. A member of the latter detachment writes: 'We reached the field a little after sunrise, having come up during the night from Port Royal where we had been engaging the enemy's gun-boats. In conjunction with Stuart's horse-artillery it was our mission to meet Burnside's movement against General Lee's right wing. With the exception of brief intervals to let the guns cool, we ceased firing only once during the entire day, and this was to move about a hundred yards to a more effective position. Excepting the few minutes thus occupied, our guns and limber-chests remained in the same position all day, the caissons plying steadily between the ordnance-train and the battle line, to keep up the stock of ammunition. I do not recall the number of casualties but our losses were heavy. When we came to make the change in position mentioned above, more than half the horses were unable to take a single step.' Pelham was obviously pleased with their efforts, for the account continues: 'Pelham came up and said, "Well, you men stand killing better than any I ever saw." The third and fourth pieces, 20-pounder Parrott guns, were on the hill west of the railway. Captain Poague told me since that the orders General Jackson gave him as he came to the place were, "to fire on the enemy's artillery till it became too hot for him, and then to turn his guns on the infantry."' [1] But the main targets proved to be the infantry as, by sweeping past Pelham's guns in line, they offered an opportunity for deadly enfilade fire of which the gunners made good use. So telling was Pelham's fire that Meade's leading brigade wavered, and he had to stop and bring up four batteries of his guns to brush Pelham aside. When the Federal gunners found Pelham's range, he rapidly changed his position to escape their shot and shell; and in this way defied them for over half an hour.

On Pelham's final retirement from his advanced position, when he ran out of ammunition and had one piece put out of action, Franklin brought forward his batteries to the Richmond road, and subjected Jackson's position to a heavy cannonade to which the Federal guns on Stafford Heights contributed.

Soon after eleven, Meade resumed his advance. In this first approach, however, he was repulsed. When his men got within 800 yards of Jackson's centre, they met such a burst of fire from Jackson's concealed guns, as well as musket

[1] Moore, 162, 163.

fire from his infantry, that they were decimated and fell back in disorder to the Richmond road.

There followed an artillery duel for the next hour and a half, and then Franklin reinforced Reynolds' Corps consisting of Meade's, Gibbon's and Doubleday's divisions with two of Hooker's divisions, Birney's and Sickle's. [1] Doubleday's division turned to face Stuart's dismounted cavalry, and the others, Meade leading, made another attack on the centre of Jackson's line. Burnside had already ordered Sumner to attack Marye's Hill from Fredericksburg to make a diversion, and some of the first of the assaults on Marye's Hill had already been made. [2] Lee's left was thus engaged as well as his right.

Now the swampy coppice, which offered a covered approach for Meade's men, comes into the story. It was one o'clock, when, with Doubleday's division holding off Stuart in the south, and 53 Federal guns posted on the Richmond road pouring shot and shell briskly on Jackson's woods, Meade with his supporting divisions advanced. The clouds of skirmishers preceding him brushed aside the Confederate skirmishers who alone manned the railway embankment; and soon Meade's brigades were within a few hundred yards of Jackson's centre again. When they reached the scene of their former repulse, Jackson's guns opened, but without the same effect, for they were hampered by Federal counter-battery fire from the Richmond road a short distance away. This time Pelham, still right of the railway but nearer Prospect Hill, could do little.

Meade's leading brigade came straight through the coppice between Archer's and Lane's brigades, and being masked by the trees, was not exposed to fire. Finding the coppice unoccupied, the men pushed their way through, and turning towards the north, fell on Lane's flank and forced him back. Meade's second brigade came the same way, but turning south, burst out of the coppice to take Archer by surprise. Two of Archer's regiments were lying on the ground with arms piled and unprepared for an attack from this quarter. They leapt to their feet, but were broken by a determined Federal charge, and gave way in disorder. Sweeping on to their front, Meade's two leading brigades now met Gregg's brigade drawn up within the wood. They wounded Gregg and threw half his regiments into confusion. Meade's other troops on the right and left of the coppice were held by Jackson's men; but the penetration through the centre of A. P. Hill's position was producing a very serious situation indeed. Jackson, however, at his observation post on Prospect Hill, seemed unmoved, even though he realised the dangerous nature of Meade's approach into the heart of his position through the coppice.

[1] Allan, army of N. Va, 484.　　　　　[2] Ibid., 485.

When a messenger galloped up to him and exclaimed in breathless haste, 'General, the enemy have broken through Archer's left, and General Gregg says he must have help, or he and General Archer will both lose their position,'[1] Jackson turned round quietly without the least trace of excitement in either voice or manner and sent orders to his second line to advance with the bayonet and clear the front. Then, with rare self-restraint, for the danger was threatening enough to justify his personal interference, he raised his field-glasses and resumed his scrutiny of Franklin's forces on the Richmond road.

He had not been studying Franklin's massed troops for long before another horseman rode up to him; and this time Jackson not only resorted to prayer, but went to see things for himself. Captain W. G. Williamson, formerly of his staff, describes the incident: 'Captain Ham Chamberlayne rode up to say, "enemy have broken through our line and killed General Gregg." Going to the spot with shot and shell and minié flying past their ears, Williamson noticed the General raise his hand and assume an expression of countenance that so impressed him that he followed, saying to himself, "I will get the benefit of that prayer."'[2]

The counterstroke was so vigorous that Meade's brigade was flung back in fierce fighting in the dense thickets, and before long its broken remnants were dispersing in panic back across the embankment.[3] As the enemy fled, the Confederate gunners poured a heavy fire into their receding mass; and although ordered not to pass the railway, two infantry brigades followed in swift pursuit. Pressing too far forward towards the Richmond road, these rash troops met with head-on canister fire from 16 Federal guns on the road, and suffering heavy casualties, they, in their turn, withdrew in disorder.

Nevertheless it was a great victory for Jackson's Second Army Corps. The Corps inflicted 5,000 casualties on Franklin's forces for a much smaller loss to themselves, and so disheartened the enemy that he made no new attempt. Burnside having witnessed several attempts by Sumner's forces to storm Marye's Hill, all of which ended in failure, now ordered Franklin to renew his attack to act as a diversion. Franklin, however, disheartened by his losses, took it upon himself to disobey.

By 2.30 p.m. the serious fighting on Franklin's front was over, and Jackson's part in the battle of Fredericksburg almost finished; but the struggle in the north continued until nightfall. Features of the battle for Marye's Hill were: the effect of the cross-fire from the Confederate guns on the ridge, and

[1] Henderson, ii, 318.
[2] Hotchkiss papers, 6.
[3] O.R., XXI, p. 632—counterstroke made by Early's troops from the second line.

the murderous musket fire from a strong Confederate position in the sunken Telegraph Road along the foot of Marye's Hill. Telegraph Road was far better for defence than any rifle pit. It was 25 feet wide, sunk about four feet below the ground on the lower side, and lined with stone fences. Troops could be readily transferred from one point in it to another, and several ranks of infantry could stand in it without crowding or confusion. In the rear of this sunken road, on the crest of the hill, at intervals on a front of about 400 yards, were nine guns. 200 yards behind the guns, and sheltered by the slope of the hill, was a brigade of Ransom's division. 400 yards in the rear of this lay another brigade of McLaws'; but Ransom[1] was specially charged with the care of the position. Behind the infantry was another battery of six guns, and two more guns were placed near the Plank road to cover direct approaches to the position.[2]

The deadly nature of the cross fire from Stansbury Hill and Lee's Hill can be seen from the map. Longstreet was made aware of the possibility of this cross-fire early on. He writes: 'an idea of how well Marye's Hill was protected may be obtained from the following incident: Colonel Alexander, my engineer and superintendent of artillery, had been placing guns, and in going over the field with him before the battle, I noticed an idle cannon. I suggested that he place it so as to aid in covering the plain in front of Marye's Hill. He answered: "General, we cover that ground so well that we will comb it as with a fine tooth comb. A chicken could not live on that field when we open on it."'[3]

The strength of the Marye's Hill position, however, did not deter the troops of Sumner. When they emerged from the streets of Fredericksburg, their first obstacle was the canal and canal ditch over which there were only two bridges. This gave them a bad start, but did not deter them; with the shot and shell from the Confederate artillery on the hills tearing through their ranks, they pressed forward with almost invincible determination, maintaining their steady step and closing up their broken ranks. When they approached the stone wall of the sunken road at the foot of Marye's Hill, musketry fire poured from the defenders of the road safe behind their breastworks. This swept the Federals down like chaff before the wind. A cloud of smoke shut out the scene for a moment, and then a clearing revealed the Federal survivors recoiling in search of cover with the Confederate artillery still decimating their retreating ranks. Some who took refuge in the unused railway cutting were caught, in a worse place than the open, by flanking fire from the batteries on Lee's Hill. This caused frightful destruction.

---

[1] Ransom considered Longstreet gave him too little credit in his report, see B & L, iii 94.
[2] Allan, Army of N. Va, 493, 494.   [3] B & L, iii, 79.

Time and time again, piecemeal, brigade after brigade, the troops of Sumner's Grand Division assaulted Marye's Hill. By nightfall seven Federal divisions had attacked, had been repulsed, and were mingled at the foot of the hill. Most of the divisions attacked one brigade at a time. In all, about 14 separate charges were made.[1]

After several of these charges had been made, Lee became uneasy at seeing the attacks so promptly renewed and pushed forward with such persistence. Turning to Longstreet who was with him on Lee's Hill, he said, 'General, they are massing very heavily and will break your line, I'm afraid.' 'General', Longstreet replied, 'if you put every man on the other side of the Potomac on that field to approach me over the same line, and give me plenty of ammunition, I will kill them all before they reach my line.'[2] Longstreet then went on to warn Lee that it was on Jackson's front that the danger lay. It was a danger, which, as we have seen, was overcome.

Repulsed on the right and left, the Federals soon afterwards reformed their lines and gave some indication of renewing the attack. Jackson writes:

I waited some time to receive it; but he making no forward movement, I determined, if prudent, to do so myself. The artillery of the enemy was so judiciously posted as to make an advance of our troops across the plain very hazardous; yet it was so promising of good results, if successfully executed, as to induce me to make preparations for the attempt. In order to guard against disaster, the infantry was to be preceded by the artillery, and the movement postponed until late in the evening, so that, if compelled to retire, it would be under cover of night. Owing to unexpected delays, the movement was not gotten ready until late in the evening. The first gun had hardly moved forward from the wood 100 yards when the enemy's artillery reopened, and so completely swept our front as to satisfy me that the proposed movement should be abandoned.[3]

During the night the Confederates strengthened their position still further by digging trenches at exposed places. The next day passed without a renewal of the attack, although the Federal batteries fired on the Confederate positions from the Stafford Heights and from positions west of the river. The following day passed in the same way, with the Federals getting themselves ready to withdraw across the Rappahannock again, and Lee coming to the decision that it would not be to his advantage to leave his strong defensive position to follow up the enemy, owing to the certainty of a deadly bombardment from the guns on Stafford Heights on any troops approaching the river and coming within easy range. On 16 December, three days after the battle, Lee

[1] *West Point Atlas*, map 73.
[2] B & L, iii, 81.
[3] O.R., XXI, 634.

discovered that Burnside had availed himself of a dark night and a violent storm of wind and rain to recross the river.

Lee had thus won a great defensive victory, and had caused the Federal troops to withdraw and think again before they renewed their march on Richmond. He was well pleased with the support he had received from both his corps commanders in the battle. He writes:

To Generals Longstreet and Jackson great praise is due for the disposition and management of their respective corps. Their quick perception enabled them to discover the projected assaults on their positions, and their ready skill to devise the best means to resist them. Besides their services in the field—which every battle of the campaign from Richmond to Fredericksburg has served to illustrate—I am also indebted to them for valuable counsel, both as regards the general operations of the army and the particular measures adopted.[1]

[1] O.R., XXI, 556.

Fredericksburg : Chain of Command [1]

Federals 116,683 available

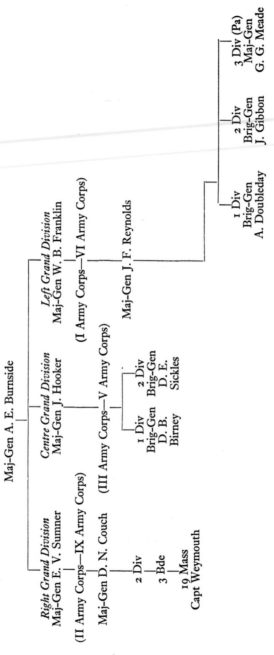

Army of the Potomac
Maj-Gen A. E. Burnside

Right Grand Division
Maj-Gen E. V. Sumner

(II Army Corps—IX Army Corps)

Maj-Gen D. N. Couch

2 Div

3 Bde

19 Mass
Capt Weymouth

Centre Grand Division
Maj-Gen J. Hooker

(III Army Corps—V Army Corps)

1 Div
Brig-Gen
D. B.
Birney

2 Div
Brig-Gen
D. E.
Sickles

Left Grand Division
Maj-Gen W. B. Franklin

(I Army Corps—VI Army Corps)

Maj-Gen J. F. Reynolds

1 Div
Brig-Gen
A. Doubleday

2 Div
Brig-Gen
J. Gibbon

3 Div (Pa)
Maj-Gen
G. G. Meade

casualties 12,653

181

[1] B & L, iii, 143–147.

Fredericksburg : Chain of Command [1]

Confederates 58,500 available, 20,000 engaged

Army of Northern Virginia

Gen R. E. Lee

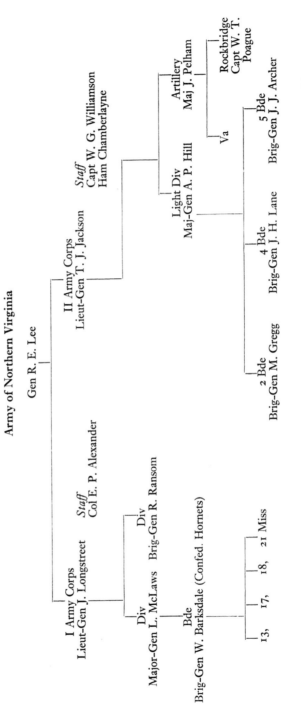

I Army Corps
Lieut-Gen J. Longstreet

Staff
Col E. P. Alexander

Div
Major-Gen L. McLaws

Div
Brig-Gen R. Ransom

Bde
Brig-Gen W. Barksdale (Confed. Hornets)

13, 17, 18, 21 Miss

II Army Corps
Lieut-Gen T. J. Jackson

Staff
Capt W. G. Williamson
Ham Chamberlayne

Light Div
Maj-Gen A. P. Hill

Artillery
Maj J. Pelham

Va

Rockbridge
Capt W. T. Poague

2 Bde
Brig-Gen M. Gregg

4 Bde
Brig-Gen J. H. Lane

5 Bde
Brig-Gen J. J. Archer

casualties 5,377

[1] B & L, iii, 143–147.

Chancellorsville

MOSS NECK

After the Battle of Fredericksburg Jackson established his headquarters at Moss Neck, 11 miles east of Fredericksburg, with his troops in winter quarters from Port Royal to Guiney's Station on the railway to Richmond. Some of them were guarding the river, and had entrenched to watch possible crossings between Fredericksburg and Port Royal.

It is said that when Jackson went to requisition for his headquarters the hunting lodge of a gentleman's house on a lawn overlooking the river, by a strange coincidence the orderly who accompanied him happened to be its owner. After his first interview with the owner's wife, Mrs Corbin, he passed out to the gate where the cavalry orderly was holding his horse. 'Do you approve of your accommodation, General?' asked the orderly. 'Yes, I have decided to make my quarters here.' 'I am Mr Corbin, sir,' said the soldier, 'and I am very pleased.' Later, Jackson became as good a friend of the Corbin family as he had been of Dr Graham and his family in Winchester.

Jackson used the upper room of the lodge for his bedroom and the lower room for his office. The latter was adorned with trophies of the chase and had sporting prints on its walls, and General Stuart, as will be mentioned later, used to tease Jackson about these. A large tent on the lawn was used as a dining room for Jackson and his staff.

While his troops were building their own winter quarters, Jackson's first task was to write up the reports of his past battles, which were getting overdue.

Many of the senior officers of the Confederate army took advantage of the lull in the operations to visit their homes, but Jackson refused to allow himself this privilege. The following remarks are extracts from a letter to his wife

written about this time: 'It appears to me that it is better to remain with my command, so long as the war continues. The army suffers immensely by absentees. If all our troops, officers and men were at their posts we might expect a more speedy termination of the war. It is important that those at headquarters set an example by remaining at the post of duty.'[1]

On the whole this period in winter quarters was a time of relaxation for Jackson. During it he found pleasure in the company of gay General Stuart, the great cavalry leader. Stuart teased Jackson about the pictures of race-horses on his walls, saying he had strange tastes for a Presbyterian. Jackson replied good humouredly that many a true word is spoken in jest, and that in his youth he had ridden in races while living with his uncle Cummings Jackson in Lewis County.

The chief advantage of his quiet time at Moss Neck, however, was the opportunity he had there for religious activities. Activities which inspired a religious revival in his own corps, and later in the whole Confederate army. Half the regiments of his corps were without chaplains, and those chaplains who were present with the forces were inefficient because their duties were completely unorganised. Jackson's view was that just as an organised Church had been found necessary for civilian communities so should there be an organised Church in the army. With this in mind, he set about founding a Corps of Chaplains in the Confederate army, and as a first step, wrote to friends of his in the Church, both to ask for pastors for his own corps, and to explain to them his ideas:

My views are summed up in a few words, which are these: each Christian branch of the Church should send into the army some of its most prominent ministers, who are distinguished for their piety, talents and zeal; and such ministers should labour to produce concert of action among chaplains and Christians in the army. These ministers should give special attention to preaching to regiments which are without chaplains and induce them to take steps to get chaplains, to let the regiments name the denomination from which they desire chaplains selected, and then see that suitable chaplains are secured. A bad selection of a chaplain may prove a curse instead of a blessing. If the few prominent ministers thus connected with each army would cordially cooperate, I believe that glorious fruits would be the result. Denominational distinctions should be kept out of view and not touched upon; and as a general rule, I do not think that a chaplain who would preach denominational sermons should be in the army. His congregation is his regiment, and it is composed of people of various denominations. I would like to see no question asked in the army as to what denomination a chaplain belongs; but to let the question be, does he preach the Gospel? The neglect of spiritual interests in the army may be partially seen in the fact that not half my regiments have chaplains.[2]

[1] Dabney, ii, 400, 401. [2] *Ibid.*, 415.

ye across the Burnside Bridge tain . 1 P.M. Sept 17 1862 . E Forbe .

26 *With McClellan as overall Commander, General Burnside's men are here belatedly taking the bridge on the south flank at Antietam (Sharpsburg), 17 September 1862. Burnside later commanded unsuccessfully at Fredericksburg. From a drawing by Edwin Forbes (1839–1894)*

27 *1st Virginia Cavalry at a halt during the invasion of Maryland. From a drawing by Alfred R. Waud (1828–1891)*

28 *Harper's Ferry, with the Shenandoah River on the left and the Potomac on the right. In the foregro*
From a painting (1863) by William MacLeod (1811–1892). In the collec

the Maryland Heights. Jackson captured Harper's Ferry with his artillery above on 15 September 1862. The Corcoran Gallery of Art, Washington; gift of Mrs Genevieve Plummer

29 *General Sumner's men building a pontoon bridge opposite Fredericksburg.*
Captain Weymouth's men eventually crossed in pontoon boats. From a drawing
by Alfred R. Waud (1828–1891)

30 *The Battle of Chancellorsville, 1–3 May 1863.*
General Howard's routed XI Corps being supported by General Couch's II Corps.
From a drawing by Alfred R. Waud (1828–1891)

One of the measures Jackson introduced was a service each Sunday at headquarters, and a place was prepared with seats and a temporary pulpit in a field nearby. There, Jackson's own example in attending so stimulated others that congregations grew from hundreds to thousands. 'Never since the days when Whitefield preached to the mingled crowd of peers and beggars in Moorfields has the sky looked down upon a more imposing worship.'[1]

Another enterprise was Jackson's encouragement of his units to build their own chapels. His suggestions met with considerable response. Trees were cut down and built up into walls of logs, chimneys were made of rough bricks and clay, and the structure was roofed with clapboards. Jackson was particularly gratified when the Stonewall Brigade was the first to begin a chapel of this kind.

Next, he introduced weekly chaplains' meetings where the chaplains chose their own chairman or moderator to organise their joint affairs. Although Jackson only intruded through the presence of his own chaplain, who kept him informed, nevertheless, his energy and will came to be exerted among his chaplains just as it was among his staff and field officers, and this communicated his own efficiency and vigour to all they did.

Jackson sought from his chaplains the same sense of duty he expected of his officers. He thought they should endure the hardships of campaigning with the troops, and should no more think of going on leave without a proper furlough than a soldier would.

Finally, Jackson appealed to the Military Committee of the Confederate Congress to bring in a law enabling quartermasters to provide chaplains, like other officers, with tents, and forage for horses, and although not adopted immediately, it was eventually brought about.

This was the time when Jackson, at the head of an army in the process of conversion, was probably nearest to the Cromwell to whom he is sometimes compared.

The last weeks of Jackson's time in winter quarters were particularly happy ones, for he yielded at last to his wife's request to be allowed to come with their little daughter to stay with him. He moved his headquarters to a tent near Hamilton's Crossing, and got rooms for his family in the Yerbys' house nearby. Although he spent the greater part of the day at headquarters, he allowed himself the evenings with his family. He had always been happy in the company of children, and it was a delight to be able to play with his own Julia. An officer's wife, who saw him often at this time, wrote to a friend in Richmond that 'the general spent all his leisure time in playing with the

[1] Dabney, ii, 417.

185

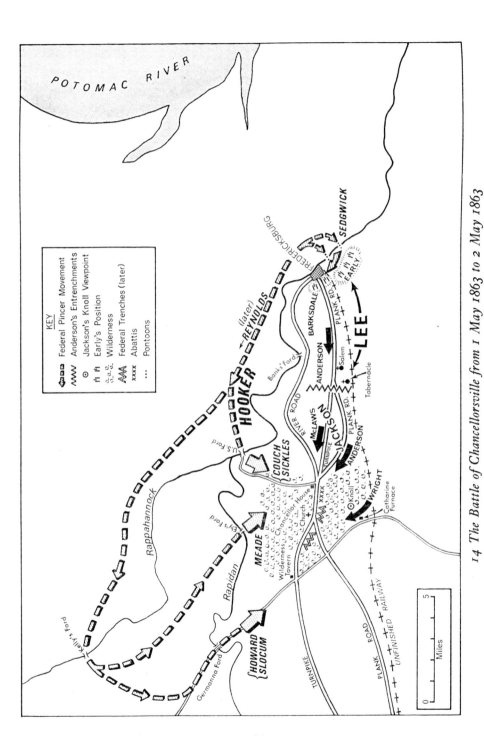

KEY
⟶ Federal Pincer Movement
ⵠⵠ Anderson's Entrenchments
⊙ Jackson's Knoll Viewpoint
ᴨ ᴨ Early's Position
ᵒᵒᵒ Wilderness
ΛΛΛ Federal Trenches (later)
xxxx Abattis
··· Pontoons

POTOMAC RIVER

FREDERICKSBURG

SEDGWICK

REYNOLDS (later)

HOOKER

BARKSDALE

PLANK RD.

EARLY

LEE

Bank's Ford

Salem

ANDERSON

Tabernacle

U.S. Ford

COUCH
SICKLES

Rappahannock

Rapidan

Kelly's Ford

Ely's Ford

Germanna Ford

RIVER ROAD

McLAWS

JACKSON

TURNPIKE

PLANK RD.

ANDERSON

WRIGHT

Catharine Furnace

MEADE

Wilderness
Tavern

Chancellor House

Church

xxxx

Knoll

TURNPIKE

PLANK ROAD

UNFINISHED RAILWAY

HOWARD
SLOCUM

0   5
Miles

14 The Battle of Chancellorsville from 1 May 1863 to 2 May 1863

186

baby.'[1] During the visit he was able to arrange for Julia to be baptised by his chaplain; but with the renewal of more active operations at the end of April 1863, Anna and Julia had to be sent away to a safer place.

BATTLE OF CHANCELLORSVILLE

The battle of Chancellorsville has been called The Perfect Battle.[2] General 'Fighting Joe' Hooker, Lincoln's new commander, had taken over a dispirited army from Burnside, but by an energetic course of training and resupply he had restored its morale. It was now a large, well organised and well equipped force of seven corps of infantry and one of cavalry. Hooker did away with Burnside's *Grand Divisions* and substituted a single corps organisation with badges evolved by General Butterfield adopted as signs for each corps.[3] General Howard's unlucky XI Corps, for example, had a moon as its badge; General Slocum's XII Corps, which helped to hold the Confederate onslaught, a large star.

Hooker was pleased with his army, and even more pleased with the plans he evolved to crush Lee's forces around Fredericksburg and move on Richmond. 'My plans are perfect,' he exclaimed. 'May God have mercy on General Lee, for I will have none.'[4] Hooker's plan consisted of a giant pincer movement. As a feint, two of his corps under General Sedgwick were to force a crossing of the Rappahannock below Fredericksburg where Franklin had crossed in the first battle of Fredericksburg. At the same time, Hooker would march three corps westwards up the Rappahannock, cross that river at Kelly's Ford (*see* Map p. 186) move down towards the south-east and cross the Rapidan at Germanna and Ely Fords, pass through the Wilderness and attack Lee's army in the rear. Slocum's, Howard's and Meade's corps were all to cross at Kelly's Ford; then Slocum and Howard would cross the Rapidan at Germanna Ford, and Meade at Ely's Ford. These three corps as they moved south-east would uncover U.S. Ford (*see* Map p. 186), and Couch's and Sickle's corps could then use this nearer ford to cross the Rappahannock below its junction with the Rapidan, thereby saving many miles of marching. Eventually, Reynolds' corps, which was one of the two left with Sedgwick, was also brought west to come over U.S. Ford. The cavalry corps (less Pleasanton's division less one brigade) under Major-General Stoneman was, meanwhile, to sweep far to the west, ride around Lee's left flank, and cut his communications with Richmond.

[1] Henderson, ii, 400.
[2] Dupuy & Dupuy, 196.
[3] An early use of Corps signs.
[4] Dupuy & Dupuy, 196.

Thanks to some good scouting work by the Confederate cavalry under Major-General Jeb Stuart, Lee was soon apprised of Hooker's tactics, and, as always, decided the best defence would be to attack, and thereby stop Hooker before he could reach the Confederate position at Fredericksburg to take them in the rear.

Thus Lee decided to move a force towards Chancellorsville, and on 29 April he sent Anderson's division westwards along the Plank Road from Fredericksburg. Anderson moved along the turnpike from Tabernacle Church and advanced to the crossroads where, in a clearing in the woods of the Wilderness, stood Chancellor House. Chancellor House and the buildings in clearings along the road to the west of it were to become key areas in the battle. Chancellor House is called Chancellorsville on most of the maps of the district. It consists of a large single brick building having buttresses, with six windows apiece at either end connected by a veranda on the ground floor with a balcony above it; and it is flanked by some wooden outbuildings. Although in an extensive clearing there are some groups of large trees around it.[1] Chancellor House was used as Hooker's headquarters, and comprises what there is of Chancellorsville. The other buildings and clearings which play such an important part in the battle were, going west along the main road (*see* Map facing p. 208): the Van Wert dwelling near which Jackson was killed; the schoolhouse; Dowdall's Tavern, the home of the Rev Melzi Chancellor[2] and XI Corps headquarters; Wilderness Church, set back a little to the north of the road; and further to the north, in a large clearing in the woods Hawkins Farm which was headquarters of Schurz's 3 Division of Howard's XI Corps. Along the turnpike still further west was Talley's Farm, and finally came Wilderness Tavern.

The dense forest of the Wilderness which covers the entire Chancellorsville battleground has few large trees, but is nevertheless very difficult to get through. The trees were mainly scrubby oak called black-jack, and it was hard to ride through the forest, and difficult even to march through with a musket in hand, unless trailed.[3] There were, however, several cleared areas; and the main ones are shown on the map (facing p. 208): Chancellorsville, Fairview and Hazel Grove in the east; Hawkins, Dowdall's Tavern and Talley's in the west. All these were important in the Battle of Chancellorsville, particularly those of higher elevation than the surrounding forest, like Fairview and Hazel Grove.

In the various accounts of the battle, a key area among the headwaters of

[1] B & L, iii, 162.
[2] *Ibid.*, 206, Dowdall's is called Chancellor's in Jackson's scribbled message.
[3] *Ibid.*, 218.

Lewis Creek is not generally described very clearly. It lay south of the Plank Road between Chancellor House and Dowdall's Tavern, with Colonel Wellford's house, Catharine Furnace, in the far south. Here a cleared knoll near Catharine Furnace formed one of the vantage points used by Jackson to view the position, and the cleared plateau of Hazel Grove was used for a position for the Federal guns to stabilise the battle in the worst period for the Federals.

The route followed by Jackson on the *Great Flank March* left the Plank Road south of Chancellor House, proceeded over an exposed ridge to Catharine Furnace, and then south-westwards (*see* Map facing p. 208). To avoid Federal fire when crossing the exposed ridge, Jackson's wagons were sent on a diversion round it. This diversion is also shown on the map.

Before 29 April, Anderson's division was extremely scattered. Some of his troops were as far forward as U.S. Ford, and Banks' Ford; other formations were around Fredericksburg.[1] Then Lee ordered Anderson to take the rest of his division westwards to Chancellorsville. Here he was met by his troops from U.S. Ford. They reported they had come back because a large Federal force was crossing at Germanna and Ely Fords, and threatened their line of retreat (*see* Map p. 186). Anderson considered it foolish to stand in the wooded country of the Wilderness around Chancellor House, where there were few fields of fire, and decided to get out of the forest and try to find a better defensive position nearer Fredericksburg. Consequently he retreated. Near Tabernacle Church he found Lee's engineer officers—sent forward by Lee who had the same idea as Anderson—examining a position with a view to establishing a line of entrenchments;[2] and between them they constructed the most extensive line of trenches until then created in mobile operations.

The next troops to be moved by Lee westwards to meet Hooker in the Wilderness were McLaws' division less one brigade and Jackson's corps less one division. Thus, only Early's division with Barksdale's brigade from McLaws' division of the First Corps, in all about 10,000 men, were left to guard the heights behind Fredericksburg.

Jackson approved of Anderson's entrenchments, when he saw them on his arrival at Tabernacle Church; but he was not prepared to make use of them. 'Stop work on the entrenchments, pack tools, and prepare to advance,' were the orders he gave. He proposed to advance on Hooker's large forces while they were still clogged in the woodlands around Chancellor House. This was an entirely different appreciation from that of Anderson, who had planned to stop the Federals as they emerged from the Wilderness by River road, the turnpike and Plank road (*see* Map p. 186). Jackson's order was for McLaws

[1] O.R., XXV, i, 849.　　　　　　　　　[2] *Ibid.*, 850.

to press up the turnpike towards Chancellor House and for Anderson's and his own troops to advance along the Plank road where there appeared to be more room to manoeuvre. Instead of waiting for Hooker to strike, Jackson proposed to hit him first.

At 11 a.m. on 1 May, the Confederate advance began, with Jackson himself in the van with Anderson's troops on the Plank road, and McLaws on the turnpike. McLaws was the first to encounter the enemy, meeting with musket and gun fire from the woods in front of him soon after he started; but Jackson's column came up against similar opposition not long afterwards. McLaws reported across to Jackson that on his front large numbers of Federals could be seen on a cleared area of higher ground among the trees of the Wilderness. He suggested that Jackson's southern flank might provide better opportunity for a turning movement.[1] Jackson ordered McLaws to hold his position. He told the artillery commander to order up guns to drive back the enemy on his front and proposed to try a turning movement only if the guns failed to do the job.

About this time a message arrived from Stuart telling Jackson that the cavalry were now on his flank and would do all they could to help. Jackson replied that Chancellor House was the objective.

Lee and his staff now rode up. Having left Early to defend Fredericksburg, he had come to see how Jackson's battle was going. Jackson explained the situation to the commander-in-chief; after which, Lee rode off to the north to see for himself how McLaws was shaping against Sykes' regulars,[2] and to find out if a turning movement was possible in the north.

Jackson's impression now was that Hooker was beginning to draw back; and he sent orders for McLaws to press on again, making sure his skirmishers and flanking parties were out to guard against ambush.[3] Whenever either column advanced, however, they were met with resistance, and Anderson sent Wright's brigade along the unfinished railway to try to get round the Federal right. Jackson, accompanied by a single orderly, rode off after this brigade.

By the time he caught up, Wright's brigade had reached Catharine Furnace, and was sweeping the woodland to the north. Stuart was in the same area, and Jackson took him and some of his guns up to the top of a knoll so that the guns might support Wright's brigade. The horse artillery found the muddy track up the hill difficult to negotiate; and when they reached the top and opened fire on a line of infantry visible in a cleared patch of woodland,

[1] O.R., XXV, i, 825.
[2] Ibid., i, 834. That Sykes was the opponent was probably only known later.
[3] Ibid., ii, 764. An order signed by J. G. Morrison, Jackson's brother-in-law.

they received more than they gave from two batteries of masked Federal guns. Major Beckham, commanding Stuart's horse artillery, describes the incident as follows:

By the direction of the major-general commanding, I moved four pieces with the view of driving back a line of enemy's infantry so that General Wright might occupy the ground with his brigade. It was supposed that the enemy had little or no artillery at this point, and that three or four guns would be sufficient for the purpose in view. The immediate effect of our fire was to scatter the enemy's lines, and at the same time to draw upon us a storm of shot and shell from eight or ten pieces of artillery, well masked by the high, rolling ground on which they were placed. I caused the fire of our guns to be directed against these batteries and, I think, with some effect, as it was not many minutes before the rapidity of the firing on the part of the enemy was so much diminished as to render it certain that some of his pieces had been compelled to retire. I do not think that men have been often under hotter fire than that to which we were exposed. One gun had every man about it wounded except one. [1]

There were ten casualties among the gunners and three horses were disabled. Jackson and Stuart and their followers had to turn about to get out of fire; but one of the cavalcade was severely wounded in the scamper down the hill.

Jackson returned to the main body on the Plank road where A. P. Hill's division from Fredericksburg had now arrived. The news from the fronts was that there was every indication that Hooker was in great strength around Chancellor House.

Jackson and Hill now rode over together to view the position on McLaws' front. They were taken up a hill where the enemy's position could be seen. Plainly visible were three lines of battle, and crude but strong earthworks. Jackson returned again to the Plank road, and just before darkness fell, encountered Lee again. With few words the two Confederate leaders rode together up a track into the woods near the Plank-Catharine Furnace crossroads.

Among the pines near the crossroads (*see* Map facing p. 208), Lee and Jackson sat together on a fallen log and considered what their next action would be. Lee's reconnaissance on the right had convinced him of the impracticability of a blow there. The forest was very thick and control of a turning movement would be difficult. They then considered the possibility of a frontal attack, and to obtain more information about the situation to the front, sent Major

[1] O.R., XXV, i, 1049.

Talcott, from Lee's staff, and Major Boswell, Jackson's engineer, to carry out a moonlight reconnaissance for them. While the engineers were away, Jeb Stuart rode up. He said that Fitzhugh Lee, commanding his Second Brigade, had reported that the Federal right was 'in the air', and offered the possibility for a turning movement. Talcott and Boswell now returned to report that the Federal line in front was very strong, and too wooded for Confederate artillery to be used against it successfully.

Lee turned to Jackson and said, 'How can we get at these people?' Jackson replied that Lee must make the decision. He quickly did so. Accepting his cavalry's report he ordered Jackson to take a force around the right flank of Hooker's force to attack the Federals in the rear. He left the details as to the route and composition of the force to Jackson.

Jackson rose quickly from the log and saluted: 'My troops will move at 4 a.m.,'[1] he said. Then he went off farther into the woods, spread his saddle blanket on the ground as a mattress, unbuckled his sword and leant it against a tree, and got ready for the night. Sandy Pendleton, his staff officer, was nearby; and seeing that Jackson had nothing to cover himself with, offered him his own greatcoat. Jackson refused the greatcoat but accepted the cape. Covering himself over with it, he prepared himself for sleep.

The chill of the night combined with his insufficient covering caused Jackson to wake up before dawn. He was shivering and felt the first signs of a cold, but got up and spread the cape over Sandy's prostrate body.[2] He discovered a little fire, which had been left by an orderly, still just burning under the trees. Finding a handy biscuit box discarded by the Federals in their retirement, he sat down, wrapped his rubber coat[3] around him, and warmed himself as well as he was able.

Mr Lacy, his chaplain, noticed him sitting there, and came over to greet him. Lacy had arrived during the night after Jackson had gone to sleep. Jackson invited him to share the box, and knowing his chaplain had served at one time in the neighbourhood, asked him if he knew of any tracks which would lead round the Federal right, and if there were any people living nearby who would act as guides. Mr Lacy suggested Colonel Wellford of Catharine Furnace as a guide, and felt confident that there were roads going round the west of the Federal position. This fired Jackson with enthusiasm. He woke up Major Hotchkiss and sent him off with Mr Lacy to contact Colonel Wellford and reconnoitre a route.

Jackson's next visitor was Colonel Long, who managed to get a cup of coffee for his major-general from a nearby cookhouse. While Jackson was

---

[1] 34 SHSP, 16, 17 (Talcott).　　　　[2] Dabney, ii, 448.
[3] Now in Edinburgh's Museum.

sipping it, for no reason his sword fell down from against the tree with a clatter. Colonel Long picked it up and handed it to Jackson. Although not unduly superstitious, he could not help thinking to himself that this was an ill omen; but Jackson buckled it on without comment. Long wrote: 'It strongly impressed me at the time as an omen of evil—an indefinable super-stition such as sometimes affects persons on the falling of a mirror. This feel-ing haunted me the whole day, and when the tidings of Jackson's wound reached my ears, it was without surprise that I heard this unfortunate con-firmation of the superstitious fears with which I had been oppressed.'[1]

Up the road from Catharine Furnace Hotchkiss now rode with the good news that a feasible way round the Federals existed. Jackson was delighted, and immediately sought Lee to tell him the details of what he proposed to do, taking Hotchkiss with him to point out the route he had chosen. Lee left all the details for Jackson to decide. 'What do you propose to make the move-ment with?' he asked. 'With my whole corps,' Jackson replied, anxious to strike with the greatest force possible. 'What will that leave me?' asked Lee, a shade despondently. 'The divisions of Anderson and McLaws,' Jackson replied. In spite of being left with only 7,000 men to hold the whole Federal force, Lee agreed to Jackson's proposal. The great flank march was on.

The route which Major Hotchkiss in consultation with the Wellfords had mapped out for Jackson's flank march began at the crossroads near which Lee and Jackson had bivouacked. Jackson's column started at 8 a.m. on the morning of 2 May 1863, led by Colquitt's brigade from Rodes' division. Following the van was Jackson himself, and at the crossroads he found General Lee waiting to wish him God-speed. Jackson pulled up Little Sorrel for a moment, said a few words to his commander, pointed dramatically down the road to Catharine Furnace and trotted off after his leading troops.

The first danger was just short of Catharine Furnace, where the road crossed an exposed ridge before dropping down to Lewis Creek. Here the column came under fire from Federal batteries on elevated cleared ground south of the main road by Chancellor House. As the fire continued Jackson gave orders that this bit of the road should be crossed at the double-quick, and sent back instructions for the wagons to turn left well short of the ridge on a diversion to avoid the shelling (*see* Map facing p. 208). Reaching Catharine Furnace the main body turned south and by noon no part of the long column had been attacked. This was too good to last. At 2 p.m., when Jackson and the main body were well on their way and out of danger, A. P.

[1] Long, 258.

193

Hill's wagon train was attacked, and Archer's and Thomas' brigades from Hill's division had to be fetched back to give support.

What had happened was that three observation balloons bobbing high over Falmouth Heights reported dust clouds sifting above the trees, and sent by the Beardslee electric telegraph news of it to U.S. Ford, from where the information travelled on by mounted orderly to Hooker. The moving columns were next observed by Sickles who also reported them to Hooker. Hooker gave Sickles orders to advance south cautiously.[1] He was not greatly worried, as he believed the Confederates must be retreating. When he met General Couch at Chancellor House, he exclaimed: 'Lee is in full retreat towards Gordonsville, and I have sent out Sickles to capture his artillery.'[2] Sickles' advance momentarily endangered Hill's wagons in the rear of the column; but thanks to the action of Archer's and Thomas' brigades the damage done was not too serious. Sickles managed to capture one regiment from the relieving brigades; but when Anderson's division on the left of Lee's holding force attacked Sickles in the flank, the Federal movement was halted.

Meanwhile, Jackson and the main body were well on their way. Crossing Lewis Creek they reached Brock road, and turned south for a short distance before reversing their direction and entering a track running northwards parallel to Brock road, but further away from the Federal position (see Map facing p. 208).

Then, down the road to meet them rode the commander of Stuart's Second Brigade, Colonel Fitzhugh Lee. 'General,' he said, stopping before Jackson and saluting, 'if you will ride with me, halting your columns here out of sight, I will show you the enemy's right, and you will perceive the great advantage of attacking down the turnpike, instead of the Plank road [the original plan], the enemy's lines being taken in reverse. Bring only one courier, as you will be in view from the top of the hill.'[3]

Jackson gave the necessary orders for the column to halt, and followed Fitzhugh Lee. What he saw from the top of the hill to which Lee led him was past believing. There before his eyes were the long lines of Howard's Eleventh Corps. The Federals were quite unaware of any danger coming from the west. Their breastworks protected them from the south and their guns pointed in the same direction. Their arms were stacked, their campfires were burning, and in the distance butchers were slaughtering oxen to provide fresh meat for the men's dinners which they were awaiting. From the hill to which Fitzhugh Lee had brought him, Jackson looked along and behind their lines. He could see Talley's Farm and its clearing, the Federal trenches south of the

[1] B & L, iii, 195. [2] *Ibid.*, 163.
[3] Freeman, LL, ii, 552.

main road, and in the distance another clearing and more trenches and rifle pits south of Dowdall's Tavern (*see* Map facing p. 208).

Jackson spent only a few minutes on the hill top. 'Tell General Rodes to move across the Plank road; halt when he gets to the turnpike,[1] and I will meet him there,'[2] he said to the courier, sending him on his way. The attack on Howard's unsuspecting corps was about to begin.

Before the assault, Jackson scribbled a message to Lee on a sheet of paper pressed against the pommel of his saddle saying that his leading division was up, his other two not far behind, and that he hoped to attack the enemy based on Dowdall's Tavern, two miles west of Chancellor House, as soon as practicable.[3]

The plan was for Jackson's corps to advance athwart the turnpike, Rodes' division leading, Colston's in the second line and A. P. Hill's on the north of the road in reserve. The famous Stonewall Brigade now under Paxton had only a minor rôle at the start of the battle.[4] They were formed up with half Stuart's cavalry to guard the Plank road. The rest of Stuart's cavalry were on the north flank.

Hampered by the undergrowth and trees of the Wilderness, the Confederate deployment was slow. It was after five o'clock before all were ready— too late, even in May, to start a battle.

Astride Little Sorrel sat Jackson, his cap pulled down over his eyes, his lips compressed, and with his watch in his hand.

'Are you ready, General Rodes?' asked Jackson.

'Yes, sir,' said Rodes, sitting his horse beside him, and impatient to start.

'You can go forward then.'[5]

A bugle sounded, and back came the sound of other bugles on right and left. The attack had begun.

Strangely heralded by a sudden rush of wild life, deer and rabbits fleeing before the Confederate advance, Rodes' division burst through the woods on the unsuspecting Union troops. Although the Confederate right lagged behind the centre, within ten minutes the Federals were in retreat towards Talley's, over the breastworks of which the Georgians of Doles' brigade leaped.

---

[1] The main road from Fredericksburg to Orange through Chancellorsville is called Plank road to Tabernacle Church, then turnpike to Chancellor House, Plank road to Talley's, then turnpike again (*see* Map facing p. 208).

[2] Freeman, LL, ii, 554.

[3] Jackson called Dowdall's Tavern, Chancellor's in this message after the Rev Melzi Chancellor its owner; it should not be confused with Chancellor House.

[4] They had some hard fighting later on. Paxton was killed and they suffered 493 casualties.

[5] B & L, iii, 208.

Meanwhile, the North Carolinians of Iverson's brigade charged through the cleared ground around Hawkins' Farm. With Jackson close to the front shouting 'Press on, press on!' the Confederates next stormed Dowdall's Tavern, emitting the blood-curdling rebel yell as they did so. A wild volley was all that met them. The few troops that attempted to make a stand were overwhelmed.

Beyond the open ground of Dowdall's Tavern the advanced troops of the Confederates entered thick woods, and the right of the line became entangled with the abbatis surrounding Slocum's XII Corps. Rodes' division was now compelled to halt; but as darkness fell A. P. Hill's division entered the fight. Jackson was riding on further still to the front, when Hill overtook him. Turning, Jackson cried out, 'Press them! Cut them off from the United States Ford, Hill! Press them!'[1]

Lane's and Pender's brigades from A. P. Hill's division were now in the forefront of the battle, stationary, making a line beyond the schoolhouse on the road to Chancellor House; Pender to the north and Lane to the south (*see* Map facing p. 208).

Jackson went slowly forward in the gloom to reconnoitre. Reaching the schoolhouse, he stopped to ask some officers what the conditions were ahead. They could not tell him, but he sent staff officers over to Hill urging him to hurry on with his night attack. In his impatience he decided to ride forward still further, to the skirmish line in front of Lane's and Pender's men, to find out what the country was like over which the Federals would have to pass on their retreat to U.S. Ford.[2]

Jackson and his cavalcade reached a junction of two tracks, Bullock Farm Road and Mountain Road (*see* Map). He asked where they led, and was told the first led to Bullock Farm and U.S. Ford, but the other only bent back to rejoin the main road to Chancellor House. Someone suggested he was too far forward and in a dangerous place.

'The danger is all over—the enemy is routed,' he replied.

'Go back and tell A. P. Hill to press right on.'[3]

Except for patches of moonlight shining on the track, nothing could be seen ahead. There was darkness: but there was also sound. Not far ahead, axes were being wielded. Trees for making more abattis were probably being felled. Voices were audible too. Union officers, apparently, were trying to get troops into line.[4] Jackson turned Little Sorrel round to ride back to the main road to the south of the track junction. Then, when he was nearly opposite

---

[1] 3 CMH, 385.
[3] J. E. Cooke, 419, 420.

[2] 6 SHSP, 265.
[4] Bigelow, 317.

Van Wert's, an unfinished, weather-boarded house in the woods on the far side of the road, a volley of shots rang out.[1]

'Cease firing, cease firing,' someone cried out, as Little Sorrel swerved off again to the north into the woods almost out of control. Jackson turned the little gelding eventually, but not before he was brushed by overhanging branches which nearly swept him out of the saddle.

'Cease firing,' Morrison[2] yelled to the invisible marksmen. 'You are firing on your own men.'

'Who gave that order?' a voice shouted back. 'It's a lie. Pour it into them, boys.'

There was another volley from the woods, and this time Jackson was hit. A staff officer, who was with him, described the nature of his wounds thus: 'Jackson was hit by three balls at once. One penetrated the palm of his right hand, and was later cut out from the back of the hand; a second passed around the wrist of the left arm and out through the left hand. A third ball passed through the left arm, half-way from shoulder to elbow. The large bone of the upper arm was splintered to the elbow-joint, and the wound bled freely.'[3]

Little Sorrel again swerved in fright and bolted towards the enemy. This time Jackson could not ward off the overhanging boughs and was badly bruised by one. By a supreme effort he managed to turn Little Sorrel towards his own lines, but he could not stop him. He was running away. Two of his staff officers, however, galloped after him, and between them stopped Jackson's mount.

'They certainly were our troops,' one of them exclaimed.

'How do you feel, General? Can you move your fingers?'

Jackson tried, but replied that he could not; the arm was broken. Carefully, they got him off his horse, and half supported, half staggering, they moved him a few yards off the road, and made him lie down under a tree, while someone fetched a surgeon.

A. P. Hill, then appeared. He told Jackson that he had tried to make the men stop firing.

'Is the wound painful?' he asked.

'Very painful,' answered Jackson. 'My arm is broken.'

This was the end of the fight as far as Jackson was concerned; but it was not the conclusion of the Battle of Chancellorsville. General A. P. Hill, whose

[1] J. E. Cooke, 420.
[2] Jackson's brother-in-law and staff officer; an eye witness.
[3] B & L, iii, 211.

brigades under Lane and Pender were now in the front line in the west, took over at first from Jackson. Then, when he in turn was wounded, Jeb Stuart, the cavalryman, took command of Second Corps. He was not, however, able to carry through Jackson's intention of cutting off Hooker's escape route towards U.S. Ford. In fact, owing to Jackson's secrecy about his plans, it is doubtful whether he was clear about Jackson's aim, although Hill, who was with Jackson at the time of his wounding, certainly was. In any case, neither that night by moonlight, nor the next day were the Confederates able to make much impression on the Federal units facing them, for, at the instigation of their corps commanders rather than their inept commander, the Federals reacted with great tactical skill to the dangers which faced them on all sides.

Owing to the positioning of the Federal Corps, by darkness on Saturday 2 May it was Jackson's force which was at a tactical disadvantage (*see* Map facing p. 208). The battlefield was dominated by the higher areas of cleared ground which gave fields of fire. In the attack on Jackson's wagons in the afternoon, Birney's division and other units of Sickles' corps, Barlow's brigade of von Steinwehr's division of Howard's Eleventh Corps, and Pleasonton's cavalry, had all moved south to attack the Confederate forces in the Catharine Furnace area from the north. They were, as has been related, stopped by the attack on their flank by Anderson's division, and by Archer's and Thomas' brigades sent back by Hill.

As the afternoon turned to evening and night, these forces were progressively withdrawn northwards again; but, after the rout of the Eleventh Corps by Jackson's divisions, starting from 5.15 p.m., two regiments[1] from Sickles' corps, Barlow's brigade, some of Whipple's division, and a large number of guns[2] were established on the plateau of Hazel Grove, where they were able to take Jackson's divisions in the flank as they advanced athwart the main road towards Chancellor House (*see* Map facing p. 208). This, with a strong line formed by Bushbeck's men, the staunchest of the routed Eleventh Corps, and the two divisions of Williams and Geary from Slocum's corps, at right angles to the road and on both sides of it, held the Confederate assault. In this stand the guns were placed on either side of the road and firing down it (*see* fig. 30).

Then, after the Federals had abandoned Hazel Grove, Howard's Eleventh Corps was withdrawn north-east to refit, and a strongly defended box of Sickles' Corps, on the west, and Slocum's Corps, on the east, was formed around the truncated Chancellor House position (*see* Map facing p. 208). Later

---

[1] 63 Pa and 37 NY of Grahams' First Brigade and Hayman's Third Brigade.
[2] B & L, iii, 188.

still, Meade's and Reynolds' corps were moved to the north-west, and a formidable bridgehead was formed around U.S. Ford.

Meanwhile, at 9 p.m. on 2 May, an imperative order was sent by Hooker to Sedgwick to cross the river at Fredericksburg, clear Marye's Heights, march upon Chancellor's House and be in the vicinity of his commanding general by daylight.[1] He was to attack and destroy any forces he might meet, and take Lee in the rear. Between them, 'they would use Lee up,' Hooker said.[2]

Lee had left Early with his division and Barksdale's brigade, a force of about 10,000 men, to hold the heights behind Fredericksburg. They were protected by strong works and supported by well-served artillery. It was a formidable undertaking that Sedgwick's men carried through: and the successful storming of the Sunken Road with its protective stone wall, followed by the scaling of Marye's Heights, may be called an epic event in its own right.

It was to no purpose, however. Dropping back in some confusion, Early's broken forces managed nevertheless to take up a new position around Salem Church on the evening of 3 May; and here they were reinforced by Lee sufficiently strongly, first to hold Sedgwick fast, and then to surround him with a horseshoe of Confederate forces and push him back towards Banks' Ford; from whence he retired to the other side of the Rappahannock.

Meanwhile, around Chancellor House, the advantage passed to the Confederates again. When Hazel Grove was evacuated by the Federals, it was used as an artillery position by their opponents. These cleared patches among the trees and undergrowth of the Wilderness were the key areas of the battle. From the dominating height of Hazel Grove's plateau the Confederate artillery was able to sweep the cleared patch around Slocum's headquarters called Fairview, and Hooker's headquarters at Chancellor House, which was also in a fairly open area. It may have been this artillery fire which decided the battle. Hooker was standing on the verandah of Chancellor House when one of the pillars supporting the balcony above was hit by a Confederate shell, and a large fragment from the pillar struck the commanding general on the head. General Couch described the incident as follows: 'A cannon-shot struck the pillar against which Hooker was leaning and knocked him down. A report flew around that he was killed.' Hooker was dazed and concussed, but he managed to mount a horse and ride with his staff about a mile north of Chancellor House. There he found a soldier's tent and stretched himself down in it. He was very confused and the will to continue to fight had left him. He could no longer grasp that with Sedgwick in Lee's rear, a strong thrust by his corps around US Ford could easily win the battle. He decided instead

[1] B & L, iii. , 165.   [2] *Ibid.*, 225.

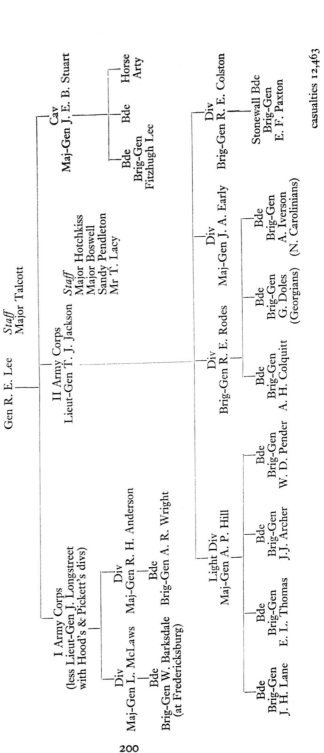

Chancellorsville : Chain of Command [1]

Confederates

Army of North Virginia 60,000   170 pieces of artillery

Gen R. E. Lee

Staff
Major Talcott

I Army Corps
(less Lieut-Gen J. Longstreet
with Hood's & Pickett's divs)

Div
Maj-Gen L. McLaws

Bde
Brig-Gen W. Barksdale
(at Fredericksburg)

Div
Maj-Gen R. H. Anderson

Bde
Brig-Gen A. R. Wright

II Army Corps
Lieut-Gen T. J. Jackson

Staff
Major Hotchkiss
Major Boswell
Sandy Pendleton
Mr T. Lacy

Cav
Maj-Gen J. E. B. Stuart

Bde
Brig-Gen
Fitzhugh Lee

Bde
Horse
Arty

Div
Brig-Gen R. E. Colston

Stonewall Bde
Brig-Gen
E. F. Paxton

Div
Maj-Gen J. A. Early

Bde
Brig-Gen
A. Iverson
(N. Carolinians)

Div
Brig-Gen R. E. Rodes

Bde
Brig-Gen
G. Doles
(Georgians)

Bde
Brig-Gen
A. H. Colquitt

Light Div
Maj-Gen A. P. Hill

Bde
Brig-Gen
W. D. Pender

Bde
Brig-Gen
J. J. Archer

Bde
Brig-Gen
E. L. Thomas

Bde
Brig-Gen
J. H. Lane

casualties 12,463

[1] B & L, iii, pp. 233–237, 238 & O.R. XXV, ii, 320.

Federals

Army of the Potomac 130,000

Maj-Gen J. Hooker

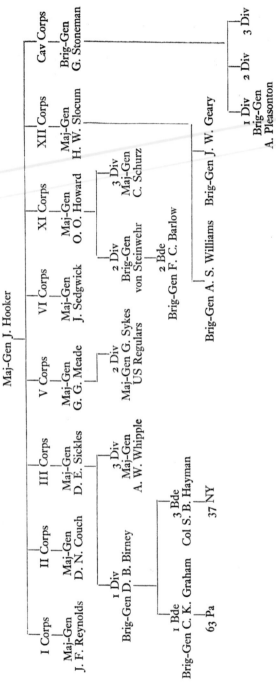

casualties 17,287

201

to leave Sedgwick to his fate and retire over US Ford. Couch continues: 'Raising himself a little as I entered, he said, "Couch, I turn the command of the army over to you. You will withdraw it to the other side of the river."' [1]

Thus, thanks to his own skill, and the spectacular genius of his principal lieutenant, Lee won the Battle of Chancellorsville. Although Hooker's plans had been 'perfect', he had not the strength of will to win the 'perfect battle', [2] and had allowed himself to be out-generalled. But, when the battle was over, Lee had lost the one man he could not spare; Jackson was mortally wounded. His last few days are recorded, following Dr Hunter McGuire's account, in the next chapter.

DEATH OF JACKSON

Supported on either side by Captain James P. Smith[3] and Joseph Morrison, Jackson moved slowly and painfully towards the rear. Occasionally resting for a moment to shake off the exhaustion which pain and the loss of blood produced, he at last reached the line of battle, where most of the men were lying down to escape the shell and canister with which the Federals raked the road. General Pender rode up here to the little party and asked who was wounded, and Captain Smith, who had been instructed by General Jackson to tell no one of his injury, simply answered, 'A Confederate officer'; but Pender recognised the General, and, springing from his horse, expressed his regret, and added that his lines were so much broken he feared he would have to fall back. At this moment the scene was a fearful one. The air seemed to be alive with the shrieks of shells and the whistling of bullets; horses, riderless and mad with fright, dashed in every direction; hundreds left the ranks and fled to the rear, and the groans of the wounded and dying mingled with the wild shouts of others being led again to the assault. Almost fainting as he was from loss of blood, fearfully wounded, and as he thought dying, Jackson was undismayed by this terrible scene. The words of Pender seemed to rouse him to life. Pushing aside the men who supported him, he stretched himself to his full height and answered feebly, but distinctly enough to be heard above the din of the battle: 'General Pender, you must hold on; you must hold out to the last.'

It was Jackson's last order on the field of battle. Still more exhausted by this effort, he asked to be permitted to lie down for a few moments; but the

[1] B & L, iii, 169.   [2] Dupuy & Dupuy, 206.
[3] Rev James Power Smith, another parson staff officer.

danger from the fire, and capture by the Federal advance, was too imminent, and his helpers hurried him on. A litter having been obtained, he was placed upon it, and the bearers moved on as rapidly as the thick woods and rough ground permitted. Unfortunately, another of the bearers was struck down, and the litter fell and threw the General to the ground. The fall was a serious one, and as he touched the earth he groaned at the pain.

Captain Smith sprang to his side and as he raised his head a bright beam of moonlight rested upon the pale face of the sufferer. The captain was startled by its great pallor and stillness, and cried out: 'Oh! General, are you seriously hurt?' 'No,' he answered, 'don't trouble yourself, my friend, about me'; and presently added something about winning the battle first and attending to the wounded afterwards. He was placed upon the litter again, and carried a few hundred yards, when Dr Hunter McGuire[1] met them with an ambulance. He knelt down by him and said, 'I hope you are not badly hurt, General.' He replied very calmly but feebly, 'I am badly injured, Doctor; I fear I am dying.' After a pause he continued: 'I am glad you have come. I think the wound in my shoulder is still bleeding.' His clothes were saturated with blood, and haemorrhage was still going on from the wound. Compression of the artery with the finger arrested it until, lights being procured from the ambulance, the handkerchief, which had slipped a little, was readjusted.

His calmness amid the dangers that surrounded him and at the supposed presence of death, and his uniform politeness, which did not forsake him, even under these, the most trying circumstances, were remarkable. His complete control, too, over his mind, enfeebled as it was by loss of blood and pain, was wonderful. His suffering at this time was intense; his hands were cold, his skin clammy, his face pale, and his lips compressed and bloodless; not a groan escaped him—not a sign of suffering except the slight corrugation of his brow, the fixed, rigid face, and the thin lips so tightly compressed that the impression of the teeth could be seen through them. Otherwise, he controlled by his iron will all evidence of emotion. Some whisky and morphia were procured from Dr Smith and administered to him, and placing him in the ambulance it started off for the corps field infirmary at the Wilderness tavern. Colonel Crutchfield, his chief of artillery, was also in the ambulance wagon. He had been wounded very seriously in the leg, and was suffering intensely.

Jackson expressed, very feelingly, his sympathy for Crutchfield, and once, when the latter groaned aloud, he directed the ambulance to stop, and asked if something could not be done for his relief. Torches had been provided,

[1] Dr Hunter McGuire's account of Jackson's last days is followed fairly closely as in S.H.S.P., V, 14, 1886.

and every means taken to carry them to the hospital as safely and easily as possible. Dr McGuire sat in the front part of the ambulance, with his finger resting upon the artery above the wound, to arrest bleeding if it should occur. When McGuire was recognised by acquaintances and asked who was wounded, Jackson would tell him to say, 'A Confederate officer'. At one time he put his right hand upon McGuire's head, and pulling him down to him, asked if Crutchfield was dangerously injured. When answered, 'No, only painfully hurt,' he replied, 'I am glad it is no worse.' In a few moments Crutchfield did the same thing, and when he was told that the General was very seriously wounded, he groaned and cried out, 'Oh my God'! It was for this that the General directed the ambulance to be halted, and requested that something should be done for Crutchfield's relief.

After reaching the hospital he was placed in bed, covered with blankets, and another drink of whisky and water given him. Two hours and a half elapsed before sufficient reaction took place to warrant an examination. At 2 o'clock on Sunday morning, Surgeons Black, Walls and Coleman being present, Dr McGuire informed him that chloroform would be given him, and his wounds examined. McGuire told him that amputation would probably be required, and asked if it was found necessary whether it should be done at once. He replied promptly: 'Yes, certainly, Dr McGuire. Do for me whatever you think best.' Chloroform was then administered, and as he began to feel its effect, and its relief to the pain he was suffering, he exclaimed: 'What an infinite blessing,' and continued to repeat the word 'blessing' until he became insensible. The round ball (as used for the smooth-bore Springfield musket) which had lodged under the skin upon the back of the right hand, was extracted first. It had entered the palm about the middle of the hand, and had fractured two of the bones. The left arm was then amputated about two inches below the shoulder, very rapidly and with slight loss of blood, the ordinary circular operation having been made. There were two wounds in his arm. The first and most serious was about three inches below the shoulder-joint, the ball dividing the main artery and fracturing the bone. The second was several inches in length; a ball having entered the outside of the fore-arm, an inch below the elbow, came out upon the opposite side just above the wrist. Throughout the whole of the operation, and until all the dressings were applied, he continued insensible. Two or three slight wounds of the skin of his face, received from the branches of trees when his horse dashed through the woods, were dressed simply with isinglass plaster.

About half past three, Sandy Pendleton, his staff officer, arrived at the hospital and asked to see the General. He stated that General Hill had been wounded, and that the troops were in great disorder. General Stuart was in

command, and had sent him to see the General. At first Dr McGuire refused to let him see Jackson, but Sandy urged that the safety of the army and success of the cause depended upon his seeing him. When he entered the tent the General said: 'Well, major, I am glad to see you. I thought you were killed.' Pendleton briefly explained the condition of affairs, gave Stuart's message, and asked what should be done. General Jackson was at once interested, and asked in his quick, rapid way several questions. When they were answered, he remained silent for a moment, evidently trying to think; he contracted his brow, set his mouth, and for some moments was obviously endeavouring to concentrate his thoughts. For a moment it was believed he had succeeded, for his nostril dilated, and his eye flashed its old fire, but it was only for a moment; his face relaxed again, and presently he answered very feebly and sadly, 'I don't know, I can't tell; say to General Stuart he must do what he thinks best.' Soon after this he slept for several hours, and seemed to be doing well. The next morning he was free from pain, and expressed himself sanguine of recovery. He sent his staff officer, and brother-in-law, Morrison, to inform his wife of his injuries, and to bring her at once to see him. The following note from General Lee was read to him that morning by Captain Smith: 'I have just received your note, informing me that you were wounded. I cannot express my regret at the occurrence. Could I have directed events, I should have chosen, for the good of the country, to have been disabled in your stead. I congratulate you upon the victory, which is due to your skill and energy.'[1] He replied: 'General Lee should give the praise to God.'[2]

About 10 o'clock his right side began to pain him so much that he asked Dr McGuire to examine it. He said he had injured it in falling from the litter the night before, and believed that he had struck it against a stone or the stump of a sapling. No evidence of injury could be discovered by examination. The skin was not broken or bruised, and the lung performed, as far as Dr McGuire could tell, its proper functions. Some simple application was recommended, in the belief that the pain would soon disappear.

All this time the battle was raging fearfully, and the sound of the cannon and musketry could be distinctly heard at the hospital. Jackson's attention was attracted to it from the first, and when the noise was at its height, and indicated how fiercely the conflict was being carried on, he told all of his attendants, except Captain Smith, to return to the battlefield and their duties. By 8 o'clock on Sunday night the pain in his side had disappeared, and in all respects he seemed to be doing well. He enquired minutely about the battle and the different troops engaged, and his face would light up with enthusiasm

[1] O.R., XXV, ii, 769. [2] B & L, iii, 214.

and interest when told how this brigade acted, or that officer displayed conspicuous courage, and his head gave the peculiar shake from side to side, and he uttered his usual 'Good, good,' with unwonted energy when the gallant behaviour of *The Stonewall Brigade* was alluded to. He said, 'The men of that brigade will be some day proud to say to their children, I was one of the *Stonewall Brigade*.' He disclaimed any right of his own to the name Stonewall: 'It belongs to the brigade, and not to me.' That night he slept well, and was free from pain.

A message was received from General Lee the next morning directing Dr McGuire to remove General Jackson to Guiney's station as soon as his condition would justify it, as there was danger at the hospital from the Federals who were threatening to cross at Ely's Ford. In the meantime, to protect the hospital, some troops were sent to this point. Jackson said he did not want to be moved, if in Dr McGuire's opinion, it would do him injury. He said he had no objection to staying in a tent, and would prefer it if his wife, when she came, could find lodging in a neighbouring house; 'and if the enemy does come,' he added, 'I am not afraid of them; I have always been kind to their wounded, and I am sure they will be kind to me.' General Lee sent word again late that evening that he must be moved if possible, and preparations were made to leave the next morning. Dr McGuire was directed to accompany and remain with him, and his duties with the corps as medical director were turned over to the surgeon next in rank. General Jackson had previously refused to permit McGuire to go with him to Guiney's, because complaints had been so frequently made of general officers, when wounded, carrying off with them the surgeons belonging to their commands. When informed of this order of the commanding-general, he said, 'General Lee has always been very kind to me, and I thank him.' Very early on Tuesday morning he was placed in an ambulance and started for Guiney's station, and about 8 o'clock that evening he arrived at Chandler house, where he remained till he died. Captain Hotchkiss, with a party of engineers, was sent in front to clear the road of debris and to order the wagons out of the track to let the ambulance pass.

The wagoners sometimes refused to move their loaded wagons out of the way for an ambulance until told that it contained Jackson, and then, with all possible speed, they gave way and stood with hats off, weeping as he went by. At Spotsylvania Courthouse and along the whole route men and women rushed to the ambulance, bringing any delicacies they had, and with tearful eyes they blessed him and prayed for his recovery. He bore the journey well, and was cheerful throughout the day. He talked freely about the late battle, and among other things said that he had intended to endeavour to cut the

Federals off from United States Ford, and taking a position between them and the river, oblige them to attack him; and he added, with a smile: 'My men sometimes fail to drive the enemy from a position, but they always fail to drive us away.' He spoke of Rodes, and alluded in high terms to his magnificent behaviour on the field on Saturday evening. He hoped he would be promoted. He thought promotion for gallantry should be made at once, upon the field and not delayed. Made very early, or upon the field, such promotion would be the greatest incentives to gallantry in others. He spoke of Colonel Willis (subsequently killed in battle), who commanded the skirmishers of Rode's division and praised him highly, and referred to the deaths of Paxton [1] and Boswell [2] feelingly. He alluded to them as officers of great merit and promise. The day was quite warm, and at one time he suffered from slight nausea. At his suggestion, McGuire placed over his stomach a wet towel, and he expressed great relief from it. After he arrived at Chandler's house he ate some bread and tea with evident relish, and slept well throughout the entire night. On Wednesday he was thought to be doing remarkably well. He ate heartily for one in his condition, and was uniformly cheerful.

Dr McGuire now found his wounds to be healthier. The stump was healing and the rest of the surface wound was covered with healthy granulations. The wound in his hand gave him little pain, and the discharge was healthy. Simple lint and water dressings were used, both for the stump and hand, and upon the palm of the latter a light, short splint was applied to assist in keeping still the fragments of the bones. Jackson expressed great satisfaction when told that his wounds were healing, and asked if Dr McGuire could tell from their appearance how long he would probably be kept from the field. Conversing with Captain Smith, a few moments afterwards, he alluded to his injuries, and said: 'Many would regard them as a great misfortune; I regard them as one of the blessings of my life.'

Captain Smith replied: 'All things work together for good to those that love God.'

'Yes', he answered, 'that's it, that's it.'

At McGuire's request Dr Morrison [3] came, and remained with him.

About 1 o'clock on Thursday morning, while Dr McGuire was asleep in a chair in his room, he directed his servant Jim to apply a wet towel to his stomach to relieve an attack of nausea, with which he was again troubled. The servant asked permission to consult Dr McGuire, but Jackson, knowing that the doctor had not slept for nearly three nights, refused to allow the

[1] The commander of *The Stonewall Brigade*.
[2] His engineer officer.
[3] A relation of Anna's and an old friend.

servant to disturb him, and demanded the towel. About daylight Dr McGuire found him suffering great pain. An examination disclosed pleuro-pneumonia of the right side. Dr McGuire believed, and the consulting physicians concurred in the opinion, that it was attributable to the fall from the litter on the night he was wounded. Jackson himself also thought it was due to the accident. The disease came on too soon after the application of the wet cloths to admit of the supposition, once believed, that it was induced by them. The nausea, for which the cloths were applied that night, may have been the result of inflammation already begun. Contusion of the lung, with extravasation of blood in his chest, was probably produced by the fall referred to, and shock and loss of blood prevented any ill effects until reaction had been well established, and then inflammation ensued. Cups were applied, and mercury, with antimony and opium, administered.

Towards the evening he became better and hopes were again entertained of his recovery. Mrs Jackson had arrived and nursed him devotedly to the end. Jackson's joy at the presence of his wife and child was very great, and for him unusually demonstrative. Noticing the sadness of his wife, he said to her tenderly: 'I know you would gladly give your life for me, but I am perfectly resigned. Do not be sad. I hope I may yet recover. Pray for me, but always remember in your prayers to use the petition, "Thy will be done."'

On Friday his wounds were again dressed; the quantity of the discharge from them had diminished and the process of healing was still going on. The pain in his side had disappeared, but he breathed with difficulty, and complained of a feeling of great exhaustion. When Dr Breckenridge (who, with Dr Smith, had been sent for in consultation) said he hoped that a blister which had been applied would afford him great relief, he expressed his own confidence in it, and in his final recovery.

Dr Tucker, from Richmond, arrived on Saturday, and all that human skill could devise was done to stay the hand of death. He suffered no pain and his breathing was less difficult, but he was evidently hourly growing weaker.

When his child was brought to him that day he played with her for some time, frequently caressing her and calling her his 'little comforter'. At one time he raised his wounded hand above his head and, closing his eyes, was for some moments silently engaged in prayer. He said: 'I see from the number of physicians that my condition is dangerous, but I thank God, if it is His will, that I am ready to go.'

About daylight on Sunday morning his wife Anna told him that his recovery was very doubtful, and that it was better that he should be prepared for the worst. He told his wife, in the event of his death, to return to her father's house. He still expressed a hope of his recovery, but if he should die,

he asked to be buried in Lexington, in the Valley of Virginia. His exhaustion increased so rapidly that at 11 o'clock Mrs Jackson knelt by his bed and told him that before the sun went down he would be with his Saviour. He replied: 'Oh, no; you are frightened, my child; death is not so near; I may yet get well.' She fell over upon the bed, weeping bitterly, and told him again that the physicians said there was no hope. After a moment's pause he asked her to call Dr McGuire. 'Doctor, Anna informs me that you have told her that I am to die today; is it so?' When he was answered, he turned his eyes toward the ceiling, gazed for a moment or two as if in intense thought, and then replied: 'Very good, very good, it is all right.' He then tried to comfort his almost heart-broken wife, and told her that he had a great deal to say to her, but he was too weak.

Sandy Pendleton came into the room about 1 o'clock, and he asked him, 'Who was preaching at headquarters today?' When told that the whole army was praying for him, he replied: 'Thank God, they are very kind.' He said: 'It is the Lord's Day; my wish is fulfilled. I have always desired to die on Sunday.'

His mind now began to fail and wander, and he frequently talked as if in command upon the field, giving orders in his old way; then the scene shifted and he was at the mess-table, in conversation with members of his staff; then with his wife and child; then at prayers with his military family. Occasionally he had a few normal moments, and during one of them was offered some brandy and water; but he declined it, saying: 'It will only delay my depart-ure, and do no good; I want to preserve my mind, if possible, to the last.' About half past one he was told that he had but two hours to live, and he answered again, feebly, but firmly, 'Very good, it is all right.'

A few moments before he died, he cried out in his delirium, 'Order A. P. Hill to prepare for action! Pass the infantry to the front rapidly! Tell Major Hawks . . . ;' then he stopped, leaving the sentence unfinished. Presently a smile spread over his pale face, and he said quietly and with an expression as if of relief, 'Let us cross over the river and rest under the shade of the trees'; and then, without pain or the least struggle, he died.

XI

Assessment

In the *Civil War Times* of October 1966, Dr Lowell H. Harrison writes:

Who was the greatest Confederate commander? This question must have enlivened many a Civil War campfire discussion; it has certainly attracted the attention of many historians since then. In 1907 Senator Charles Allen Culberson of Texas sought an answer by asking the surviving Confederate generals their opinions. While their choice was overwhelmingly Robert E. Lee, a few other generals were named, and a number of those who responded added interesting explanations of their selections.

Lee's closest rivals for this honour were Thomas J. Jackson, his great lieutenant, and Joseph E. Johnston; but each of them received but two votes for the top position. Thomas L. Rosser gave his vote to Jackson with little comment. Robertson added a brief explananation of his vote:

Beyond the question of doubt, Stonewall Jackson was by long odds the most wonderful military genius developed on either side during the Civil War. All his campaigns except Kernstown, his first, were bold, strategic, skilful, and invariably successful. He never knew defeat. He had utter confidence in himself. The death of the Southern Confederacy dates from Chancellorsville.

Although Jackson received only these two votes for first place, he was mentioned prominently in 15 other replies—more secondary notice than was received by any other general. The comments were generally laudatory. William R. Cox conceded that Jackson was unequalled as a strategist, but he insisted that Jackson was less considerate of the lives and comfort of his soldiers than any other Confederate commander. General M. C. Butler felt that Jackson was a military genius although Lee was his choice as greatest commander of the war, but he would probably have agreed with George B. Cosby (and others) that Jackson's meteoric career was cut short by his death and that there was no opportunity to ascertain just what he could have accomplished.

This seems to be a sensible, balanced appraisement, as far as it goes; and the views of his brother generals are obviously worth careful consideration. This present book, however, has been concerned almost entirely with Jackson as a general; and a recapitulation of what has emerged may help to fill in the gaps in his colleagues' estimation of his worth.

At First Manassas, Jackson displayed leadership qualities of a high degree. His brigade reached the field of Bull Run from the Valley after the brigades of Bartow and Bee. By the time he was moved north to help face the Federal troops surging down from Sudley Ford, Bartow's and Bee's brigades had been well-nigh routed.

The first thing of note done by Jackson at Manassas was to march to the sound of the guns, thereby following a principle of war approved of and practised by Napoleon. Next, he chose a good defensive position on the top of Henry House Hill, with woods on his flanks and cavalry poised to strike. On the hill he placed his guns as a rallying line, making use of the slight swell of the ground to give his gunners some protection.[1] Major Imboden's battery, lent to Bee, was left defenceless by the rout of the infantry and galloping back in confusion, was stopped, and added, for a time, to the artillery line. From then on, Jackson and his brigade formed a rock on which the other routed brigades were able to form. For example, General Bee's men were inspired to stand when he pointed and likened Jackson's brigade to a stone wall, and General Beauregard was able to prolong Jackson's line by rallying other units to their colours in the continuation of it. Finally, ordering all about him to use his favourite arm the bayonet, Jackson inspired a series of charges of such vigour that the Federals were driven from the field.

Promoted to the rank of major-general after the battle, he was moved back to the Valley to what was, in all but name, an independent command. He proved himself more than worthy of this promotion.

Always aggresive, Jackson attempted a winter campaign in his new command; and there followed the successful but unhappy Romney operation in the north-west of the Valley. During this expedition Jackson showed himself to be a disciplinarian who expected much of his commanders and his men. He rebuked Loring for not seeing personally that his troops were properly encamped. He ordered Garnett to move on and not wait to let his men cook their dinners. He put his own shoulder to many a wheel when guns got stuck on hills. He urged on his men by example, and rebuked his officers, where necessary, for lack of energy. In this way, although many fell by the wayside, he forced his column forward by sheer will-power. One must conclude that

[1] This swell is clearly seen at the Battlefield Park by standing by Griffin's and Rickett's guns on Henry House Hill, and looking toward Jackson's line of guns.

although attentive to the comfort of his men in quarters, where duty or victory were concerned he was indifferent to their suffering; and it did not matter to him if the weak and sickly fell. It was instances like this which William R. Cox was probably thinking about when he remarked that 'Jackson was less considerate of the lives and comfort of his soldiers than any other Confederate commander'; but more will be said at the end of this chapter about Jackson's human relationships.

In the first battle of the main Valley campaign Jackson was defeated. Believing that the Federal forces were leaving the Valley, and informed by Ashby's cavalry that only a small force lay before Winchester, he advanced boldly on that town. His tactics at the Battle of Kernstown which followed cannot be criticised. He made no frontal attack where he was watched and expected, but sent his columns to climb up the low wooded ridge on his left to turn the Federal position. If the Federals had not been so strong, and if they had not reacted so quickly, he might well have been successful. Because he failed, and had come along way before the battle, he is accused of attacking with tired troops on insufficient information. The results, however, were surprising, and suggest that Jackson possessed another attribute of a good general, luck. His aggresive thrust so startled the authorities in Washington that they sent reinforcements to the Valley, and retained McDowell to guard the capital instead of letting him join McClellan in the Peninsula. The result of the Battle of Kernstown was thus a strategic victory for the Confederates.

Jackson's retreat down the Valley to Elk Run after Kernstown is usually considered one of the most brilliant of his moves. Strategically placed on the flank of General Banks' advance southwards, just by waiting to pounce on Banks' flank, he halted that general at Harrisonburg. Next, Jackson carried out one of the most complicated and bewildering of his many marches. Proceeding first up-river, to give the impression of an intended direct attack on Banks, he swung suddenly east over Blue Ridge to Meechum's Gap; and then, going into reverse, he put his infantry on the train back to Staunton. As so often with Jackson, everyone was surprised, friend and foe alike. And it produced the results required. Attacked unexpectedly at M'Dowell by a superior force, Frémont's advanced troops under Milroy and Schenck were forced right back into the Mountain Department. Having followed this by blocking all the routes down from the Mountain Department by which Frémont might have joined his colleague further north, Jackson turned to pursue a now retreating Banks towards Strasburg.

The next operations, before and about Front Royal, provide further examples of Jackson's strategic and tactical skill. Banks had returned to Strasburg and was entrenching. He had a small outpost at Front Royal. There

followed movements of Jackson's troops almost as puzzling as those before the Battle of McDowell. First, he brought some of Ewell's forces from the east valley to the west; and then he marched them back again, with most of his own forces, through the Newmarket Gap. Next, with great superiority in numbers, he assaulted the surprised garrison of Front Royal. After Front Royal he struck westwards to cut Banks' line of retreat on Winchester, and having captured most of Banks' supplies, proceeded to fight a successful set-piece battle short of Winchester with the result that the Federals fled northwards across the Potomac.

The next episode in his extraordinary adventures in the Valley show him in the unusual position of near-victim of a Federal trap. Frémont pressed down on Strasburg from the west; McDowell sent a strong force under Shields to attack across the Blue Ridge. It seemed certain that Jackson would be caught between the two approaching arms. Nevertheless, he escaped; and with much of his booty in the form of wagons loaded with Federal stores. By forced marching and skilful delaying actions he got away just before the pincers closed.

In the last act in the Valley, Jackson maintained his standard in the preceding ones. Having retreated down to Port Republic, where a single bridge separated the western valley from the eastern, he set Ewell the task of holding back Frémont at Cross Keys while he prepared to meet Shields approaching Port Republic. Both battles, although not going quite according to plan, were Confederate successes. Both Federal columns were not very long afterwards retreating back northwards.

From the Valley to Richmond; and Jackson was at his most secretive during the slow march of his divisions eastwards. But in the battles around Richmond Jackson was not at the top of his form as a general. His troops were worn out from too much fighting and too much marching. They were slow to start in the morning and late in arriving at their destinations. Jackson's expert cartographer, Hotchkiss, had been left behind in the Valley, and Jackson found the swampy forests of the Chickahominy very difficult to get through. He was late at arriving at Hundley's Corner, and did not march to the sound of the guns at Mechanicsville. He was late again entering the fight at Gaines' Mill, and although Hood's Texans and D. H. Hill's division, both under his command, achieved the first breaks in the enemy's strong defensive position, Jackson personally added nothing to his reputation there.

All that is remembered about Jackson at Gaines' Mill is that he was late in entering the battle. Unfortunately for his reputation it is forgotten that he was delayed on the way by taking the wrong turning; that he held back D. H.

Hill to catch the Federals to be driven into his arms by A. P. Hill as they sought to retreat along their line of communication to the north; and that by not entering the battle immediately he was following the plan formulated originally by General Lee.

But it was the same at Savage's Station, Frayser's Farm and Malvern Hill. Slow to cross the Chickahominy, he could not help Macgruder; unable to get across White Oak Swamp, he made no attempt to move round to the west to assist A. P. Hill because he had been given orders by Lee to follow the direct route. Here, perhaps, is seen a repetition of the rigidity which at times possessed Jackson in an executive position. It brings to mind the Jackson of the VMI days: pacing the pavements outside the superintendent's office in the rain in order to deliver his reports exactly at the proper time; refusing to remove his heavy clothing in a heat-wave because no direct order allowed it; and at Harper's Ferry refusing to hand over to Johnston without written instructions. At Malvern Hill, no criticism can be directed at Jackson personally for the massacre of the Confederates when they attacked. Longstreet, who made the plan, thought that the crossfire from batteries to the west, combined with the fire of Jackson's artillery from the north, would soften up the defences sufficiently to warrant a direct attack. He was wrong. The swampy forests of Jackson's approach made it almost impossible to bring enough of his guns into action. Without sufficient artillery support, the Confederates were beaten back with heavy casualties.

Cedar Run, Jackson's next battle, shows him at his best again. He displayed his strategic insight by moving forward to defeat Pope's advancing corps in detail before they could concentrate at Culpeper. He made a sound tactical plan to turn the Federal position at Cedar Run by a double flanking attack; and he displayed personal bravery, leading his men with drawn sword in the forefront of the battle during its climax. One of his failings, however, is also illustrated. He did not inform all his senior officers of his battle plan. When Winder was killed, Taliaferro on taking over was not fully cognisant of what the Confederate left wing was supposed to be doing.

Although the Second Battle of Manassas (Bull Run) was a triumph achieved by Longstreet's flank attack on Pope's left, nearly all its successful preliminary engagements can be credited to Jackson. His march up the west bank of the Rappahannock, and then through Thoroughfare Gap to Bristoe Station and Manassas; his raid on the Federal store at the latter place; his mystifying withdrawal to Groveton Ridge; and his costly ambush of King's division as they marched unconcerned up the turnpike to Stone Bridge: these were quite in the tradition of the great marches and countermarches, and battles, of the Valley; and all in all as successful.

There followed the Confederate invasion of Maryland. Jackson was given the task of capturing Harper's Ferry, the last engagement in which he had supreme command. His brother-in-law, D. H. Hill, considered that Jackson was at his best when he was the supreme commander. 'Jackson's genius never shone when he was under command of another;' he wrote, 'it seemed then to be shrouded and paralysed. Compare his inertness at White Oak Swamp with the wonderful vigour shown a few weeks later at Cedar Run, in the stealthy march to Pope's rear, and later still, at the capture of Harper's Ferry.'[1] This is not altogether true, however, as regards Jackson's last three battles, and does not tally with Lee's view as witnessed by his comment, 'such an executive officer the sun never shone on.'[2] All that can be said is that when Jackson was on his own, he never failed, while when under the command of others, he was not up to his best form on all occasions.

Harper's Ferry he captured with his artillery: a suitable method for one commissioned from West Point into the artillery arm, and a task well and quickly done.

At Sharpsburg Jackson proved himself a staunch leader in the defence of West Wood and Dunker Church, and a skilful tactician when he struck at Sedgwick's flank.

At Fredericksburg Jackson received the first blow and was nearly defeated when his centre was penetrated by Meade's troops approaching through the swampy coppice which joined the opposing positions. Only his foresight in massing his guns on his flanks and establishing his defence in depth, and the vigorous counter-attack by Early's troops from the well-placed second line, saved the day.

Finally at Chancellorsville, Jackson was at his very best again. Scorning Anderson's carefully dug entrenchments at Tabernacle Church, he did not wait to be attacked by Hooker; but attacked himself to such good effect that the Federal leader faltered, and the initiative passed to the Confederates. Then Lee and Jackson evolved the boldest operation of the war; the further division of the Confederate forces so that Jackson could move round and strike Hooker's right flank, which, according to Stuart, was 'in the air'. The flank attack was successful, and much of the credit for its success was Jackson's. The complete fulfilment of this daring operation was not achieved because of Jackson's death; for his successor did not know what Jackson's plan had been; but the *Great March* was sufficient to cause Hooker to withdraw his armies across the Rappahannock again.

Enough has been said to show how good Jackson was as a strategist and

[1] B & L, ii, 389, 390.   [2] Henderson, ii, 477.

tactician—he has been called 'the greatest flanker and rearer' the world has ever seen. His virtues were many; his failings few.

'Jackson is said to have a passion for artillery, and to superintend its handling whenever he has an opportunity,' writes J. E. Cooke.[1] This is what one would expect from one who, having been placed in the West Point class list high enough to choose his arm of the service, 'requested assignment to the artillery—an honoured and active arm which had also been Napoleon's choice'; but, nevertheless, Jackson is not often recorded as playing a personal part in placing his artillery.

In this book there are four battles where his skilful use of artillery is manifest: First Bull Run, Port Republic, Harper's Ferry and Fredericksburg; but only at Bull Run is Jackson seen in personal control of his field pieces during a major action. There, as mentioned above, he used his six-pounder Napoleons to form a rallying line and employed Captain Imboden to go from battery to battery, even from piece to piece, to make sure each gun was properly aimed and all fuses cut to the standard and correct length. Here indeed is the sort of attention to artillery detail which Cooke postulates.

At Port Republic, when the town and his own headquarters were overrun by Colonel Carroll's men, Jackson guarded the bridge over North River with Lieutenant Brown's six-pounder from Captain Poague's battery, and personally ordered the first round to be fired to disperse his enemies. Later in the same operation he sent off Captain Imboden's 12-pounder Parrott to Poague, and personally ordered the placing of Imboden's mule battery—to little effect owing to the misbehaviour of the mules.

Harper's Ferry was probably Jackson's most successful artillery battle; but here it is his senior artillery officer, Colonel Crutchfield who is recorded as placing the artillery on the Bolivar front, and transferring pieces across the Shenandoah[2] to enfilade the Federals' entrenched position from the east. The resulting lines of fire are shown on the sketch map (p. 154). With fire from the Maryland Heights, the Loudoun Heights, the batteries west of the Bolivar Heights and from the lower position across the Shenandoah just mentioned, the Federals at Harper's Ferry were in a sad state indeed; and Jackson made the greatest use of his advantage by subjecting them to such a severe and sustained bombardment that they surrendered without waiting for the Confederate infantry to assault. Here then, Jackson controlled the artillery fire and won a battle with it.

Fredericksburg is the greatest artillery encounter of the Jackson period of

[1] *Stonewall Brigade*, 3.   [2] Wise, 290.

31 *The Sunken Road at the foot of Marye's Heights which featured in the Batt of Fredericksburg, 13 December 1862, and the Battle of Chancellorsville, 1– May 1863. This is what it looked like after the second battle.*

32 *Battle of Chancellorsville, 1–3 May 1863. Federal reserves by Chance* quarters, *and on the verandah of which he was hit on the head by a fragm*

33 *General Howard's XI Corps Headquarters at Dowdall's Tavern—Battle*

...ouse (on right of sketch) which was General 'Fighting Joe' Hooker's Head-...a pillar struck by gunfire. From a drawing by Alfred R. Waud (1828–1891)

...hancellorsville, 1–3 May 1863. From a drawing by Alfred R. Waud (1828–1891)

the war. In it, acting through his artillery commanders, he placed his artillery extremely effectively. First, there was young Pelham enfilading Meade's advance from the south, and weakening Meade's attacks. Next, Jackson's massed artillery on the flanks of his narrow front on Prospect Hill held back Meade's new attacks in which Pelham had been less effective; and although not all his artillery was in position, the 53 guns[1] used were well placed.

The lines of fire of the artillery on Jackson's front and over the whole battle area at Fredericksburg are clearly displayed on the map on page 173, and that battle, and those preceding it mentioned above, show something of the way in which Jackson used his artillery.

Not much has been said in this book about Jackson as an administrator. He changed his camp after First Manassas because the water was bad and the site a poor one; he 'chased up' his men's pay for them, and got them new tents, weapons, clothes, and food. He rebuked Loring in the early Valley campaign because he left his troops to be settled in by his inspector-general instead of doing it himself; but attentive as he was to the health and comfort of his men in quarters, on the line of march and in battle he looked only to the success of the Confederate arms. The well-being of an individual, or even of his corps, was as nothing compared with the interests of Virginia. When he asked Major Harman whether the wagons were up after Front Royal, and was told that only the ammunition caissons were forward, he was more than satisfied. He paid little attention to the commissariat, but woe to the man who failed to bring up the ammunition. Taylor says: 'In advance his trains were left behind; in retreat he would fight for a wheelbarrow.'[2]

The Confederates were desperately short of all the means of making war, and Jackson was as good as any of his brother generals at getting what was required from the enemy. In fact he acquired the reputation of being a wagon hunter. He was always on the lookout for U.S. wagons loaded with stores; principally for the lemons that might be in them, his soldiers said, knowing his habit of constantly sucking a bit of that fruit!

Jackson was least successful in his relationships with his senior commanders, and this weakness was noticeable at an early stage in his career. He was junior to Major French at Fort Meade in Florida; but, he held the same brevet rank, and was not satisfied with the responsibilities French allowed him. Then he took it upon himself to investigate French's love affair with the French's

---

[1] Wise, 378, 380. Wise says that Jackson had 14 guns on the right of Prospect Hill, and 21 on the left, and that Pelham had 18 guns.
[2] Taylor, 56.

54 *The wooden house at Guiney Station south of Fredericksburg where Stonewall Jackson died. He is shown being carried in after being wounded at the Battle of Chancellorsville, 1–3 May 1863. He died on 10 May 1863 and the house is now a shrine to him, preserved as shown here. The other building has gone. From a modern painting by Sidney King*

nursemaid. Charges and countercharges were passed to headquarters bearing a close resemblance to the course of events following later quarrels between Jackson and brother commanders.

After the Romney operation Brigadier-General Loring's troops were moved by the order of the Secretary of War without Jackson's permission; and a quarrel developed which led to Jackson's resignation. When Jackson was persuaded to stay on, he still preferred charges against Loring for indiscipline in promoting the move. There followed another period when charges and countercharges were passing: and a waste of valuable time and energy which could have been better employed.

Next came the case of Brigadier-General Garnett at Kernstown. Having run out of ammunition, Garnett ordered a withdrawal when Jackson considered he should have fought on with the bayonet. Garnett had behaved with conspicuous gallantry. The officers of his brigade declared that he was perfectly justified in ordering a retreat. Jackson thought otherwise, and almost immediately after the battle relieved him of his command, placed him under arrest, and framed charges for his court-martial. Henderson says that in arresting Garnett at Kernstown Jackson had lost a good general, but he had taught his officers a useful lesson. They realised that as long as cold steel was left to them, they were expected to hold their ground. But when we read that Garnett was only about to be brought to trial as long afterwards as Cedar Run, and that even then the field court-martial had to be abandoned because of the impending battle, the whole matter does not show Jackson in a good light.

The most famous of the generals to be involved was Major-General A. P. Hill. This quarrel started on the march to Cedar Run, when Hill's wagons became intermingled with those of Ewell, and he only succeeded in marching two miles in a day. After this, in Jackson's eyes, Hill was a bad marcher, and generally placed in the middle of his columns so that the good marchers of Ewell's division in front could hurry him by their example, and the Stonewall Division from behind could press him on. Jackson did not prefer charges against Hill at once, but he noted down his failings before Cedar Run, and much later made use of these records along with others. The first Specification under the Cedar Run charge of 'Neglect of Duty' read:

In that Maj-Gen A. P. Hill when he was directed by Maj-Gen T. J. Jackson to move early on the morning of August 8th, 1862 from Orange C.H. towards Culpeper C.H. by way of Barnette ford did fail to move in obedience to said order but did continue in the vicinity of Orange C.H. until night, thus remaining a day's march in rear of the position which he should have occupied. All this near Orange C.H. on or about Aug 8th, 1862. [1]

[1] Virginia State Library, Early Papers, Box 2.

There were other arrests made and other charges preferred against several commanders, including Winder, but the case of A. P. Hill was the dominating one; and it continued to drag on until Jackson's death, for further dereliction of duty on Hill's part occurred on the march to Maryland. This time it was the failure of Hill's division to start its march at dawn, combined with the fact that Hill paid no heed to Jackson's strict march instructions to halt his troops every hour, that led to Hill's arrest; and, for a time, to his marching in the rear in disgrace. Fortunately he was allowed to return to his command for Harper's Ferry and Sharpsburg.

These unfortunate happenings were noted with regret by Jackson's old friends. Maury, for example, as we have seen, wrote: 'His arrest of Hill, Winder and General Richard Garnett, three of the noblest officers in our service, were inexcusable, especially of Garnett, whom he arrested for not charging Shields' victorious army with the bayonet when his ammunition failed.' Jackson was on better terms with his staff officers than with his senior commanders. Major the Rev R. L. Dabney served Jackson loyally as adjutant-general until his resignation after the battles around Richmond. An example of the valuable work he did is recorded on page 112, where he is seen getting Whiting's and Winder's division moving before the battle of Gaines' Mill. He was chief of staff during the successful movement of Jackson's divisions in the Valley as well as during the less satisfactory period of the battles around Richmond. He was at all times extremely loyal and on good terms with his master. In his biography of Jackson he lauds him to the skies and is more partisan even than Henderson.

Dr Hunter McGuire, Jackson's medical director, was another who gave Jackson his full support. He is mentioned several times in this work and the account he wrote and published in the S.H.S.P. was followed for Jackson's last days and death in the last chapter.

Jackson's assistant adjutant-general, Major A. S. Pendleton, was a splendid young staff officer. In his early twenties, he was more than willing to gallop off in all directions, on any occasion to carry Jackson's terse orders to his units. Familiarly known as 'Sandy' or 'Sandie'[1] he was a great favourite of the General's. Another of his right-hand men among the juniors of his staff was Henry Kyd Douglas, the author of the most readable contemporary account of the Civil War quoted in this book. Douglas was a great admirer of his distinguished master, and much liked by Jackson.

Two technical members of the staff, who may be considered together, were Majors Boswell and Hotchkiss. Boswell, his engineer officer, checked distances, delivered messages—like all of the staff—and reconnoitred the enemy's

---

[1] According to Freeman, his family called him Sandie ; Douglas calls him Sandy.

positions and prepared those of Jackson. Gallant and chivalrous, and the best of companions, is how Douglas describes him. Major Jed Hotchkiss was Jackson's topographical officer, and a brilliant one. His ready pencil speedily mapped any area Jackson desired. His value was even more appreciated after the disastrous spell without his services in the battles around Richmond. Hotchkiss' manuscript diary and maps are valuable sources of information on Jackson's campaigns.

Major Harman, Jackson's quartermaster, and Major Hawks, his commissary, were of a different type. Harman was one of the proprietors of a line of stage coaches and a large farmer. Hawks owned a carriage works. Both served Jackson well, and appear regularly as recipients of praise in his official reports; but Harman, although he knew all about wagons, was no disciplined, trained staff officer. He had several quarrels with Jackson, and resigned and was reinstated at least once.

Last, but by no means least, of the gentlemen around Jackson, who are mentioned in this book, is Beverley Tucker Lacy, the Presbyterian minister appointed general chaplain at Jackson's headquarters at Moss Neck. Lacy put into practice Jackson's idea of supplying chaplains to regiments lacking them. He also coordinated the work of the chaplains of different churches throughout the army. He succeeded surprisingly well in this task, and from Jackson's and Lacy's work a revival of religion swept through the army. Mr Lacy, like Dr McGuire, was with Jackson at the end.

In the realm of human relationships Jackson was most successful with his ordinary soldiers. His bravery, his eccentricities and his success combined to win him a place in their hearts. Although he was the strictest disciplinarian in the Confederate army, there is no doubt that the men loved Jackson and followed him willingly. The hold he had over them was seen as early as the end of the First Manassas operation, when he bade farewell to his First Brigade. [1] When he finished his speech there arose cheer after cheer, and from this developed the habit of cheering Jackson wherever he appeared. If he rode down a column he was followed by cheers all the way. If men were standing about in camp and heard cheers in the distance, they would say to one another, 'There goes a hare—or "Old Jack"'. His brigade and his division were soon unofficially called 'Stonewall' after the glory they jointly won at First Manassas; later the brigade was officially so designated. [2] His men were proud to call themselves his 'Foot Cavalry'. The dying soldier after Second Manassas exemplifies the bond between Jackson and his men. 'I belong to

[1] p. 27 and see Appendix on *Stonewall Brigade*.
[2] O.R., XXV, ii, 840 and Appendix.

the Fourth Virginia, your old brigade, General,' the man said. 'I have been wounded four times but never before as bad as this. I hope I will soon be able to follow you again.' 'You are worthy of the old brigade,' replied Jackson in a low and husky voice, placing his hand on the man's head. 'I hope with God's blessing, you will soon be well enough to return to it.' [1]

The pattern of Jackson's generalship now begins to emerge: brilliant strategic ideas; bold but sound tactical planning and execution; a secrecy which confuses the enemy, but at times brings near disaster to his own side when subordinates find themselves in command without knowing his plans; an insistence on strict obedience from his senior commanders which results in arrests and courts-martial; personal bravery which combined with eccentricities endear him to his men; but, above all, a Faith which gives him rock-like confidence and impels him to convert and discipline his men in a manner other than military, and thus to create a noble fighting corps led by a Southern Cromwell. Yet Jackson was more than a Cromwell. It would be fairer to call him an American Napoleon.

[1] Douglas, 150.

APPENDIX 1

Jackson's Artillery[1]

In order to study the types of the various pieces used by Jackson it is essential to know something of the organisation of the field artillery of the time.

There were a few concrete rules laid down as to the number or size of the pieces used in formations. The field guns were grouped into batteries, and each battery had between four and six guns. These batteries were a formation in their own right, with each two guns forming a section with a lieutenant in charge. Each gun was towed by a limber drawn by six horses with a quantity of ammunition ready for immediate use in a chest on the limber. Further supplies of ammunition were carried in a caisson carrying two chests of ammunition, towed by a limber, similar to the one attached to the gun, having one chest of ammunition on it. The caisson was also drawn by a six-horse team.[2] The gun and limber and the caisson and limber were all under the command of a sergeant and two corporals, the whole unit being termed a platoon. Each platoon had a crew consisting of nine men, and each team of horses had three drivers who rode the horses on the left side. During moves, the cannoneers either rode on the limbers and caisson or walked behind their guns. In batteries designated 'Horse Artillery' the cannoneers rode horses.

Once in action, when the gun had been unlimbered the caissons and limbers were moved to a position three to six yards respectively to the rear. The greatest problem whilst in this formation was the protection of the horses, and often every horse was killed. This led to the practice of removing all horses as far to the rear, and under as much cover, as possible. Often, especially in the CSA, the teams were cut down to only four horses, and sometimes the caissons were dispensed with. This was due wholly to the lack of available horses.

The CSA organised their field artillery and infantry with one battery to each infantry brigade. This was not a good system, as the CSA found to their cost. It meant that the artillery strength was dispersed amongst the whole army in small groups, making impossible any form of concentrated bombardment. This state of affairs seems intolerable, but it was not until 1863 that the system was changed to allow more concentration.

---

[1] By Peter Everingham.   [2] Wise, 111.

Artillery tactics had in fact taken a turn for the worse. The guns were now used more and more as a weapon of support, whereas they were originally used as assault weapons. Commanders often showed little enterprise in the placing of their artillery, though to some extent blame can be laid on the difficult country, which, being wooded, was not conducive to effective use of artillery. The method of placing pieces amongst or to the rear of the infantry was useful when the enemy made a final assault. An assaulting enemy, however, or an enemy being assaulted, would be unshaken by any preliminary bombardment, which was difficult to organise from scattered guns.

There were of course exceptions to such tactical employment of artillery; and Jackson, indeed, often placed his artillery differently. He preferred to mass his batteries on a flank, both to protect his own men and to bombard the enemy prior to attack. That his methods were successful is made abundantly clear during such actions as Harper's Ferry and Fredericksburg. Speedy movement, too, was much approved of by Jackson who liked to see his guns in the very best positions, even if it meant moving them in the middle of a battle.

Batteries were moved into position at a trot, a gallop being reserved for extreme emergencies. Covering five miles an hour or more, they could easily keep up with infantry and sometimes with cavalry. Of course this sort of speed only applied to the light field artillery; the heavier guns, such as 30-pounder Parrott rifles and the siege artillery were moved extremely slowly and laboriously.

But what of the field guns themselves? It is not intended to deal with every piece used during the war: that would be an impossible task. Those which will be dealt with in detail are the most important, and refer specifically to Jackson's own field artillery pieces.

The most widely used piece of the war was the Napoleon smoothbore. This was produced in a gun-howitzer combination, being shorter and lighter than the old 12-pounders and firing a slightly smaller charge. Its full name was the 12-pounder Gun-Howitzer M1857. Changed slightly, its full weight, both gun and carriage, was 2,355 lb. The tube itself weighed 1,227 lb and had an overall length of 66 inches.[1] Cast in bronze, it was a smoothbore muzzle-loader firing black powder charges at a rate of two, or for canister, four to five aimed rounds a minute. Surprisingly, it was very quick to load, and accurate when well aimed up to ranges of 2,000 yards. Greater ranges could be achieved by using increased charges, but this reduced accuracy alarmingly.

The tube was mounted on a wooden carriage and held in place by iron bands bolted over the trunnions. At the rear and base of the tube attaching it to the carriage was the elevating screw to raise or lower the tube—a 'hit or miss' method of elevation. The whole gun was mounted on cart-like wheels, and could be moved laterally by sticking a handspike into slots in the trail, by which it could be moved sideways. At this time there was no form of recoil mechanism, and the gun ran back,

[1] Coggins, 66.

Comparative Gun Sizes (tube)

Scale 1 inch to 2 feet

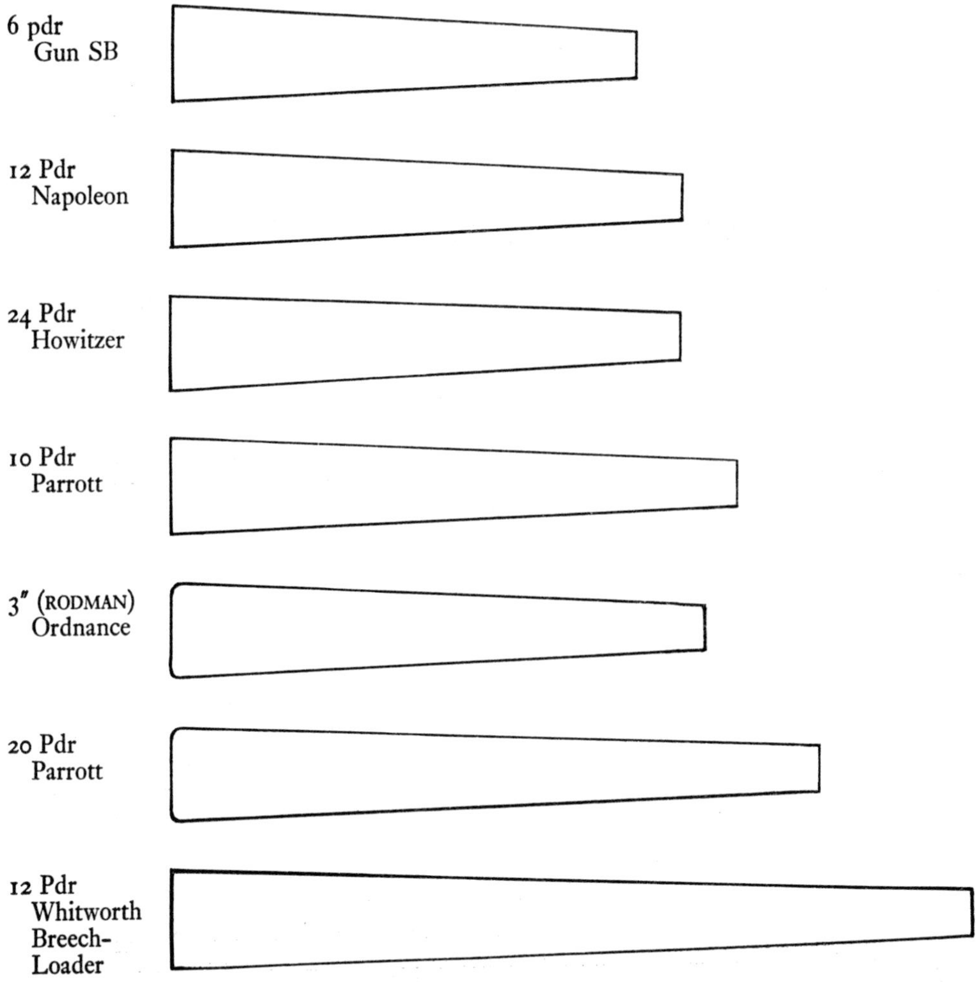

6 pdr
   Gun SB

12 Pdr
   Napoleon

24 Pdr
   Howitzer

10 Pdr
   Parrott

3″ (RODMAN)
   Ordnance

20 Pdr
   Parrott

12 Pdr
   Whitworth
   Breech-
   Loader

Model	Tube Weight Pounds	Tube Length Inches	Cal Inches	Weight Charge (pounds)	Weight Shot (pounds)
6 Pdr Gun Smoothbore	884	60	3·67	1·25	6·10
12 Pdr Napoleon	1,227	66	4·62	2·50	12·30
24 Pdr Howitzer	1,318	65	5·82	2·00	18·40

RIFLED FIELD PIECES

Model	Tube Weight Pounds	Tube Length Inches	Cal Inches	Weight Charge (pounds)	Weight Shot (pounds)
10 Pdr Parrott	899	74	3·00	1·00	9·5
3 Inch Ordnance (*Rodman*)	820	69	3·00	1·00	9·5
20 Pdr Parrott	1,750	84	3·67	2·00	20·0
12 Pdr Whitworth Breech-Loader	1,092	104	2·75	1·75	12·0

making tracks. The smoke created by the gun on firing was such that it was difficult to resight the gun. Then the tracks came in useful, as the gun could be realigned by pushing it back up its tracks. But this again was a rather uncertain method.

The ammunition for the 12-pounder Napoleon was standardised smoothbore shot. There were several types used, such as: solid shot, shell, spherical case or shrapnel and canister. Solid shot was generally used at long distance against masses of troops. The shot was not attached to the charge, and the powder bag was placed in the tube for the shot to be rammed on top of it. Shell on the other hand was manufactured as a complete round containing both shell and powder in a linen bag. This type of round was used against troops who were entrenched or against buildings. It was never very successful because the powder charge contained in the shell was so small (a 12-pounder shell contained only $\frac{1}{2}$ lb of black powder) that the effect of the explosion was almost negligible. Often the charge did not even explode, simply because the time fuse in the shell depended on ignition from the flash at discharge, and was more often than not blown off, or out, during flight. Spherical case or shrapnel was much the same as shell, though it contained musket balls which scatter on exploding. The 12-pounder round contained some 78 musket balls, but, as in the shell, the fuse was so crude that it seldom produced the expected devastating effect. Perhaps the most useful round used at about 300–400 yards was

canister. This came both as a complete round or with powder and canister separate. The shot which filled the canister, shaped literally like a can, was large, often two inches in diameter. Its effect was devastating and is often described as cutting great swathes in the lines of approaching enemy. The CSA artillery often resorted to canvas bags filled with bits of chain, which could be extremely effective.

In a full battery formation a 12-pounder battery had four 12-pounders and two 24-pounder howitzers. This was by no means fixed, however, and Jackson, for example, preferred to have all six-pounder Napoleons.

The second of the smoothbore muzzle-loading guns used mostly by the Confederates was the 6-pounder. The carriage for this was basically the same as for the 12-pounder, the tube being secured in the same manner. However, because the tube was slightly thinner, the cheeks of the carriage were placed closer together. The length of the tube was 60 inches and it weighed 884 lb. With the carriage the total weight was 1,784 lb. The carriage was mounted again on cart-like wheels, and it is interesting to note that the wheels of all the field pieces were of standard size and thus interchangeable.

The maximum effective range of the gun was 1,523 yards [1] although this decreased quickly as the gun became fouled. Shot was classed in the same manner as for the 12-pounder except that spherical case contained only 38 balls and canister 54 balls. Loading, as on the other muzzle-loaders, proved to be very fast; and experienced teams could unlimber, load and fire within seconds of arrival at their positions.

The whole gun and limber was normally towed by a six-horse team with quick release traces to allow for the speedy removal of any killed or injured horse. Because of is relatively light weight, it was an extremely manoeuvrable field piece. Its position could be changed very quickly and, if necessity demanded, it could be towed by only four horses.

The more sophisticated guns used by Jackson belonged to the Parrott [2] family. These were rifled muzzle-loaders ranging in size from 10- to 30-pounders. The most popular field artillery pieces were the 10- and 20-pounders. These had a cast-iron tube with a wrought-iron band wrapped round the breech. This form of casting could also be used for breech-loaders; and Parrott himself in 1861, in his first patent, had said the band could be made movable to allow for breech loading.

Unfortunately for the Confederates, Parrott was a patriotic Unionist, and in consequence his pieces were in short supply in the South. Copies were of course made, and proved, surprisingly enough, very effective.

Of the Parrotts the 10-pounder was of 3-inch calibre with a tube 74 inches long.

---

[1] Coggins, 66.

[2] The Parrott gun was invented by Robert Parker Parrott (1804–77), who graduated from West Point in 1824. After some years spent as a professor at that institution and as a member of the Ordnance, he became superintendent of an iron foundry at Cold Springs, New York. Here he perfected his gun, a cast-iron rifle which was cast hollow and was strengthened by shrinking wrought-iron bands over the reinforced section.

It had a light tube weighing 899 lb, only slightly heavier than the 6-pounder smooth-bore Napoleon. Its range was about 1,900 yards, and it was extremely accurate at any range up to this. The tube was mounted on a carriage similar to the 6- and 12-pounders, being secured in the same way. Elevation and sighting gear were a little more elaborate on the Parrotts, which had a pendulum sight on the rear of the piece instead of open sights. The 20-pounder was mounted in precisely the same manner as the 10-pounder on a slightly wider carriage. The tube weighed 1,750 lb and had a calibre of 3.67 inches, having five lands [1] instead of the three in the 10-pounder. [2] Range was also in the region of 1,900 yards. Both rifles fired smooth shells which relied on the expansion of a band of either copper, brass or lead to connect with the lands. These proved far more successful than shells which already had grooves or lands on them.

There were some disadvantages, however, since Parrotts showed a disturbing tendency to explode at the breech after having been in constant use. There are instances, too, of the muzzle being blown off; although this was rare. All in all, the Parrott was a highly successful piece, but its use was confined to the Civil War, and it did not have much influence on the future of ordnance.

There was a further piece of rifled artillery used mainly by the Confederates, the 3-inch rifled Rodman cannon. There is very little information about this, or the way it was mounted. With the standardisation of both carriage and wheels, however, it is safe to say it was mounted on the same type of carriage as the 6-pounder and 12-pounder, and in the same manner. The tube had a length of 69 inches. It weighed 820 lb and had a range of 1,830 yards. The round fired, like that from the Parrotts, was smooth, depending on an expanding cup on the base to fit in the rifling. This was quite a successful muzzle-loading rifle; often used but little mentioned.

Having described some of the pieces, both smoothbore and rifled, and shown some of their merits and defects, it may be wondered why the rifle was not used more than it was, because of its greater accuracy. The basic reason was in fact manufacture. It was difficult to produce a serviceable rifled piece, and its production took far longer than a standard smoothbore. In use the rifled piece proved slower to load because it fired separate shot, that is shot and charge loaded separately; whereas the smooth-bore had usually fixed shot and charge.

Another disadvantage of the rifle was that at close range it could not inflict the damage of the larger-bore smoothbores. Here accuracy was of secondary importance: speed and size of shot taking its place. There were, however, differing views about it; and arguments both for and against. Perhaps the most convincing argument against rifled cannon was that at a time when both sides were short of artillery the rifle was more slowly produced than the smoothbore.

Of breech-loading pieces there is little to be said. Few were used in the war, mainly because of difficulty of production of both piece and ammunition, and also the relatively complicated and clumsy breech mechanisms required. Perhaps the

---

[1] Projections. [2] Coggins, 77.

best example of a breech-loader used by both Confederate and Union batteries was the British Whitworth. This had a hexagonal bore and could send a shell some five or six miles. This sounds a real advantage. However, in days of imperfect means of observation and sighting, added to doubtful exploding charges, it had few advantages over the standard 12-pounder Napoleon, and it was slightly slower to load.

APPENDIX II

Jackson's Cavalry

Jackson's cavalry and the cavalry working with Jackson were superior to the Federal cavalry. Turner Ashby and Jeb Stuart, the two cavalry commanders most closely associated with Jackson, were outstanding in many respects; and the rank and file, many of them Valley planters and farmers, were born horsemen with a natural flair for reconnaissance and long range penetrations into enemy territory as well as for straightforward fighting. Many brought their own horses and it was no rare thing for a Virginian gentleman to resign a commission in another arm to join his friends as a private in the cavalry. Most of the Virginians were well acquainted with the countryside which was to provide their battleground. They knew every country lane and woodland track and had friends in every village.

By contrast the Federal cavalry were outmatched. Although there were some exceptions from among those recruited from the Western States, throughout the North generally horsemanship was practically an unknown art. 'As cavalry,' says one of Banks' brigadiers, [1] 'Ashby's men were greatly superior to ours. In reply to some orders I had given, my cavalry commander replied, "I can't catch them, sir; they leap fences and walls like deer; neither our men nor our horses are so trained."' The Federal cavalry were badly trained and unprepared for war: after Front Royal, Taylor records, 'The Federal horse was from New England, a section in which horsemanship was an unknown art, and some of the riders were strapped to their steeds. Ordered to dismount, they explained their condition and were given time to unbuckle.' [2]

But if the Federal cavalry were badly trained, Ashby's cavalry were badly disciplined. They were short of officers and did largely what they wanted, sometimes only half of them being available for duty while the remainder were back visiting their homes and friends. Many of them followed Ashby from personal devotion, and when Jackson attempted to discipline and organise them on proper military lines, Ashby threatened to resign. Jackson then left them as they were, although their lack of discipline had serious consequences. For example in the pursuit of Banks after Front Royal, by the time Newtown was reached nearly the whole of Ashby's cavalry had turned aside to pillage and carry off Federal horses back to their homes, a mission which took a day or two to complete. To the misconduct of

[1] Henderson, i, 225.   [2] p. 79.

Ashby's troopers the escape of the Federal Army on this occasion must be partly attributed. 'Never have I seen an opportunity when it was in the power of cavalry to reap a richer harvest of the fruits of victory,' wrote Jackson in his report. 'Had the cavalry played its part in the pursuit, but a small portion of Banks' army would have made its escape to the Potomac.'

On the other hand Jackson usually demanded and got much from his cavalry, and during this period of the war few of the Federal commanders except Pope used their cavalry nearly as well as he did. After Front Royal—before the indiscipline of Ashby's men—Jackson personally ordered 250 Virginian horse to charge Kenly's rear-guard at Cedarville, and infused Flournoy's cavalrymen with his own aggressive spirit to such a degree that a 'gallant and effective charge' resulted.[1] On the march from the Valley to Richmond Jackson's cavalry provided so impenetrable a screen that no information of his movements passed to the Federals, and he was able to arrive in the Richmond area and play his part in the defeat of McClellan in the Seven Days' Battles, largely unheralded. Before the Battle of Chancellorsville, Stuart, after ranging ahead on the Confederate flank, came up to report that the Federal right was 'in the air'.[2] The commander of Stuart's second brigade, Fitzhugh Lee, trotted up to Jackson a little later when the famous turning movement was well under way, and led him to a hill from which he saw what was past believing: the long lines of Howard's XIth Corps in enfilade before him. From such examples as these it can be seen that Jackson was well served by his cavalry commanders and knew how to get the best out of them. In fact, in the employment of his cavalry Jackson was in advance of his age as well as being as skilful as the best generals of the past. Such masterly use of horsemen, particularly for watching enemy movements two or three marches to front or flank, had not been since the days of Napoleon.[3]

[1] p. 78.   [2] p. 192.
[3] Henderson, i, 422.

APPENDIX III

The Stonewall Brigade[1]

Jackson's first contact with his brigade of the Army of the Shenandoah[2] was at Harper's Ferry. He began the war by taking a contingent of cadets from the Virginia Military Institute to Richmond to act as drill instructors.[3] After a short spell there, he was posted to train Virginia troops at Harper's Ferry. When superseded by General J. E. Johnston at Harper's Ferry, he was given command of the First Virginia Brigade consisting of: 2nd Va, 4th Va, 5th Va, 27th Va, 33rd Va, and a battery of artillery raised in Rockbridge County in the Shenandoah Valley.

The 2nd Va and the 33rd Va came from Winchester and the northern end of the Shenandoah Valley. The 4th Va, on the other hand, came from the southern end of the Valley, from around Pulaski and Wytheville. Units from Staunton and Lexington area, a little further north, made up the 5th Va and 27th Va.

Unofficially each regiment had a nickname. The *Innocent* 2nd Va was so called because it refrained from pillaging on the march. The *Harmless* 4th Va received its nickname because of its good conduct in camp. The *Fighting* 5th Va was less well behaved, but a good fighting regiment all the same. A large number of unruly Irishmen gave the *Bloody* 27th Va its name. The *Lousy* 33rd Va received its title after being the first regiment to collect lice.

The Stonewall Brigade was composed of recruits of all ages, from boys to old men. A survey of the muster rolls reveals that 54 per cent of the Brigade were farmers; 13 per cent were blacksmiths, masons and machinists; 11 per cent were clerks and merchants; and 9 per cent were college students. The remaining 13 per cent were carriage-makers, teachers, lawyers, carpenters, cabinet-makers and distillers, while four men called themselves, simply, Gentlemen. The Brigade contained a number of non-English foreign-born men in its ranks. One company of the 5th Va consisted almost entirely of Americanised German boys. Out of its 87 original members, 84, including a captain, were 18 years old or under. The 33rd Va had an Irish company known as the *Emerald Guards*, and because of its fondness for fighting and liquor, it became the problem child of the Brigade. There were several other unusual units. A company in the 4th Va was known as the *Liberty Hall Volunteers*.

---

[1] Based on a paper by M. J. Steel.
[2] The Virginia troops were merged in the army of the Confederate States on 6 June 1861.
[3] p. 45.

Of this company's original 69 members, 57 were students of Washington College, Lexington, and their professor of Greek became the first company commander. In the course of the war, it had a total enrolment of 161 and suffered 203 casualties, showing that several soldiers received more than one wound. The Rockbridge Artillery[1] was so popular that Jackson had to restrict its membership. It was recruited largely from college graduates and theological students, and its four guns were at once christened Matthew, Mark, Luke and John. [2] During the war 45 of its members received commissions, and 147 men were killed.

Many members of the same family served together in the Stonewall Brigade. In C Company of the 5th Va were 18 members of the Bell family, of which six were killed in action, and five died of disease. All six sons of David Barton of Winchester served with the 33rd Va: two were wounded and two killed, one within sight of his own home.

The men of the Stonewall Brigade were by no means soldierly in appearance. The only thing bright about them was their rifles. There were no definite orders about what clothing should be worn. At first it was forbidden to wear Federal uniform; but even this was relaxed as time went on. Clothes were all shades of grey from light blue to butter-nut, and soft felt hats soon replaced kepis. Long boots also disappeared and were replaced by strong brogues which were found to be more comfortable; but a shortage of footwear on the Confederate side was a feature of the whole war, and men were generally only too pleased to wear anything that came to hand. Greatcoats and knapsacks were soon abandoned as too cumbersome for the long marches the Brigade had to undertake. All that was kept was a blanket and waterproof sheet slung over the shoulder (see sketch of 'Reb'). Spare kit was carried in a small haversack.

One of the great achievements of the Stonewall Brigade was its marching. In the Valley in 38 days it marched 400 miles, fought three major battles and took part in numerous skirmishes. Several marches were over 25 miles long.

Jackson had strict rules for marches. He rested his men for several minutes in every hour, and it was because Major-Gen A. P. Hill of the Light Division did not pay any attention to Jackson's march regulations in the Maryland campaign that he was put under arrest. [3] At a halt Jackson liked to see his men lie flat on the ground to rest. Certainly, although there was straggling in the Stonewall Brigade as in all the other Confederate units, the Brigade carried out some prodigious marching feats. The table[4] gives some of the details of the famous Valley marches for Jackson's force as a whole; and the Stonewall Brigade went even farther than most—for example, after the Battle of Winchester, they went from Winchester to Harper's Ferry and back, and they were the last to escape Frémont's and Shields' pincer movement. [5]

---

[1] Commanded originally by the Rev Dr W. N. Pendleton, rector of Grace Episcopal Church, Lexington and an old West Point Graduate.

[2] Henderson, i, 123, note.

[3] p. 148.

[4] Henderson, i, 403: given at end of this appendix.

[5] p. 84.

Jackson commanded the Stonewall Brigade in person at the Battle of Falling Waters[1] and First Bull Run;[2] and afterwards in the Valley and later except at M'Dowell the Brigade fought under him as its divisional commander or corps commander. He was always interested in their achievements and, what was more, always expected great things of them. For example, when in the Romney operation Brig-Gen Garnett said it was impossible for the men of the Stonewall Brigade to march further without halting to cook their rations, Jackson replied: 'I never found anything impossible with this brigade.'[3] He was never soft with them. When a part of the men of the 27th Va mutinied, he ordered Colonel Grigsby to have them shot.[4] He remained proud of the Brigade throughout. When the Stonewall regiments passed him on the flank march to Manassas junction, and although forbidden to shout, heralded him with a wild rebel yell, he said: 'Who could fail to win battles with such men as these?'[5] And at Second Manassas, when asked for help from a brigade, Jackson enquired, 'What brigade, Sir?' and when told the Stonewall Brigade, replied: 'Tell the Stonewall Brigade to maintain her reputation.'[6]

Led by Jackson personally, or under Jackson's general command, the Stonewall Brigade was a fine fighting unit, in spite of its disciplinary lapses. Like other units of Jackson's command they were proud to call themselves his 'Foot Cavalry'; but they were even prouder of the title *Stonewall* which they shared with their leader, a title which they bore unofficially throughout the battles following First Bull Run, and officially, after Jackson's death, in the Confederate order No 129, Richmond, May 30 1863.[7] They were great marchers and stout fighters, and it may truly be said that the Stonewall Brigade, like the Tenth Legion of Caesar and the Old Guard of Napoleon has made its name forever famous.[8]

[1] p. 47. [2] p. 13. [3] p. 51. [4] p. 72.
[5] p. 135. [6] p. 142.
[7] O.R., XXV, ii, 840; quoted on page 238 at end of Appendix.
[8] J. E. Cooke, 3.

The Marches in the Valley Campaign
March 22 – June 25, 1862

		Miles	
March 22	Mount Jackson – Strasburg	22	
23	Strasburg – Kernstown – Newtown	18	Battle of Kernstown
24–26	Newtown – Mt Jackson	35	
April 17–19	Mt Jackson – Elk Run Valley	50	
30– May 3	Elk Run Valley – Mechum's River Station	60	
May 7–8	Staunton – Shenandoah Mt	32	Battle of M'Dowell
9–11	Bull Pasture Mt – Franklin	30	Skirmishes
12–15	Franklin – Lebanon Springs	40	
17	Lebanon Springs – Bridgewater	18	
19–20	Bridgewater – Newmarket	24	
21	Newmarket – Luray	12	
22	Luray – Milford	12	
23	Milford – Front Royal – Cedarville	22	Action at Front Royal
24	Cedarville – Abraham's Creek	22	Action at Middletown and Newtown
25	Abraham's Creek – Stevenson's	7	Battle of Winchester
28	Stevenson's – Charlestown	15	Skirmish
29	Charlestown – Halltown	5	Skirmish
30	Halltown – Winchester	25	
31	Winchester – Strasburg	18	
June 1	Strasburg – Woodstock	12	Skirmish
2	Woodstock – Mount Jackson	12	
3	Mount Jackson – Newmarket	7	
4–5	Newmarket – Port Republic	30	
8	. . . .	30	Battle of Cross Keys
9	Cross Keys – Brown's Gap	16	Battle of Port Republic
12	Brown's Gap – Mount Meridian	10	
17–25	Mount Meridian – Ashland Station (one rest day)	120	
		676	miles in 48 marching days. Average 14 miles per diem

The Stonewall Brigade
Army of the Shenandoah

First Bull Run [1] 19 July 1861

First Brigade, Brig-Gen T. J. Jackson

2nd Va	Col J. W. Allen
4th Va	Col J. F. Preston
5th Va	Col Kenton Harper
27th Va	Lieut-Col J. Echols
33rd Va	Col A. C. Cummings

Captain Imboden's battery of artillery;
Rockbridge Artillery under Lieut Brockenborough;
Leesburg Artillery under Lieut H. Heaton

Brigade loss: k, 119; w, 442 = 561

Kernstown [2]

First Brigade, Brig-Gen R. B. Garnett

2nd Va	Col J. W. Allen
4th Va	Lieut-Col C. A. Ronald, Major A. G. Pendleton
5th Va	Col W. H. Harman
27th Va	Col J. Echols (w), Lieut-Col A. J. Grigsby
33rd Va	Col A. C. Cummings
Va Bty, Rockbridge	Captain W. McLaughlin
Va Bty, West Augusta	Captain J. H. Waters
Va Bty	Captain J. Carpenter

Brigade Loss: k, 40; w, 168; m, 153 = 361

Operations about Front Royal and Port Republic [3] 20 May to 10 June 1862

First Brigade, Brig-Gen C. S. Winder

2nd Va	Col J. W. Allen
4th Va	Col C. A. Ronald
5th Va	Col W. S. H. Baylor, Lieut-Col J. H. S. Funk
27th Va	Col A. J. Grigsby
33rd Va	Col J. F. Neff

(all Jackson's artillery under Col S. Crutchfield)
Captain Imboden's mule Bty
Captain J. [4] Carpenter's Bty (Alleghany)
Captain W. T. Poague's Bty (Rockbridge)

Brigade Loss: k, 23; w, 181; m, 32 = 236

[1] B & L, i, 195. [2] B & L, ii, 300. [3] B & L, ii, 301. [4] Joseph.

Seven Days' Battles [1]

First Brigade, Brig-Gen C. S. Winder

2nd Va	Col J. W. Allen (k) Lieut-Col L. Botts
4th Va	Col C. A. Ronald
5th Va	Col W. S. H. Baylor
27th Va	Col A. J. Grigsby (w) Captain G. C. Smith
33rd Va	Col J. F. Neff
Va Bty, Alleghany	Lieut J. [2] C. Carpenter
Va Bty, Rockbridge	Captain W. T. Poague

Brigade Loss: k, 30; w, 149 = 179

Cedar Run [3]   9 August 1862
(Brig-Gen C. S. Winder killed in command of First Division)

First Brigade, Col C. A. Ronald

2nd Va	Lieut-Col L. Botts
4th Va	Lieut-Col R. D. Gardner
5th Va	Major H. J. Williams
27th Va	Captain C. L. Haynes
33rd Va	Lieut-Col E. G. Lee
Va Bty, Alleghany	Captain J. Carpenter (w), Lieut J. C. Carpenter
Va Bty, Rockbridge	Captain W. T. Poague

Brigade Loss: k, 10; w, 48 = 58

Second Bull Run [4]   16 August to 2 September 1862

First Brigade, Col W. S. H. Baylor (k)
   Col A. J. Grigsby (w)

2nd Va	Lieut-Col L. Botts (w)
	Captain J. W. Rowan
	Captain R. T. Colston
4th Va	Lieut-Col R. D. Gardner
5th Va	Major H. J. Williams
27th Va	(Col A. J. Grigsby (w))
33rd Va	Col J. F. Neff (k)
Artillery massed	

Brigade Loss: k, 65; w, 346 = 411

[1] B & L, ii.   [2] John.   [3] B & L, ii, 496.
[4] B & L, ii, 500.

Maryland Campaign [1]

First Brigade, Col A. J. Grigsby, (do/w), Lieut-Col R. D. Gardner,
   Major H. J. Williams

2nd Va	Captain R. T. Colston
4th Va	Lieut-Col R. D. Gardner
5th Va	Major H. J. Williams
27th Va	Captain F. C. Wilson
33rd Va	Captain J. B. Golladay,
	Lieut D. H. Walton

   Brigade Loss at Antietam: k, 11; w, 77 = 88

Fredericksburg [2]

First Brigade, Brig-Gen E. F. Paxton

2nd Va	Capt J. Q. A. Nadenbousch
4th Va	Lieut-Col R. D. Gardner (w)
	Major W. Terry
5th Va	Lieut-Col H. J. Williams
27th Va	Lieut-Col J. K. Edmondson
33rd Va	Col E. G. Lee

   Brigade Loss: k, 3; w, 44; m, 1 = 48

Chancellorsville [3]

First Brigade, Brig-Gen E. F. Paxton (k)
      Col J. H. S. Funk

2nd Va	Col J. Q. A. Nadenbousch
4th Va	Major W. Terry
5th Va	Col J. H. S. Funk, Lieut-Col H. J. Williams
27th Va	Col J. K. Edmondson (w), Lieut-Col D. M. Shriver
33rd Va	Col A. Spengler

   Brigade Loss: k, 54; w, 430; m, 9 = 493

[1] B & L, ii, 602.   [2] B & L, iii, 147.   [3] B & L, iii, 238.

This is the special order giving the title *Stonewall Brigade* to the First Brigade of Jackson's old division of the Army of Northern Virginia:

Special Orders,   Adjt and Inspector General's Office,
No 129   Richmond, May 30, 1863

XVIII   The following resolution has been submitted to the Secretary of War from the officers and soldiers of the brigade formerly commanded by Lieut-Gen Thomas J. Jackson:

Resolved, that in accordance with General Jackson's wish, and the desire of this brigade to honour its first great commander, the Secretary of War be requested to order that it be known and designated as the "Stonewall Brigade", and that, in thus formally adopting a title which is inseparably connected with his name and fame, we will strive to render ourselves more worthy of it by emulating his virtues, and, like him, devote all our energies to the great work before us of securing to our beloved country the blessing of peace and independence.

XI   The Department cheerfully acquiesces in the wish thus expressed, and directs that the brigade referred to be hereafter designated the "Stonewall Brigade". It commends the spirit which prompts the request, and trusts that the zeal and devotion, the patience and courage of the fallen hero, whose name and title his earlier companions in arms desire so appropriately to honour and preserve, may attend and animate not only the "Stonewall Brigade" but each brigade and every soldier in the armies of the South, now struggling to drive back from their borders an implacable and barbarous invader.

By command of the Secretary of War   JNO. WITHERS
                                                      Assistant Adjutant-General

Commentary on Sources and Bibliography

The works found most useful in writing this book were the *Official Records*, which I was fortunate to have at hand in the Staff College Library, Camberley, the three volumes of *Battles and Leaders* and Henderson's classic biography. During a short visit to the United States, I was able to see some of the manuscript collections listed below; but found very little new material. Most of the original letters and documents relating to Stonewall Jackson have been sifted through most thoroughly already, first by Henderson, and more recently, not only by the late Colonel W. Couper and the Jackson Memorial Association, whose collections are now at the Virginia Military Institute, Lexington, but also by D. S. Freeman, F. E. Vandiver, Burke Davis, Lenoir Chambers, Bruce Catton and other American scholars. I was, however, able to find some West Point Records not previously used.

A tour of the Jackson battlefields, so admirably sign-posted by the National Park Service, and visits to museums with pertinent exhibits, provided background material. I found the VMI Museum, the Jackson Museum in his old Lexington home, and the museum at Winchester in his old headquarters particularly valuable in this respect—and their lady custodians uniformly charming and helpful.

Among eye-witness account of Jackson's campaigns and Jackson's generalship—the theme of my book—I found R. L. Dabney's biography of Jackson very useful. As he was there, one must accept most of what he says, and if one is forbearing about his unctuous style, much can be got from his book. Kyd Douglas's now well-known little book is probably the most readable on the Civil War, although a shade inaccurate. It has much colourful information about Jackson. W. Allan is first-rate on the Valley campaign. I have repeated the traditional extracts from R. Taylor, leader of the Louisianians; but found little else in his *Destruction and Reconstruction*. Maury, Worsham, E. A. Moore and J. E. Cooke provide valuable information concerning the appearance, character and leadership qualities of Jackson, as does Longstreet in a more critical way. The *Southern Historical Society Papers*, Richmond, 1876–1944, 49 volumes, provide many articles by participants like Dr Hunter McGuire and others, which have been used in this book; and I was fortunate to have sent me the Centennial editions of the Hagerstown *Herald-Mail* which I found a useful source of information on the battle of Antietam.

Together, T. J. Arnold and Roy Bird Cook (not to be confused with J. E. Cooke)

cover Jackson's early life very well indeed. Bigelow's *The Campaign of Chancellors-ville* gives a full account of this battle with excellent maps. Freeman's *Lee's Lieutenants* is a very well documented secondary source on Jackson. Henderson, with his mass of eye-witness testimony personally collected and collated, ranks higher than a secondary source for me. He also treats the subject in the way I have tried to do, and most exceptionally for a biographer of Jackson, past or present, has good maps, many drawn by his favourite Hotchkiss, who himself provides much valuable information about Jackson in his papers in the Library of Congress.

It was comforting to learn from Mr Monroe Cockrell, who answered a query of mine through the Jackson Memorial Association, about errors in Henderson's book, that in his opinion Henderson remains a leading authority on Jackson as a general, and that even that mighty researcher D. S. Freeman could find few errors in Henderson. Incidentally, Burke Davis claims to have found at least one error even in Freeman!

Finally, I found that many of the articles in past and present issues of *The Civil War Times* provided valuable information on Jackson and the Stonewall Brigade.

Some Manuscript Collections in the United States having materials by or about Stonewall Jackson

Duke University, North Carolina, Durham
  P. G. T. *Beauregard* (1818–93) Papers.
  Alexander R. Boteler (1815–92) Papers. Includes correspondence with Jackson.
  Dunlap Family Papers. Civil War letters from William A. Dunlap, a Confederate soldier, contains comment on Jackson.
  Thomas Jonathan Jackson (1824–63) Papers, 1855–1906. Correspondence, commissary papers, vouchers, soldiers' leave requests, etc.
  Hector McNeill (d. 1871) Papers. Jackson is mentioned in correspondence.
  Munford Family Papers. Correspondence and personal papers concerning Jackson

Library of Congress, Washington
  Early (1816–1894) Papers. Includes correspondence with Jackson.
  Henderson Papers. Letters to Henderson from participants in the Civil War for his book.
  Hotchkiss Papers; *Harman* Papers. These are very valuable sources.

University of North Carolina, Chapel Hill
  Dabney Family Papers. Dabney (1820–98) wrote a biography of Jackson and these papers include some of his research materials.

University of South Carolina, Columbia
   William Dunlap Simpson (1823–90) Papers. Correspondence with or mention of Jackson.

University of Virginia, Charlottesville
   John Esten Cooke (1830–86) Papers. Includes correspondence with Jackson, also details about his own biography of Jackson.
   Fishburne Family Papers. Includes data on Jackson's teaching career and his marriage. The ledger which Jackson used when he was a youthful constable is here.

Virginia Historical Society, Richmond
   Henry Brainerd McClellan (1840–1904) Papers. Includes correspondence with Jackson.
   Langhorne Family Papers. Includes letters written by Langhorne while serving with Jackson.
   Patton Family Papers. Includes correspondence with Jackson.
   Conrad Family Papers. Includes correspondence with Jackson.

Virginia State Library, Richmond.
   A small amount of correspondence, battle reports and other material relating to Jackson.

Virginia Military Institute, Lexington.
   Original letters and photostat letters by Jackson held on behalf of the Jackson Memorial. In the process of being catalogued and not fully available during my visit.

West Virginia University, Morgantown.
   Charles Henry Ambler (1876–1957) Papers. Mention of Jackson.
   Roy Bird Cook (b. 1886) Papers. His is probably the best book on the early life of Jackson.
   Thomas Jonathan Jackson (1824–63) Papers. Letters by Jackson from various parts of the United States, Mexico, and at sea to his sister and niece. Also the script of a radio programme on Jackson broadcast on 21 August, 1951, by Radio Station WLW, Cincinnati, Ohio.

U.S. Military Academy, West Point.
   Class standings and records of Jackson while a Cadet at the Military Academy, 1842–46. Some of these do not appear to have been used before.

Some Biographies of Jackson

Adams, J. D.   *Stonewall Jackson*   Dutton, 1931
Addey, Markenfield   *Life and imprisonment of Jefferson Davis together with the life and military career of Stonewall Jackson*   New York, 1886

Addey, Markenfield *Stonewall Jackson* New York, 1863

Anderson, J. H. *Notes on the life of Stonewall Jackson and on his campaigning in Virginia, 1861–63* London, 1904

Arnold, Thomas Jackson *Early Life and Letters of General Thomas Jackson (Stonewall)* Reprint, Richmond, Va, 1957 This is a handy source of some of Jackson's letters

Chambers, Lenoir *Stonewall Jackson* 2 vols New York, 1959

Cook, Roy Bird *The Family and Early Life of Stonewall Jackson* 3rd ed. Charleston, W.Va, 1948

Cooke, John Esten *The Life of Stonewall Jackson* New York, 1866

Cooke, John Esten *Stonewall Jackson and the Old Stonewall Brigade* Reprint, Charlottesville, 1954

Dabney, Robert L. *Life and Campaigns of Lieutenant-General Thomas J. Jackson* 2 vols New York, 1866

Davis, Burke *They called him Stonewall* New York 1954. This is fine writing in the best sense, and contains a brilliant description of the execution of John Brown in the presence of Jackson and his VMI cadets.

Douglas, Henry Kyd *I Rode with Stonewall* Chapel Hill, N. C. 1940

Gittins, John G. *Personal Recollections of Stonewall Jackson* New York, 1899

Henderson, G. F. R. *Stonewall Jackson* 2 vols Longmans Green & Co., London, 1904

Jackson, Anna (Morrison) *Life and Letters of General Thomas J. Jackson* New York, 1891

Jackson, Anna (Morrison) *Memoirs of Stonewall Jackson* Louisville, Ky, 1895

McCabe, J. D. *The life of Jackson* (VMI Library, Lexington)

Maguire, Thomas Miller *Jackson's Campaigns in Virginia, 1861–62* London, 1913

Nash, E. *Jackson's Strategy* London, 1904

Tate, Allan *Stonewall Jackson the Good Soldier* New York, 1930

Vandiver, Frank Everson *Mighty Stonewall* New York, 1957. Very fully documented and making full use of D. S. Freeman's researches, but with poor maps.

White, Henry Alexander *Stonewall Jackson* Philadelphia, 1900

Some Other Books Used

Allan, W. *Stonewall Jackson's Campaign in the Shenandoah Valley of Virginia* London, 1912

Allan, W. *The Army of Northern Virginia in 1863* Cambridge, Mass, 1892

Bigelow, J. *The Campaign of Chancellorsville* New Haven, 1910

Blackford, C. M. *Letters from Lee's Army* New York, 1947

Catton, Bruce *Picture History of the Civil War* New York, 1960. (American Heritage). A spendid pictorial record with a good text

Coggins, J. *Arms and Equipment of the Civil War* New York, 1962. A new book on weapons in which the drawings are better than the text

Cooke, J. E. *Wearing the Gray* Indiana, 1959

Couper, W. *100 years at the VMI* 4 vols Richmond, 1939

Daniel, L. C. *The Confederate Scrapbook* 1893

Donald, David *Divided we fought* (Pictorial History) New York, 1956

Dupuy, R. E. & Dupuy, T. N. *The Compact History of the Civil War* New York, 1962. A very good outline history and winner of the 1960 Fletcher Pratt Award for outstanding Civil War history.

Freeman, D. S. *Lee's Lieutenants* 3 vols New York, 1942–44. The most fully documented work on Jackson which the author came across

Hamlin, P. G. *The Battle of Chancellorsville* Bangor, Maine, 1896. Valuable maps showing the cleared areas west of Chancellor's House which played such an important part in the battle.

Honig, Donald (Editor) *Blue and Gray* New York, 1886

Johnston, R. M. *Bull Run* Boston, 1913

Long, A. L. *Memoirs of Robert E. Lee* New York, 1886

Longstreet, James *From Manassas to Appotomax* Philadelphia, 1896. Detailed but dull

Luvaas, Jay *The Military Legacy of the Civil War* Chicago, 1959. This book has an interesting chapter on Henderson

Maury, D. H. *Recollections of a Virginian* New York, 1894

Moore, E. A. *The Story of a Cannoneer under Stonewall Jackson* Lynchburg, Va, 1910

Palfrey, F. W. *Campaigns of the Civil War V: Antietam and Fredericksburg*

Ripley, R. S. *History of the Mexican War* 2 vols New York, 1849

Ropes, J. C. *The Story of the Civil War* 4 vols New York, 1894–1913

Rywell, M. *Confederate Guns* Harriman, Tennessee, 1952. Pistols, muskets and carbines; not cannon

Taylor, R. *Destruction and Reconstruction* New York, 1900

Vandiver, Frank Everson *Ploughshares into swords* Austin, Texas, 1952. This describes the supply of Confederate ordnance

Wiley, Bell Irvin *The Life of Johny Reb* Indianapolis & New York, 1962

Wise, J. C. *The Military History of the VMI* 1839–65. Lynchburg, Va, 1915

Wise, J. C. *The Long Arm of Lee* 2 vols Lynchburg, Va, 1915. This gives a very thorough description of the Confederate field batteries, and where and how they fought.

Official Records and Semi-official Records

Battles and Leaders 3 vols New York, 1956

Confederate Military History, editor Evans, C.A. 12 vols Atlanta, 1899

Southern Historical Society Records   49 vols Richmond, 1876–1944
War of the Rebellion   Official Records   70 vols Washington, 1880–1901
West Point Atlas   vol i New York, 1959

Journals and Newspapers

Historical Handbooks, National Park Service   Current issues. Superintendent of
   Documents. Washington, 25, D.C.
Civil War Times   Harrisonburg, Pa
Hagerstown Herald-Mail   Centennial copies
Richmond Times
Charleston Mercury

Index

The numerals in **bold** type refer to the **figure** numbers of the illustrations

245

By the same author

The Second World War (George Allen & Unwin) 1966
Famous Sieges (Arthur Barker) 1966
Sergeant Morris (Longmans) 1967 (Editor)

STONEWALL JACKSON
as Military Commander